CREATING STRATEGIC PARTNERSHIPS

CREATING STRATEGIC PARTNERSHIPS

A Guide for Educational Institutions and Their Partners

Pamela L. Eddy and Marilyn J. Amey

Foreword by
Debra D. Bragg

STERLING, VIRGINIA

Published by Stylus Publishing, LLC
22883 Quicksilver Drive
Sterling, Virginia 20166-2102

Library of Congress Cataloging-in-Publication Data
Eddy, Pamela Lynn.
Creating strategic partnerships : a guide for educational institutions
and their partners / Pamela L. Eddy and Marilyn J. Amey;
foreword by Debra D. Bragg. – First Edition.
   pages cm
Includes bibliographical references and index.
ISBN 978-1-57922-754-8 (cloth : alk. paper)
ISBN 978-1-57922-755-5 (pbk. : alk. paper)
ISBN 978-1-57922-756-2 (library networkable e-edition)
ISBN 978-1-57922-757-9 (consumer e-edition)
1. Universities and colleges–Business management. 2. Strategic
alliances (Business) 3. Public-private sector cooperation. I. Amey,
Marilyn J. II. Title.
LB2341.92.E33 2014
378.1'06–dc23
                                                    2014007784
13-digit ISBN: 978-1-57922-754-8 (cloth)
13-digit ISBN: 978-1-57922-755-5 (paperback)
13-digit ISBN: 978-1-57922-756-2 (library networkable e-edition)
13-digit ISBN: 978-1-57922-757-9 (consumer e-edition)

Bulk Purchases

Quantity discounts are available for use in workshops and for
staff development.
Call 1-800-232-0223

First Edition, 2014

10   9   8   7   6   5   4   3   2   1

To my mother, Vickie Eddy, who epitomizes the ideal of connecting with others. To Marilyn—this journey would not have been possible without you. I continue to draw on the model you have provided of what it means to be a true collaborator.

To Dennis, with whom I first wrote about organizational collaboration, and to Caitlin and Megan, who have grown up hearing partnership stories. To Pam—we have lived this partnership in all its positive and challenging phases, and throughout, you have been a wonderful colleague and friend.

CONTENTS

Throughout my career as director of the Office of Community College Research and Leadership (OCCRL) at the University of Illinois, I have studied partnerships but never as systematically or as creatively as Dr. Pamela Eddy and Dr. Marilyn Amey. Bravo to these two dynamic scholars for taking on an incredibly complex phenomenon and helping readers to make sense of it. There are rewards for practitioners, policymakers, and scholars who read their book because they are bound to gain a better understanding of how partnerships work and how to make them work more strategically. For more than a decade, Drs. Eddy and Amey have collaborated—dare I say partnered?—to better understand how partnerships form, how they operate under the best and worst of situations, and, most important, how they affect the institutions and people who are touched by them.

Through the authors' careful analysis of dozens of partnerships that have been conducted for myriad purposes, this book points out that partnerships have become ubiquitous to the educational environment. By contrasting "traditional" partnerships from "strategic" partnerships, readers begin to understand how partnerships that take on a more strategic form offer the promise for achieving greater impact through deeper and more long-lasting change. Not to diminish the value of traditional partnerships, which are more targeted and limited in scope, Drs. Eddy and Amey suggest that strategic partnerships have the potential to generate better education and economic effects and, therefore, greater social good. Ultimately, in their view, the most successful partnerships have the potential to enhance the public good that all of P–20 (primary through graduate) education seeks to create for its many diverse stakeholders. While much of the focus of this book is on higher education and community colleges in particular, its importance extends to all of P–20 education and beyond, including workforce training and employment.

So why are partnerships important? What makes this issue increasingly important for educators and those who wish to collaborate with them? According to the authors, partnerships create the opportunity for educational institutions to increase capacity to bring about positive change. When working at their peak, partnerships are transformative for the institutions and people involved. For example, partnerships generate communication within and between organizations and people that generates further creative thought and more concerted action. The best strategic partnerships produce better results than the individual partners could have achieved independently. Sharing ideas and resources often achieves greater efficiencies and has other positive effects for the organizations and individuals who are involved or touched by the partnership.

Building on the notion of social capital, Eddy and Amey introduce the idea of "partnership capital" to exemplify how partnerships (and the people who make up and occupy them) build on networks and resources that exist to varying degrees in institutions and communities. This idea holds promise for helping practitioners, policymakers, and researchers to better understand the ways wealth, power, and prestige are accomplished through collective relationships to bring about larger systemic change. By capitalizing on prior knowledge, experience, and other tangible and intangible assets, partnerships find and also generate capital to sustain their efforts. By contrast, when partnerships lack capital of various kinds, they tend to be more limited and more uneven in their efforts to grow a collective enterprise, at least at the start. Certainly new partnerships, including those that lack common experiences and assets, can be successful, but the concept of partnership capital helps to explain why they are more difficult to start up and sustain over the long term.

It is important to note that the contrast between traditional and strategic partnerships that defines many of the concepts in this book is largely about the availability of partnership capital, which is more limited for traditional partnerships and more expansive for strategic ones. Drs. Eddy and Amey carefully portray these ideas in case descriptions in each chapter to bring life to their conceptual framing of partnerships. For those of us who teach courses in higher education leadership, organization, governance, and policy, this aspect of the book represents an especially important intellectual gift. Cases that come from the field, that are generated through deep associations with practitioners who are working in actual, living partnerships, add meaning and utility to the book. Through the experiences and lessons learned from people who are part of real partnerships, the cases allow others to experience grounded learning that can be applied to new situations.

As noted earlier, as a researcher who studies transitions throughout the P–20 pathway, particularly those that involve the community college, I have studied policies, programs, and practices that are associated with partnerships formed for various purposes, constructed in numerous ways, and achieving a multitude of results, both positive and negative. I have observed that, whereas some partnerships exemplify what Drs. Eddy and Amey label traditional and strategic, some so-called partnerships never really become partnerships at all. Because partnerships—or collaborations of some sort—have become the coin of the realm for attracting external funding, the idea of partnerships is adopted without understanding the complexity of what partnering is really all about. In an environment that increasingly awards applicants with federal or state grant funding when they adopt a partnership approach, the likelihood of organizations coming together under a "partnership" arrangement is also increasing. For applications without this commitment to collaborate on paper, the potential to obtain the resources that are needed to engage in the work is slim to none, and yet, awarding funds to a collection of institutions does not guarantee that a partnership will form.

The notion of a partnership that conveys the meaning and characteristic functionality described by Drs. Eddy and Amey—either traditional or strategic—is not made through securing a grant, but what follows through the complex interweaving of ideas, commitments, and intended results. If the organizations lack a shared vision of what is possible together, if their leadership remains locked into institutional perspectives rather than a larger, collective view, and if resources are not shared for the betterment of the whole, then partnerships do not exist. And the danger is that successes and failures may be tied to the notion of partnerships when, in fact, partnerships were never implemented in the first place. Their potential has never been realized—cannot be realized—because they never existed. This failure is a shame because, as Drs. Eddy and Amey point out, there are countless reasons why partnerships are important to educational institutions and their students and other stakeholders, and it is important that the opportunities for success be maximized.

Luckily, my colleagues and I at OCCRL have seen partnerships do amazing things, even though we readily admit the advantages have been hard to quantify and are often mostly understood through anecdotal accounts. Working as a researcher and policy evaluator, this difficulty in measuring benefits is an admission of both fact and frustration. To capture the effects of a collective partnership that simultaneously implements policies, programs, and practices intended to bring about either incremental or transformative change is very difficult. So, while complexity of circumstances, goals, and intended outcomes drives the formation of partnerships in the first place, this complexity renders almost all standard research designs inadequate and ineffectual. Certainly, the notion of rigorous research that relies on experimental or quasi-experimental methods is difficult to envision as a design for understanding the impact of partnerships. More promising is to use qualitative studies, as Drs. Eddy and Amey have done, to provide insights into cases of success and failure under different circumstances. Through this methodology, a foundation can be laid for theory building about how partnerships work that can be followed by further empirical study. For those of us who study education, this book is the ultimate gift that Drs. Eddy and Amey have provided, and for which I express deep gratitude.

Moving forward, I express my sincere hope that Drs. Eddy and Amey continue their partnership in the study of collaborations in the form of education partnerships. Their contribution to the literature is important and sure to inspire others to think more carefully and critically about how institutions and people combine forces to bring about strategic change. Whether you are a practitioner involved in partnering, a policymaker incentivizing partnering, or a researcher studying partnering, this foundational book provides the impetus to think about partnerships in new ways, and it also helps us understand how our work can contribute to making partnerships operate more productively and effectively in the future to ultimately bring about change.

Debra D. Bragg
April 23, 2014
Gutsgell Endowed Professor
Director
Office of Community College Research and Leadership
University of Illinois

ACKNOWLEDGMENTS

The path from conception of a book topic to the final copy that readers hold in their hands is often circuitous. We initially started thinking about partnerships while discussing with a group of colleagues the type of partnerships they participated in, how these relationships worked, and who was involved. This first meeting involved colleagues working at different organizational levels in colleges, in community organizations, and in businesses who saw fit to invest time in telling their stories and in our fledgling project. They were willing to offer their thoughts, share examples of partnerships, and react to different partnership models we developed over time, challenging our thinking, testing our ideas in their respective partnering experiences, and offering constructive analyses that helped us deepen and revise our thinking. In the intervening years, we have had several coauthors who helped us work on various conference presentations, research articles, and writings—Jessica Rehling, Casey Ozaki, Jesse Watson, Tim Campbell, and many others who contributed to edited volumes by sharing their partnership stories in ways that helped us expand and refine. What remains unseen in these public venues is how our thinking was influenced by conversations in conference sessions, hallway dialogues, poster and roundtable discussions, and comments made by many discussants and reviewers reacting to our proposals and presentations at national conferences over the last 10 years.

A muse for our thinking throughout this process was Debra Bragg. We owe her a great deal of gratitude for her ongoing commentary, her well-placed questions, and her ability to help us advance our work since we began. We are grateful to her for writing the foreword; it is only fitting to have her present as our work culminates in book form. Another colleague who provided similar remarks was our departed colleague Barbara Townsend. You knew you were in for an intellectually stimulating conversation when both Debra and Barbara were in the session audience! A word of thanks also goes to Todd Treat for his comment that we should consider the role of slack in our model. This suggestion helped us to see the critical role of this construct and how considering slack helps us understand organizational context and possibilities better.

A special thanks to Tehmina Khwaja, PhD student at the College of William and Mary, who read several versions of this volume, helped conduct literature reviews, and provided feedback to questions such as, "So, does this make sense?" Her good humor, strong editing skills, and well-placed comments helped us achieve a stronger outcome. Yet, any errors or shortcomings in the material remain our own. Finally, as collaborators working on a long-term project like this, we have found joy in our thinking and writing time together. We are grateful to John von Knorring for his patience, belief, and support of this project.

PROLOGUE

The Increasing Role of Partnerships in Education

C alls for partnerships are on the increase as a means to leverage resources and to create programs that best prepare students for a changing labor market that is increasingly global in nature (Bastalich, 2010). Yet, think about partnerships you were involved in that did not work out. Did you ever wonder about the various forces and actors at play that contributed to the failure of the collaboration? This book helps you to understand the building blocks of partnerships and distinguishes between traditional and strategic partnerships. The various chapters lead you through a series of reflective questions that can help with partner selection and intentional steps to build a successful partnership.

The fallout from the Great Recession created added incentive to develop partnerships because of tight budgets. We know that collaborations provide a platform to address individual organizational goals and to meet state education and economic goals (Eddy, 2010a). When they work, resources are optimized, individual organizational needs are met, and outcomes are greater than a single entity could achieve (Baus & Ramsbottom, 1999; Flora & Hirt, 2010). When they do not work, time and resources invested are ultimately lost, even when accounting for short-term gains (Kolowich, 2009). Additionally, other potential opportunities may have been bypassed that eventually would have been successful.

Push for Partnerships and Conflicting Frameworks

Given the prospect of positive outcomes of partnering and the underlying belief that partnering results in better outcomes than what can be done individually, policymakers increasingly promote partnerships to address state and federal issues (Fowler, 2012). Institutional leaders often do the same to accomplish different external mandates and to meet internal agendas. On the one hand, partnering is increasingly a required activity through policy, grant requirements, or accreditation demands. On the other hand, because partnerships are built on relationships, partnering often emerges because people want to work together to accomplish a common goal.

A significant component of partnerships involves working with others. Research on group work attests that more learning is possible when pairing with others (Nilson, 2010), proving true the adage that two heads are better than one. Greater outcomes may emerge due to the synergies created when working with more people because of the added knowledge base and experience individuals bring to the joint work.

Yet, despite their potential, many partnerships fail (Eddy, 2007; Fear, Creamer, Pirog, Block, & Redmond, 2004). Partnerships are sometimes considered "fringe activities," risky, difficult to negotiate, political, and easily challenged by the institutional status quo (Bruffee, 1999; Fear et al., 2004). Despite perceived initial benefits, partnerships are often difficult and time-consuming to sustain and almost always more complicated to manage than at first appears. Many partnerships fail to obtain desired results, cannot be sustained for long periods, or cease to benefit both parties (Eddy, 2007; Fear et al., 2004), even when mandated to achieve specific outcomes. The assumption that educational institutions can readily collaborate due to similar educational goals proves false. It is not enough to have common goals; the systems involved in the partnering organizations often build on different cultural assumptions and operating standards that contribute to the complexity of partnering with others. It is critical to understand the motivations to partner and how these initial parameters affect the ongoing nature of the partnership (Amey, Eddy, & Campbell, 2010). Motivations to collaborate typically coalesce around three areas:

1. economic potentials
2. value alignment
3. policy mandates (Eddy, 2010a)

But, other factors may affect decisions to partner and should be accounted for in laying the foundation for strategic partnerships between organizations.

How partnerships are integrated into the existing system of operations differs by the framework in place; and complicating collaborations are the fact that organizations operate in a range of frameworks. For instance, one institution may function within a structural framework (Bolman & Deal, 2008) in which rules and structures guide the work; another institution may use a human resource frame (Bolman & Deal, 2008) that values relationships and employee needs above protocols. Knowing the type of frame in use (structural, human resource, political, and symbolic; Bolman & Deal, 2008) helps provide a map of how partnerships may be best aligned. Organizational operations concern the inner workings of process and relationships within institutions and differ depending on the type of organizational framework in place. The frame in place guides what motivates each organization to want to partner.

Looking Forward

In this volume, we first identify potential types of partnerships with particular emphasis on those we characterize as strategic. We point out the differences between strategic and traditional partnerships, drawing the distinctions in motivation to partner, alignment of goals and objectives, context and policy environment, intentionality of purpose, action, decision making, leadership required, and the potential for resulting change, including second-order systemic change. We return to these strategic partnership themes in each chapter as we explore examples of domestic and international educational collaborations and their sustainability and challenges.

This text can help policymakers and educational leaders, college administrators, and their governing boards support the creation of strategic partnerships, facilitate organizational change, and sustain effective partnerships. We do not presume that every collaboration is inherently beneficial, that all partnerships should be sustained, or that every pairing results in transformational change for all partners. Similarly, we do not assume that trust appears because organizations have chosen to partner, power is evenly distributed, or those involved achieve shared meaning within the partnership. Yet, we know from examining distinct partnerships in many states and countries, which we use as illustrations of key concepts throughout the book, that cross-sector collaborations can benefit each partner organization as well as the state or nation. Historically, members of educational partnerships often identify shared values and goals, active participation, aligned processes, successful outcomes, mutual respect, highly focused passion, and good working relationships as reasons partnerships continue to exist (Baus & Ramsbottom, 1999).

Each chapter addresses a critical component for partnering, and we use case studies to highlight the various concepts. Readers will find a case study at the end of each chapter that helps illustrate the topics covered in that chapter. These cases may provide more understanding of the ideas presented and may be used in training sessions or classes to aid in learning. Chapter 1 presents a typology of traditional and strategic partnerships, ultimately providing a model for strategic partnering. Chapter 2 delves into the motivating factors for individuals and organizations to partner. Many partnerships emerge as a result of the need to get something done (Lattauca & Creamer, 2005) and are built on existing relationships or shared experiences. Moving along the continuum of motivation from being purely based on task or resources to a shared vision or alignment of values contributes to how partners treat the joint venture and how long-term planning occurs. Given their critical role in the partnership process, we review relationships in chapter 3. Here, we explore individual social capital to showcase how the connections between people begin to establish the process by which partnerships emerge. Power and position contribute to how relationships operate in practice.

Chapter 4 begins to look at communication within the partnership and how framing by leaders or champions sets the stage for others to understand what is going on with the new collaboration. Framing for outside stakeholders and community members plays an increasingly important role, particularly as funding is sought for sustainability and influencing public understanding of the partnership. Framing occurs on multiple levels and may be done differently for an internal audience than for an external one. Just as individual social capital is a key element for the partnership, so is the impact of organizational structure and the associated organizational resources at the disposal of the group. Chapter 5 outlines the structural implications of partnering. Framing by the leader or champion helps others understand more fully the intentions and goals of the partnership, particularly how it fits into existing operations.

As in many change initiatives, leadership represents a pivotal component for partnering. The role of leadership at various levels of the partnership is covered in chapter 6. As funding becomes tight, leaders must decide how to use their limited resources, how to leverage their resources with other areas, and how the partnership supports and advances the strategic mission of the college or organization or how it detracts from this central ideal. Next, chapter 7 showcases what might emerge from a partnership. The group process creates partnership capital and, in cases of sustainable partnerships, stands apart from what the individual partners bring to the arrangement. The main components of partnership capital are trust, networking, and shared vision.

This volume concludes in chapter 8 with a template for those who aspire to create or sustain an existing partnership. Each chapter contains a summary of key points and a set of case examples to illustrate concepts. Themes that run throughout the remainder of the book include:

- the influence of policy on the partnership process
- examples from both domestic and international contexts
- the role of leadership in each of the partnership model stages
- the role of individuals as champions and gatekeepers to resources

If the formed collaborations are mutually beneficial, are achieving their desired outcomes, and are important in the long run, then leaders need to find ways to stabilize and sustain partnerships beyond temporary funding and advocacy of a single champion/leader. As many partnerships find the seeds of inception sown by the availability of funding that stipulates collaboration, money and resources are often motivations to begin working together. Once funding disappears, only those partnerships built on more than sharing resources are poised for sustainability. Generating a broader base of commitment in personnel, resources, time, and motivation are required for long-term viability. This book intends to support leaders and institutions seeking long-term sustainability for partnerships.

Summary Points

- Pressures to partner are increasing, due to both policy mandates and economics.
- Grant funders, foundations, and donors are calling for more collaborations to increase efficiencies and scale up innovations.
- Motivations to partner differ among participants; however, most successful partnerships are built on a shared value system and alignment of goals.
- Top-level leaders are important champions for partnering.
- Partners most often operate from different organizational frameworks, which complicate collaborations.
- Framing the reasons to partner and the rationale for dedication for resources toward the partnership is critical for campus and community buy-in. How leaders help frame change matters to ultimate success.

I

CREATING A STRATEGIC
PARTNERSHIP

Partnerships are in the news, topics of conversations for policymakers looking to save costs, and the focus of college leaders trying to leverage influence. Yet, a source of confusion in discussing partnerships is definitions. Various terms are often used interchangeably when considering partnerships. Indeed, Clifford and Millar (2008) note that an issue with research on partnerships is that *partnerships* is commonly not defined. *Collaborations, alliances, consortia, joint ventures, teams,* and *partnerships* all describe situations in which individuals and organizations join together for some purpose. Thus, it is important to be clear on how we use terms to describe partnerships. Here, we make the distinction between traditional partnerships and strategic partnerships. We argue that traditional partnerships are often the outcome of individual efforts, pursuing singular interests that eventually involve others (Amey, 2010), or are formed to meet a targeted outcome (Johnson, 2007), likely as a result of meeting a mandate that either emerges from a top-down decision or a policy requirement. Strategic partnerships instead are formed based on a sense of purpose and for what they contribute in helping leaders meet institutional goals and objectives.

A central feature of traditional partnerships is the happenstance origins of these pairings. The resulting partnership typically is not integrated into organizational operations; rather, it is person-centric and peripheral to campus operations. Strategic partnerships, on the other hand, originate in a different context and for different purposes. Strategic partnerships are intentionally formed based on goal alignment among partners that helps create more staying power. Like traditional partnerships emerging out of individual

1

interests, individuals may initiate strategic partnerships. But the difference is that in strategic partnerships individuals pursue connections based on how the partnership helps meet institutional strategic goals.

Traditional partnerships form by happenstance, whereas strategic partnerships are intentional.

Individual motivations behind pursuing a partnership matter. On the one hand, individuals may become involved in or start a partnership due to self-centered motivating interests (traditional partnership). On the other hand, individuals may be aware of their institutions' strategic goals and seek out partners that can help obtain these goals. In this case, self-interests may also be fulfilled because contributions at the individual level are rewarded as a result of helping to meet strategic initiatives. Strategic partnerships intentionally engage institutional members in critical examination of priorities and organizational strategies that often lead to real change rather than collaborating to reinforce the status quo. Adaptive or second-order change (Argyris & Schön, 1992; Heifetz, 1994) requires institutions to question their current operations and actions, ultimately deciding what they must do differently for deep changes to occur. Strategic partnerships build on deeper rationales for partnering than individual self-interest or happenstance and are not based on whims or fads (Birnbaum, 2000). In contrast, traditional partnerships create first-order change; they make only incremental adjustments and do not question underlying systemic assumptions associated with operations. Also, traditional partnerships do not propose new goals or outcomes for the individual organizations involved.

First-order change creates incremental, surface changes.
Second-order change questions underlying assumptions,
ultimately resulting in deep change.

The role of leaders in strategic partnerships is to create meaning for campus members that underscores why the partnership is important and how it supports organizational strategy. The creation of a shared understanding of the partnership helps everyone involved realize why it is important to support. In some cases, newly formed partners begin their first meetings by defining expectations and creating common language or terms

(Eddy, 2010b); in other cases leaders create more conceptual understandings about the new partnership. As with other forms of institutional actions, organizational leaders may frame to followers the work under way as strategic alignment after the fact. Irrespective of the timing of the framing, leaders create a vision of the future with the partnership for institutional members (Smircich & Morgan, 1982). How leaders help campus members make sense of the partnership influences reactions to campus commitment to the project and use of scarce resources.

How leaders frame the partnership creates ownership and buy-in for people beyond senior leaders, especially when leaders use communication networks that invite participation and are inclusive (Hickman, 2010). Typically, the type of communication found in traditional partnerships remains distinct for each partner. For example, a school partner may use the term *student*, whereas a business partner may refer to *employees*. Even though individuals may have multiple roles and be both a student and an employee, the language conveys different intentions. A strategic partnership may think instead of the student/employee as a key end user or client, which conveys a very different shared meaning.

Leaders frame change for stakeholders and create meaning for institutional staff.

The types of relationships involved in the two forms of partnerships also differ. Traditional partnerships, given their emergent nature, typically involve dyads and small groups and draw on social networks only peripherally invested in the partnership. This type of loose coupling (Weick, 1976) benefits the embryonic phase of partnership development as groups have more latitude because they are not tightly connected to organizational operations. Strategic partnership relationships include connections that are more central to organizational operations. Here the partnership goals are tied to the mission and vision of the partner organizations.

Partnership capital (Amey et al., 2010) can emerge from both traditional and strategic forms of partnerships. The creation of partnership capital occurs when the partners develop a set of shared norms, shared beliefs, and networking that aligns processes among individual collaborators. In the case of traditional partnerships, once created, this type of capital remains static and is easily diminished if partners change. Much like a bank account, once the partnership's capital is used up, no resources remain because nothing is being added. For strategic partnerships, however, partnership capital

TABLE 1.1
Typology of Partnership Definitions

Traditional Partnership	*Strategic Partnership*
• Individually driven [3] or top-down leadership [6] • Organizationally circumstantial [2] • Creates first-order change [5] • Builds on status quo [5] • Discrete and static partnership capital [7] • Technical communication; distinct [4] • Loose and small social networks not always tied to the partnership [3]	• Intentional leadership actions [6] • Tied to institutional goals or strategies [2] • Creates second-order change [5] • Capacity building [5] • Dynamic and blended partnership capital [7] • Multidisciplinary vocabulary [4] • Dense and central networks tied to partnership; thinking community [3]

is dynamic and changes over time due to deepening relationships, ties to organizational operations, and a strong foundation of shared norms. In this case, continuous additions are deposited into the partnership bank account. Table 1.1 outlines a typology for the definitions we ascribe to *traditional partnerships* and *strategic partnerships*. The numbers in brackets correspond with the chapter in this book that reviews the concept.

In this book, we established this typology to reflect central characteristics of collaborative work, though we recognize that these definitions exist on a continuum. We draw distinctions between traditional and strategic partnerships that represent the opposite end points of the range of factors. At the same time, we acknowledge that at any point, a partnership may or may not include all of these characteristics; as well, the characteristic may fall in various places across the continuum, and all members of the partnership may not view it similarly. We recognize the evolving nature of partnerships from traditional to strategic, and that some partnerships fall predominantly in one category or the other almost from the start.

It is also important to note that we see blurred definitions of *partnerships* often occurring as relationships and contexts change, partnerships develop, and individual leaders and members turn over. A partnership may have started quite by happenstance and over time, but grows into a key contribution (strategic partnership) for current organizational operations as a result of how the partnership helps achieve strategic objectives. Thus, there is a shift from a traditional partnership to a strategic partnership as the group's goals align with the organizations' strategies. Another partnership that initially met strategic goals may no longer be needed as organizational plans change;

however, if the initial partnership reformats to meet the new organizational strategy needs and vision, it might once again become strategic. Assumed in this scenario is ongoing attention to feedback loops and the partnership's ability to be nimble enough to accommodate shifting priorities. By now, an obvious point is that partnerships are dynamic in nature. The following cases are examples of both traditional and strategic partnerships to illustrate our definitions.

A Case of Traditional Partnering

An individual faculty member at a research university in the Midwest was a Fulbright scholar in Europe. The time he spent in the host country allowed him to build relationships with institutional leaders at his in-country university and with centrally located policymakers. As a result of these connections, the faculty member was able to reciprocate visits with members of the European university by hosting members on his U.S. campus. As well, he continued to make return trips to the host country to champion outreach activities and was able to bring another departmental faculty member along to help study the organizational and policy environment. Outcomes of this original individual interaction include faculty exchanges, creation of a comparative education course, and publications for the initial faculty member.

The traditional formation of this partnership builds on the initiation by a single faculty member that emphasizes a person-focused research agenda. Beyond the individual faculty member, there are inferred commitments by the faculty member's department and university. First, there are time demands, both for the individual involved and for coverage of duties in times of absence from the home institution. Second, there are pressures for institutional commitments to establish sister-school relationships, contribute resources for the joint project, and allocate energy to supporting the venture. Decisions like these are often made ad hoc without investigating how they align with the values and mission of the department or college and have long-term ramifications. In addition, because the project is so vested in an individual, when the person stops working in the area due to changes in research focus or retirement, the entire partnership is jeopardized.

Key Points

- This partnership was based predominantly on the social capital of the initial faculty member.
- The emerging partnership was not central to the U.S. university's departmental or college goals, so resources were not committed within

the annual budget and had to be acquired ad hoc to help support the initiative. In addition, adjuncts had to be hired to fill in for the faculty's absence.

- The partnership outcomes were not central to the vision of the department and took the faculty away from more critical projects.

A Case of Strategic Partnering

The Bologna Process spurred on institutional partnerships and collaborations due to its goal of providing seamless educational opportunities for students based on agreed-upon learning outcomes. This background enabled countries that signed the Bologna agreement to begin to address their systems of higher education and to question traditional patterns of operation. Recently, the Higher Education Authority in Ireland released its *National Strategy for Higher Education to 2030* report, commonly referred to as the Hunt Report (Higher Education Authority, 2011). This strategic plan promotes changes in a number of institutional operations, including teaching and learning, research, engagement with the wider society, internationalizing higher education, system governance with a coherent framework, and a sustainable and equitable funding model. In 2011 the Irish higher education system comprised 7 universities, 8 third-level colleges, and 17 institutes of technology (IoTs). The calls for the creation of a coherent framework of postsecondary education advocate for system-wide collaboration among institutions. In particular, the report points to the IoT sector's need to consolidate to achieve economies of scale. A new designation of technological university accommodates for these newly created types of institutions.

Dublin Institute of Technology (DIT) represents a unique case in the IoT system as this college sought university status in the past and now offers a range of degrees from certificates to doctorates. The push for a cluster model that pulls regional colleges into collaborations would have a newly envisioned technological university located in the Dublin area. The potential for designation as a technological university allows DIT a change of status, while also meeting national goals of consolidation. The other IoTs in Dublin would gain resources and leverage in a newly configured operation. The Hunt Report (Higher Education Authority, 2011) and subsequent policies from the Higher Education Authority of Ireland outline specific criteria for obtaining the newly designated status that reinforces the ultimate alignment of institutional goals and national priorities.

Key Points

- The *National Strategy for Higher Education to 2030* (Higher Education Authority, 2011) in Ireland recognizes the critical role of collaboration in the postsecondary system. The push for a coherent framework builds on achieving strategic objectives versus merely identifying saved resources.
- The overall move for consolidation recognizes the contributions of the diverse institutions but also acknowledges the need for economies of scale. Thus, partnerships will emerge rather than being mandated.
- The small size of the country results in a high level of familiarity and social capital among partners.

Organizational Change and Partnerships

We approach partnerships using a lens of organizational change. Essentially, change models look at the motivation for change, bringing people together, creating a plan, and, potentially, institutionalizing the initiative. Kotter and Cohen (2002) created a popular linear model of change that includes eight steps that they argue must be followed in order. These steps include creating a sense of urgency, building a guiding coalition, creating a vision, communicating the change vision, empowering broad-based action, generating short-term wins, not letting up, and making change stick. The concept of a force-field analysis (Lewin, 1951) uses the same premise of change, namely, unfreezing the current situation, moving, and refreezing in a new configuration or organizational operation. Partnerships often fail before reaching the final stage of making change permanent because one or more partners have achieved their goal and they bail on the collaboration as their needs have been met. In the end, no real organizational change occurs. What both of these change models fail to consider are the moving parts of the partnership, which involve individuals and organizations having different access to power and resources to support change; they also do not account for how the change initiative aligns with an institution's strategic goals. We argue that this alignment is most critical to the change process and helps distinguish strategic partnerships from their more traditional counterparts.

Collective or collaborative change practices, compared to first-order change built on individual actions, focus on institutionalized leadership and change practices, shared power and empowerment, and organizational learning (Hickman, 2010). A number of critical levers for collective change exist. First, leaders must frame change for others and, by doing so, may influence how others approach the proposed change. Second, the focus in these cases is not on a single leader at the top but rather on the roles of the systems or operations in the institution. The attention on the process moves thinking beyond what might advance a single individual and toward looking at the overall system. Finally, distributed leadership (Peterson, 1997) moves decision making to lower levels, at which the most information and knowledge is known about organizational processes. The lower levels are also the location of most decision and policy implementation. The ideal of collaborating for change does not imply that top-level leaders become irrelevant. Instead, these leaders serve as advocates and framers of the overall process, but they also allow champions of change to emerge from multiple levels and locations. Leaders as meaning makers help others interpret campus actions. This type of leadership provides ownership and buy-in for people beyond top-level leaders (Burns, 1978; Hickman, 2010).

Collaborative change practices create buy-in by sharing power—and responsibility

---

Change occurs along a continuum that ranges from incremental or surface change to deep or substantial change. "First-order changes are incremental and modifications that make sense within an established framework or method of operating. Second-order changes are modifications to the framework itself" (Bartunek & Moch, 1987, p. 484). Central to this concept is how feedback is used to help understand underlying systems of operation and to change these systems as required. Second-order change assumes that double-loop learning occurs (Argyris & Schön, 1978), meaning that participants challenge core assumptions and question underlying reasons for operations. This deep reflection represents a form of organizational learning (Argyris & Schön, 1996). According to Huber (1991), "An organizational entity learns if, through its processing of information, the range of its potential behaviors is changed and an organization learns if any of its units acquires knowledge that it recognizes as potentially useful to the organization" (p. 89). In strategic partnerships, we assume that organizational learning leads to second-order change because of the feedback process in which underlying structures and operations are questioned and new processes emerge due to the partnership. The incremental nature of change most typical in traditional partnerships is still change and results in advancement for one or more of the partners. But the level of first-order change does not result in substantive differences from business as usual, within either the partnership or the organizations of the individual partners.

More frequently, state and national policies require collaboration as part of mandates. At the heart of many policies is the desire to create change and to solve problems (Fowler, 2012). Yet, policy rarely articulates the type or range of change desired. In some respects, policymakers may intend for second-order change to occur, but the policy process instead outlines a protocol that only supports first-order change.

Policymakers have a number of tools at their disposal in creating policy, and the ultimate policy formation may differ depending on the goals. McDonnell and Elmore (1987) outlined four types of policy instruments used in practice: (a) mandates that result in compliance based on a set of regulations and rules; (b) inducements in the form of transactions to motivate particular outcomes (often, funding is the main inducement); (c) capacity building in which funding serves as an investment to expand either physical plant or human capital to achieve greater outcomes; or (d) system-changing actions in which authority among individuals and agencies is enhanced to change the system that delivers public goods and services (p. 134). Links are evident between the type of policy instrument used and the resulting form of change. Mandates and inducements are tools for transactional leadership actions (Burns, 1978), and once incentives are removed, the change ends (Kelman, 1961). Capacity-building and system-changing policy actions instead can help support longer-lasting and deeper levels of change. Having an awareness of these underlying linkages helps in better understanding the reasons behind policy formation and outcomes and the forms of partnerships created.

Policymakers seek change, but mandates rarely result in intended outcomes.

Increasingly, we also see international partners joining in college partnerships, yet institutional policies and plans are still emerging regarding these efforts. The desire to increase global competency of college graduates (Slimbach, 2010), to address global challenges (Selsky & Parker, 2005), and to create economies of scale and efficiency (Altbach & Knight, 2007) all drive seeking out international partners to meet these goals. Rationales for partnering abroad may emerge in traditional ways based on individual interest or happenstance opportunities. For instance, some partnerships start due to faculty research in another country (Amey, 2010) or interest in offering college programming to a wider market (Holland, 2010). Linking these individually driven motivations to partner to institutional goals

(Cooper & Mitsunaga, 2010) may result instead in a fundamental shift to operations or second-order change. Central to these differences are motivations for the initial partnership and the strategic goals of the institutions.

The metaphor of *matryoshka,* or nesting dolls, helps illustrate levels of change. One might envision the largest doll as representing the system or institution. Certain levels of change initiatives might emerge here, but, as is more likely, initiatives may be started by any of the smaller units within the matryoshka. If links only occur among lower levels in the system, deeper second-order change will not occur in the larger system. However, connections between the levels may allow ideas to be transmitted throughout the system, and in the process, feedback between the levels can result in questioning the underlying operations and the creation of organizational learning (Argyris & Schön, 1996).

Partnerships that are integrated into the fabric of the organization are more successful.

Morgan (2006) used the metaphor of the holographic brain to illustrate organizational learning. He argued that this "system has an ability to self-organize and regenerate itself on a continuous basis" (p. 97). The capability to rebuild is based on the following underlying principles: (a) build the whole into the parts; (b) importance of redundancy; (c) requisite variety; (d) minimum specs; and (e) learning to learn (pp. 99–112). The capacity to evolve and learn allows the feedback loops into the system a route to alter underlying patterns given new information from the environment. For partnerships, the metaphor is useful in understanding how individual partners at lower levels of operation are able to represent the larger culture of the organizational values and mission, but still bring in some variety, and to have more freedom for experimentation given the level of operation and the loose coupling (Weick, 1976) to the larger organization. Many traditional partnerships operate at this lower level. Strategic partnerships, on the other hand, begin at the larger organizational level and then become part of the lower holographic levels of operations, integrating the partnership concepts into the fabric of the system of operations. Critical to operations in practice is the context in which partnering occurs.

Context for Partnering

Partnerships occur within the dynamic environment of higher education. Long-standing collaboration between college teacher preparation programs and public schools, between school districts and colleges for dual enrollment, and between colleges and businesses showcase the benefits of partnering. Most of these arrangements, however, have built on traditional conceptions of partnering and have been limited in their reach to obtain fundamental change. The current economic climate and increased calls by the public for accountability in education change the rules of partnering and leading change (Hickman, 2010). Institutional leaders must consider how best to use the resources at their disposal as leverage for the greatest advantage (DiMaggio & Powell, 1983). Policymakers are increasingly flexing their influence via mandates and targeted funding opportunities (e.g., Race to the Top and the American Graduation Initiative) to require educational collaboration. The goal of obtaining more college graduates and the national completion agenda drives much of the conversation as well. Therefore, college leaders must make informed choices about how to approach partnership opportunities.

The context of partnering underscores differences in institutional resources and control of these resources, especially as institutions compete for resources, prestige, and legitimacy (DiMaggio & Powell, 1983). Yet, the presence of normative pressures—"keeping up with the Joneses"—also pushes for conformity. These pressures come in the form of coercive pressure (i.e., government regulations and mandates that must be followed); normative pressure (i.e., pressure to meet cultural norms or societal/organizational member expectations); and mimetic pressure (i.e., copying other institutional practices in a desire to conform) (DiMaggio & Powell, 1983). The control over resources (Pfeffer & Salancik, 1978) often affords power in the decision-making process. Thus, during the formation of partnerships, several competing variables are operating at the same time. On the one hand, institutions seek to keep up with their peers and increase prestige. On the other hand, individual partners operate within different contexts, which may have contrasting associated norms and expectations for operations. Further, access to needed resources is dependent upon who is involved in brokering the initial partnership and the level of institutional resources that are available.

Institutions seek partners to meet mandates, in search of prestige, or to keep pace with competitors.

Research on partnerships typically has been normed on domestic partnerships, but the global orientation of the world (Friedman, 2005) and the prospects of expanded educational markets (Levin, 2001) require consideration of international educational partnerships. Although different from domestic collaborations in many ways, cross-border collaborations are becoming more frequent and can be addressed using the strategic partnership principles that are the foundation of this text and the partnership model. Several public failures in the international arena (e.g., Michigan State University in Dubai, George Mason University in United Arab Emirates, Suffolk University in Senegal; Lane & Kinser, 2011) have made college leaders give more thought to how best to approach international partnering and underscore the need for more intentionality in these types of collaborations. The use of our strategic partnership model also applies to creating international partnerships, and examples throughout this volume highlight this application.

The context of partnering also contains a temporal element. Traditional partnerships have a time-bound nature. In this case, the partnership may dissolve once it has accomplished the original reason for partnering or when the initial champions for the partnership move on and the partnership has not been institutionalized enough to remain viable. A strategic partnership, however, is marked by the ability to remain viable even when key players move on. The social capital and relationships of the initial champion may not be replaced, but there is a skill set that others can replicate. New champions develop as a result of the embedding of the partnership in the organization's culture, and different social networks create expanded opportunities for collaborators.

Conflict always emerges within the context of partnering. Often, traditional partnerships are unable to weather these struggles and will disband. In strategic partnerships, some form of conflict negotiation is created to resolve issues. A shared sense of operations or created process helps forestall larger contentious problems. Thinking of a strategic partnership like a helix helps underscore the dynamic nature of these relationships. Conflict is accommodated in this view by the flexible nature of the process and a wider agreement about goals and values for the partnership. Feedback into the partnerships

Sustainable partnerships require continuous communication, environmental scanning, and attention to conflict resolution.

helps address conflicts or disagreements before they blow up. It is important to consider, however, the risk of strategic partnerships becoming routine and no longer addressing organizational strategies. If changes stop occurring within a strategic partnership, and the group no longer reacts to feedback that questions assumptions and accommodates changes in external contexts, the collaboration may be jeopardized. Therefore, central to sustainable partnering are participatory communication, attention to feedback, continuous environmental scanning, and a process for addressing conflict and change.

Strategic Partnership Model

Four important points underlie our argument for strategic partnerships. First, partnerships can be useful in achieving sound educational outcomes, can be of benefit to each organization involved, and can support student learning and program completion. Second, partnerships that are intentional in formation and goal alignment between partners operate differently from those built by happenstance. Third, leadership in strategic partnerships helps to create meaning for campus members by providing a framework that shows alignment with organizational strategy; this type of leadership provides ownership and buy-in for people other than senior leaders (Hickman, 2010; Peterson, 1997). Fourth, partnerships are often difficult to establish and sustain because of fundamental differences between educational organizations themselves (P–12 and higher education institutions) and with partners from other sectors (government, business, and nonprofit sectors). At the same time, it is possible to construct strategic alliances between sectors that appropriately address state and regional education needs when we understand the essential components of partnerships stimulated by public policies and the challenges faced when engaging in these activities.

We also present a theoretical model that lays out the development process for educational collaborations, incorporating the strategic partnership themes and resulting in a toolbox for those interested in partnering and leading organizational change. We will introduce a review of the three phases of the strategic partnership model, namely, pre-partnership, partnership development, and partnership capital (see Figure 1.1). In phase one, we focus on the role of antecedents and motivations for each partnering organization, reviewing reasons for joining with others, and factors to be considered in selecting viable prospective collaborators. In particular, we examine the contribution of individual social capital and power as they affect relationships created in the partnership. We also note the importance of considering organizational capital invested by the institutions linking together.

In phase two, what often begins with a formal process (e.g., contracts, external mandates) increasingly relies on a social process (trust, networks of relationships) as the partnership progresses and becomes more institutionalized. Trust among individuals within the partnership grows through interacting and obtaining mutual benefit. Presumably, this trust develops among sufficient numbers of individuals to sustain the activity and form a kind of social network attributable to the partnership. Over time, the rigidity of a formal partnership contract gives way to a more informal and flexible working relationship that is likely to weather the need for ongoing negotiation and changes characteristic of developing organizations (Todeva & Knoke, 2005). Another key element during the development stage is institutional

Figure 1.1 Strategic partnership model

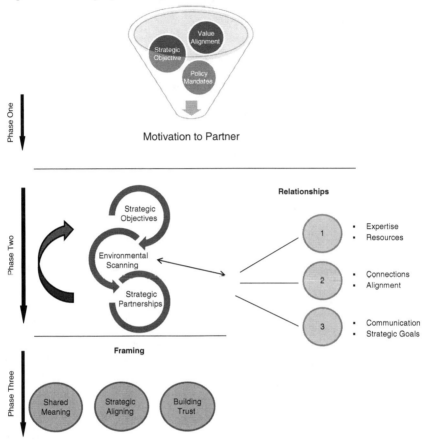

compatibility. When P–12 and higher education systems try to work together, one consideration is the norms and culture of the faculty and P–12 staff who control the curriculum, the level of governing board oversight, and the organizational structure that may affect decision making. Likewise, partnerships between colleges and business or community associations often have to address different cultures and organizational processes to establish more productive and effective working relationships.

Finally, in phase three, the partnership model evolves and creates partnership capital. By partnership capital, we mean the existence of shared norms, shared beliefs, and networking that align processes among individual collaborators. Each arrangement may not result in partnership capital, but if the goal is for an educational collaboration to be sustained over time, amid competing priorities, different cultures, reward systems, decision-making structures, or challenging environments, we believe partnership capital is fundamental to achieving this end. Therefore, we present our perspective on partnership capital, how it is formed, how it works, and its benefits and drawbacks to organizational collaboration as a critical next step in cultivating effective partnerships.

Summary Points

- Partnerships are becoming increasingly critical to campus operations.
- Traditional and strategic partnerships differ in terms of the initial motivations and intentions.
- Traditional partnerships based on individuals historically have had limited shelf lives and long-term sustainability.
- Strategic partnerships differ from traditional partnerships in the rationale for startup. Strategic partnerships require goals aligned with institutional mission and vision. Intentionality and alignment are cornerstone features of strategic partnerships, which provide greater leverage for change.
- Change occurs in both forms of partnerships, but the type of change differs. Traditional partnerships create first-order (surface) change, whereas strategic partnerships create second-order (deep) change.

CASE #1: A VIEW FROM THE BALCONY

The position held in the organization influences the view one has of potential partnerships. Faculty members desiring to partner look for collaborators that help advance their research interests and projects, whereas upper-level leaders must contend with choices among competing opportunities. Dr. Scott Hendrickson is the new vice provost of international affairs at Founders College, a mid-size liberal arts college. Hendrickson is the first person to fill this new position. Traditionally, the leadership role in the international office was filled by a faculty director on a three-year rotating basis. Over time, international work expanded beyond the traditional study-abroad trips to include programs that brought international faculty and students to campus for both short- and long-term projects. In fact, the recent university strategic plan listed internationalization of the campus as one of its six goals. The demand for faculty grants for international work was on the upswing as more of the national dialogue turned to graduating global citizens and internationalizing the campus. Factions on campus argued over who had access to this funding and how decisions were made regarding programming, and they operated under the perception that there was money "hidden" in the office. In addition, the lack of coordination of programming and events meant that even faculty in the same department did not know when someone invited in a visiting scholar or was working with partners in another country.

Hendrickson knew he was in for some challenges during his interview. In the small group meetings with faculty from across campus, he was peppered with questions about how he was going to make decisions, whether this new role meant that faculty were losing a voice in the process, and how he was going to reconcile perceived injustices. The provost was clear in his charge regarding the role of the new vice provost—the new leader must bring together all programming under one umbrella. No area "owned" international work or the traditional study-abroad programs.

The first action Hendrickson took was to create an advisory committee. This committee included members from across campus—some of whom were elected by their areas, others were chosen by area deans. The second activity Hendrickson undertook was visiting with each of the college's three deans to determine their vision for international work on campus. He was savvy enough to realize early on that a handful of faculty held strong informal power on campus, and he worked with them to determine their goals and to understand their perspectives. He quickly learned how past committees investigated what was needed to strengthen internationalization and how the final reports gathered dust on a shelf, only to be pulled off every few years and updated.

Against this internal backdrop were increased opportunities to partner around the world. Individual faculty work in Southeast Asia created a platform for work in India. When the Obama-Singh grant initiative was accepting proposals, this group wanted to put together a program to partner with some colleges in India. Yet, little historical relationship existed beyond personal faculty connections. Another group wanted to work in China to create a joint degree program. The Hispanic Studies program wanted to expand its study-abroad program in South America, in particular; as Brazil was offering funding for student and faculty exchanges, the program wanted to jump at this opportunity. Finally, the business and education programs were clamoring to offer international experiences for their students, many of whom were adult learners in graduate degree programs. Because of the historic lack of attention to its needs in the past, the business school created its own infrastructure for programming and faculty members were skeptical about the efforts to centralize administration of international programming.

After six months on the job, Hendrickson was pondering his options. He now had a better idea of the funding available for various initiatives, he knew the players on campus, and he had a sense of the international stage. He faced some tough choices. How was he going to maintain some of the historic programming partnerships that were no longer moneymakers but were important to the undergraduate curriculum? He was deluged almost daily by offers of international partnerships. What were the most important to pursue? Because of his conversations across campus, he knew there were faculty members and programs with shared interests in a region but with no awareness of what the others were doing. The provost just asked for next year's strategic plan for the international office. Hendrickson started writing.

Case Questions

- How can existing partnerships be best leveraged to lead to partnerships that would benefit more areas of the college?
- How might the college's strategic objectives drive decision making for international partnerships?
- How do the internal barriers to collaboration influence the type of international partnerships sought?
- What tactics might leaders use to help others understand the "big picture" of choices for institutions?
- How does framing by leaders help campus members accept final decisions that may not include a place for them at the table?
- How can some traditional partnerships transition to strategic partnerships? What forums are required to get campus members to question underlying assumptions?

2

PARTNERSHIP MOTIVATIONS
AND ROLES

Various rationales for partnering ground emerging partnerships (Baus & Ramsbottom, 1999; Tedrow & Mabokela, 2007). As such, the motivations leading individuals and organizations to partner may influence the staying power of the collaboration. In some instances, finding the right partners depends on shared understanding of goals and outcomes (Gardner, 2011). Traditional partnerships, on the one hand, are organizationally circumstantial and not necessarily tied to long-term institutional goals other than by happenstance. In this case, the motivation to partner is contextual and localized with individuals as opposed to linked to institutional goals. For example, a new request for proposals stipulates that funding is contingent on individuals or groups partnering. Or existing relationships or friendships might create situations ripe for partnering because of the desire to work together on a project. In strategic partnerships, on the other hand, partnerships are tied to institutional goals or strategies (Barnes, 2011a; Gardner, 2011). Here, particular motivations align for more successful outcomes in which relationships can be fostered and the goals of the partnership are intentionally linked with college priorities. The desire to fulfill institutional goals and mission motivates how partners are sought for strategic partnership.

Reflecting on motivations to partner helps uncover some initial assumptions about the partnership and begins to lay the groundwork for anticipated outcomes. Questions to ask at the initial stage of partnership formation are made both at an individual level and at a collective organizational level. Some of these preliminary questions may include:

- What do we hope to get out of this partnership?
- What do we need in a partner to help us achieve our goals?
- Are we hoping to reach short-term goals?
- Are we hoping to obtain strategic objectives?
- Can we achieve these goals with one partner or are multiple partners beneficial?
- What does an environmental scan show regarding potential partners?
- What are the motivations of these potential partners?

We group the motivations behind partnerships into four themes, each of which involves particular roles for leaders and operates differently depending on context and organizational mission. The four themes are:

1. economic goals
2. policy mandates
3. value alignment
4. strategic leadership

First, economic goals for the development of projects (Kearney & others, 2007) and available funding drive the creation of many partnerships (Gazley & Brudney, 2007), particularly in traditional models. Included in this arena are ways for partners to share resources to create economies of scale (Daniel, 2002) or to aid in the economic development of a region or country (Fluharty, 2007). International partnerships, responses to national or state grant availability, and institutional budget cuts all instigate the desire to work with others. Second, mandates and policy initiatives often frame how partnerships develop. Currently, a focus on persistence and increasing graduation rates pushes institutions to reflect critically on the options they have to succeed in obtaining these objectives. The interconnectivity between P–12 and higher education provides a natural starting point for partnering opportunities to achieve these outside benchmarks and demands (Rochford, O'Neill, Gelb, & Ross, 2005, 2007).

Leaders initiating partnerships due to economic motivations or mandates typically view outcomes as meeting short-term needs.

Third, goals and values motivate individuals and organizations to partner (Connolly, Jones, & Jones, 2007). Sharing fundamental guiding principles, on both a personal and institutional level, creates an environment in which alignment comes more readily as partners operate with the same cultural understanding, have similar goals, and generate less conflict due to their shared understandings (Kruss, 2006). Desires to partner based on these underlying similarities are particularly important in strategic partnerships that intentionally look to connect strategic missions; for instance, possessing the common goals of access and student learning can create a platform ripe for working together. Finally, institutional priorities motivate leaders to look outward to other organizational partners that can support these objectives (Hickman, 2010). Individuals can be strategic leaders and provide the source of motivation to institutions to look outward and seek particular types of partners (Peterson, 1997). Seeking partners in this fashion requires a clear understanding of internal priorities and an awareness of potential partners that share or complement these positions.

> Leaders initiating partnerships due to value alignment or strategic goals are able to connect to individuals and the collective, creating the opportunity for transformational changes.

Precursors to Partnering—Phase 1

The context in which partnering occurs influences not only the formation of the partnerships, but also sets the foundation for sustainability or long-term viability of the initiative (Barnes, 2011b). What often begins as an individually driven, informal relationship mushrooms into larger projects with institutional commitment resulting in dedication of resources to the project. Here, "the challenge lies in translating these formal expressions of collegiality into vibrant, meaningful, and lasting partnerships that contribute to the core missions of both institutions" (Barnes, 2011b, p. 178). Understanding more about the initial motivations behind partnering contributes to planning tactics to make the partnership long-lasting. As outlined earlier, the following sections focus on four rationales for partnering, namely, economic goals, policy mandates, value alignment, and strategic leadership.

Economic Goals

A central motivator for partnering is sharing resources to save money and create efficiencies. Philadelphia serves as an example of one large-scale partnership effort based on economics. The superintendent of the public school system advocated for sharing facilities and resources when he required, as part of his reform effort, that all schools connect with community-based organizations, and he campaigned to bring more volunteers into the schools. One such effort linked public schools and religious institutions (Mundell, 2003). Here, volunteers were sought from the religious community to fill roles in the schools to support student learning and to address shortages in teaching staff due to budget cuts. The schools gained human resources to fulfill their mission of educating students and the volunteers connected students with the community and community-based programs. Yet, the reliance on volunteers in this relationship makes longer-term sustainability of the program questionable. As well, a new leader in Philadelphia may focus efforts on another initiative and this traditional partnership may founder.

Colleges also increasingly look abroad when thinking of ways to contribute to the bottom line. A collaboration between Houston Community College and the Qatari government built on the need to train a skilled workforce in the Middle East (Violino, 2011). The college gained in providing coursework and training to businesses overseas, and the foreign country benefited by acquiring training resources that were not available in Qatar. This new arrangement for partnering, however, is not viable for all colleges. Even when resources are the root of other countries seeking to partner with a U.S.-based institution, there is an assumption that a certain resource base and institutional capacity exists that makes the college look more attractive to an international audience.

A central motivator for partnering is sharing resources to save money and create efficiencies.

As universities seek to increase their revenue streams, different forms of contract training or continuing education programs help to accomplish this goal as well as meeting community and business training needs (Stevens, 2010). Community colleges have a long history of providing communities with cost-effective training that also adds revenues to the college. For example, a partnership between a community college system and a state-extended health care industry was motivated by the desire to share resources (Correia, 2010). In this case, the partners communicated via face-to-face meetings and created a distinct organizational structure for the new partnership in which they used a variety of data to monitor outcomes, all of which contributed to the success of the partnership.

Abramo, D'Angelo, and Di Costa (2011) analyzed universities' capability for collaboration with industry as a function of size, location, and research quality and found that the research quality of universities had a greater impact than did the geographic distance between the university and business on the capability for collaborating with industry. Thus, in thinking of economic development and resource connections, institutions with less capability need to look more in their immediate community environment for partners, whereas research universities with higher prestige and research abilities may cast a wider net to locate compatible partners. Research institutions can use this advantage for strategic selection of partners in a different way from other institution types.

Location matters when identifying potential partners. Institutions with less capability need to look closer to home, whereas more prestigious institutions have a wider range of options.

Universities in Australia are increasingly turning to partnerships with industry in response to the relative decline in federal government funding of higher education. The Australian Research Council (ARC) Linkage Projects, an organization that brokers partnerships with researchers and external stakeholders, provides examples of collaborations created for economic reasons (Berman, 2008). Many of the emerging partnerships started at an individual level where academics maintained contact with a former graduate student or postdoctoral fellow who ultimately obtained a senior position in a public or private company. Additional connections resulted when academic researchers approached companies with research proposals. However, very few of these partnerships were successful unless there was a history of contact at an individual level.

In the ARC, the university entered into these partnerships seeking economic support for research, whereas the industry partner's interest in research was ultimately linked to achieving commercial success. Further benefits to businesses included opportunities to scout future employees, value to the community, and enhancement of public image (Berman, 2008). The resulting innovative research supported both the university academics and the business partners. Yet, challenges emerged due to the mismatch of organizational structures and inherent university bureaucracies that impeded the quick turnaround industry required. As with other cross-sector partnerships, bridging the cultural divide requires higher education institutions to forgo some of their traditional academic practices and to become more flexible (Andrews & Entwistle, 2010). Likewise, business partners must recognize that the academic culture results in a particular reward system for faculty and administrators that does not align with the reward system in a for-profit workplace.

Time also presented a challenge as academics were not as familiar with the need for fast turnaround for project completion as their industry partners were. Here, researchers focused more on knowledge building, but industry partners were vested in moving final products to commercial venues. The lack of consistent and frequent communication between partners also created problems. The written products produced disconnects as academic writing and scholarly approaches held little value for business application. The initial motivation to partner to achieve economic benefits was strained by the cultural divide between academics and industry.

Cross-sector partnerships may encounter a cultural divide that, without intervention, can sow the seeds for ultimate failure.

We can draw several conclusions from the example in Australia in which economic motivations provided the impetus for partnering (Berman, 2008). First, the most successful collaborations were based on long-standing individual relationships. In this case, relationships were at the core of the ability to build effective partnerships. Second, incremental successes led to increased trust over time, which resulted in increased funding. Here, relationships developed and trust built, given the amount of time the partners spent on the projects. Third, even though economic reasons drove partners to collaborate, different underlying values and goals for the partnership created strain. What the university valued and rewarded differed from the reward structure in business that was built on profits. The divide between the operational cultures of academics and business created tensions that contributed to partnership failure.

Cross-sector partnerships all involve some of the same fit and sustainability concerns. Traditional forms of consortia originally focused on improving institutional efficiency by sharing resources and services, whereas current consortia often emphasize improving effectiveness by encouraging innovation (Forcier, 2011). Here, resource and economic drivers may provide the starting point for motivation, but outcomes may change to create joint innovations and partnership capital. Thus, partnerships that start based on economic motivations may evolve to form different relationships over time, which assumes that the partners understand and agree to the differences. When partnerships are strictly motivated by economic savings or facilities sharing, once the financial health of one of the partners improves, the original reason for partnering may no longer be relevant and the partnership may dissolve (Eddy, 2007).

Figuring out planning strategies when economics motivate the partners requires answering the following types of questions:

- What is the cost benefit for us to engage in this partnership?
- Does this partnership meet only short-term resource issues, or might it contribute to long-term strategic goals?
- What does this partnership commit us to over time?
- Am I in a position to make the commitment to partner?
- What existing relationships exist between or among the potential partners?
- What are the goals for each partner in the collaboration?
- What, if any, history exists among the partners?

Policy Mandates

Policy formation is a dynamic activity built on values and ideological perspectives with the ultimate goal to address a public problem (Fowler, 2012). As noted in chapter 1, there are a variety of policy instruments used that range from mandates and rules dictating behavior to changes to the underlying system and operations (McDonnell & Elmore, 1987). In addressing challenges, institutions may seek partners to fulfill the obligations of policies or the policies themselves may require collaborations. Public sector education, in particular K–12 education, has a long history of reform efforts, notably with the publication of *A Nation at Risk* (National Commission on Excellence in Education, 1983). Increasingly, calls for accountability have moved into the domain of higher education (Lumina Foundation, 2012; U.S. Department of Education, 2006). This section reviews some of the ways in which policy motivates individuals and organizations to partner.

Preparation of quality teachers was a cornerstone of educational reform in the policy of No Child Left Behind (2002). Research highlights how better trained teachers create a learning environment in which students obtain higher evaluation outcomes (Cochran-Smith, 2005). One strategy to better educate classroom teachers relies on partnerships with university schools of education. Yet, actual transformation of educating practices often does not occur or become sustainable. Two decades of professional development school research (Yendol-Hoppey, 2010) found that merely mandating a requirement to hire qualified teachers did not change the system of teacher preparation. Disconnects still exist among the classroom, student outcomes, and university training; yet, institutional change focused on improving teacher preparation remains and brings hope. Professional development schools (PDS) provide a great example of a partnership that may have outlived its utility as the fad of this format of connecting educational institutions passed. Once the reward structures created by the policy ended, there was not enough institutionalized into the school systems to keep these partnerships viable. A more recent version of PDS is found in the San Francisco Teacher Residency (SFTR) program, which represents a partnership among the San Francisco Unified School District, the University of San Francisco, Stanford University, the United Educators of San Francisco, the San Francisco Education Fund, and AmeriCorps (see www.usfca.edu/soe/programs/ted/teacher_residency). This residency program is similar to that in the medical profession in which teacher candidates apprentice with master teachers and university academics to learn best practices for success in low-performing school districts and in tough subject areas like math and science.

Policy mandates seldom achieve their targeted objectives or changes to the system.

Predating the focus of No Child Left Behind (NCLB) on teacher preparation was a program in Connecticut to promote partnerships (Bliss & Lisi, 1990). In 1987, Connecticut's Department of Higher Education established the Institute for Effective Teaching (IET) to promote the state's teacher preparation programs. That same year, Connecticut State University's Center for Educational Excellence (CEE) was founded. Both organizations supported and funded partnership activities. In 1989, IET and CEE collected data on the partnerships that revealed that only a third of the institutions covered by the new policy in Connecticut had working partnerships (Bliss & Lisi, 1990). One of the promising partnerships was between Hillhouse High School in New Haven and Yale University. Hillhouse High School was one of four magnet schools funded in 1989 by the U.S. Department of Education. It was designated the International Studies magnet school with the objectives of providing a curriculum in three languages—Chinese, Japanese, and Russian—and promoting voluntary desegregation. Despite some early successes, the act was repealed in 2011.

On the student side of the educational spectrum, Kansas changed admission requirements for resident high school students to attend one of the six public institutions in the state (K.A.R. 88-Article 29); historically, the state legislated open access to all public universities for all graduates of Kansas high schools. The increased admission standards translated to some students' not meeting admission criteria to start in one of the state's public four-year universities. Pittsburg State University (PSU) and Fort Scott Community College (FSCC) overcame historic barriers of four-year and two-year college collaborations and instituted a program at PSU in which FSCC courses were offered, enabling local students to travel less and get a start on their education at the community college level even when there was no two-year college in the local community (Tatro & Hodson, 2011). This program generated more credit-hour production at the college and had a positive economic impact on both communities.

Changes in policy often shift the playing field and create new requirements, which can result in organizations partnering to build bridges and pathways for student success.

Another area of policy oversight includes the preparation of school administrators in university programs. Kentucky instituted a new policy regarding principal preparation programs administered by the Education Professional Standards Board (16 KAR 5:020); this policy created a mandate regarding the partnership between university programs and school districts. Historically, mutual need and benefit drove institutions to partner. Institutionalization of the new requirement regarding program accreditation brings a new dynamic to the partnerships that are now mandated (Browne-Ferrigno, 2011). Buy-in to the process may be influenced by the required feature of the policy instead of the organic nature of partnering in the past. Rules now govern how institutions partner; however, so little time has elapsed since implementation of the new requirement that outcomes remain unknown.

State and federal policymakers create policies in an effort to motivate change, address public community issues, and regulate programming. The Canadian system of higher education traditionally was separated into discrete sectors, with two-year colleges and universities having few students moving between them. In 1996, the Ontario Ministry of Training, Colleges, and

Universities created the College-University Consortium Council (CUCC) to promote and coordinate more collaboration among the educational sectors (Monahan, 2004). An outgrowth of this push for collaboration was shared programs for nursing education. Despite some success in the collaborative efforts, Kirby (2007) documented the challenges inherent in the initiative. He noted that areas of contention concerned program accreditation, effective governance, student admissions, interpersonal relationships, program funding, and faculty roles. The combined use of mandates and inducements in this instance resulted in some positive outcomes, but long-term viability is questionable (Kirby, 2007). This traditional partnership model shows that change resulted, but that underlying organizational cultural differences were not addressed to allow for deeper change to occur.

Traditional partnerships can exhibit short-term results as a result of policy mandates, but when underlying organizational cultural differences are not addressed, deeper change does not occur.

The context of policy implementation matters as urban and rural communities differ in resources, challenges, and community needs. Often, rural colleges are a major employer in the region and an engine for community development and change (Miller & Kissinger, 2007). Chesson and Rubin (2003) argue that state policy can take advantage of rural community colleges to promote economic development and small-business assistance. Specifically, they advocate for states to create policies removing barriers to education by keeping costs low, better preparing low-income youth for college, supporting student diversity, and ensuring funding to colleges for adequate staffing and support of developmental education and basic literacy. In urban settings, educational institutions may still be major employers and engines for community development and change, but the array of potential partners may be more abundant.

Policy creation occurs due to the public definition of issues and the legislative formation of a policy agenda. Yet, educational leaders are not among the biggest lobbyists in putting forth the issues that are most important to them (Fowler, 2012). The Brookings Institution found that only 1.4% of news articles deal with educational issues (Dionne, West, & Whitehurst, 2009). This low rate of coverage signifies two main points: One, the public has scant information or background on the work occurring within the education sector; and, two, educators are not getting their story out to the public or using media to help frame their message. Thus, if colleges and universities hope to have an impact on policy creation, more engagement in the process and highlighting links between the work of colleges and state problems is critical (Weerts & University of Wisconsin, 2011).

If colleges and universities hope to have an impact on policy creation, they must become more engaged in the process and emphasize links between their work and solving state problems.

Policy mandates do not always translate into practice in the ways intended or result in anticipated impact on practice. The level of implementation of policy influences actions. Thus, success of mandates is driven by actions from individuals and leaders embracing and committing to change. How individuals are rewarded for their involvement in implementing policies can influence the success of the mandates. In general, funding is an inducement to follow mandates (Fowler, 2012). But the greatest factor influencing implementation of policies is when the goals of the mandated partnership align with the university's mission. In this case, multiple forms of motivation help assure that the changes stick.

Particular questions are raised in determining whether it is best to link up with partners and in picking those partners when policies figure into decisions to partner. The following types of questions emerge:

- What types of rewards are in the policy mandate to partner?
- If the policy requires a partnership, can we easily build on an existing arrangement?
- How central is the required partnership to our core operations or long-term goals?
- Does the policy create enhanced capacity for our organization?
- How does the policy change any of our existing systems? What are the repercussions of these changes?
- How will we pick a partner based on the policy requirements?

Value Alignment

When organizations have similar missions, core values, and goals, a coalition is easier to create as partners have a shared ethos and partnering requires little change from their standard forms of operation and understandings of mission. As opposed to partners that may complement one another's strengths, partnerships built on value alignment reinforce the status quo and allow quicker progress and partnership formation because of shared understandings of concepts and objectives. The caution here is to avoid getting stuck with the status quo and to question processes or be open to changes. Sharing a common starting place regarding direction of the project and seeking similar goals places these partnerships on firmer ground (Cooper & Mitsunaga, 2010). Common goals may coalesce around issues concerning student learning (Eckel & Hartley, 2008; Hebel, 2007), service learning (Sandy & Holland, 2006), community engagement (Moore, 2008), and shared research areas (Eddy, 2010a).

Shared values and common goals among partners provide a jumpstart for new partnerships. Yet, getting stuck in the status quo is a risk.

Partnerships may help support academic curricula. Eckel and Hartley (2008) investigated curricular joint ventures of three different alliances and identified four factors supporting coordination, namely: "(a) identifying partners, (b) developing and delivering the curriculum, (c) making operational decisions and resolving emergent conflicts, and (d) balancing individual and collective partner interests" (pp. 623–624). Building partnerships on shared objectives resulted in better outcomes in their case study, as did personal face-to-face interactions among partners. Developing a sense of collective identity, what we would call partnership capital, created a space in which conflicts over individual partner needs versus collective needs could be negotiated. Another example of a curricular-driven partnership involved various colleges and the Green Power Partnership (GPP). Here, the involved campuses had high levels of awareness for the environment as evidenced by strong environmental academic programs and sustainability efforts on campus (Ghosh, 2011). This shared value of concern for environmental issues helped jump-start these partnerships. Social justice issues provide another venue to partner around shared values. One example of this involved the partnership between Catholic Relief Services and Cabrini College (Laver, 2008). Here, Cabrini created a social justice–centered curriculum that helped provide opportunity for authentic student learning via the connections with Catholic Relief Services.

In all of these examples of curriculum-based partnerships, there was a shared interest around a particular issue that aligned the institutions involved to seek similar outcomes. Often in these situations, individual partners are

familiar with one another given their shared interest in a topic, thus beginning the partnership with a level of trust and shared vision.

Value alignment around partnering builds on shared interests and
creates levels of initial trust that can be leveraged for partnership
changes.

Service-learning opportunities provide another gateway for colleges to
partner with community organizations. As with partnerships built on curricular issues, a commitment to student learning is central to these arrangements. Yet, bridging academic and agency cultures is still required (Sandy &
Holland, 2006). Understanding more about the individual organizational
cultures aids in knowing what each holds as norms (Helms Mills & Mills,
2000). Eckel and Hartley (2008) used a social rules system framework for
their research on alliances, which allowed closer examination of "the development of rules that reconcile the organizational values and cultural assumptions of the partners" (p. 617). Yet, in practice, individuals involved in
emerging partnerships rarely probe into these assumptions or recognize the
underlying tensions created when cultural assumptions differ.

The issue of differences in culture was highlighted in Maletzke's (2009)
research of U.S. universities and USAID that sought to support foreign assistance policies. Maletzke found that the partners were motivated by more
than monetary support or project outcomes; instead, common philosophical
values drew them together. Yet, despite these strong relationships, barriers to
success emerged due to lack of institutional understanding about the project
and misalignment of bureaucratic systems in the partnering organizations.

Even when shared values and goals are evident among partners, differences in organizational culture and histories can create barriers.

A common area of interest for collaboration by community stakeholders,
industry employers, public education leaders, and colleges is student access
as a pathway to higher education. The use of technology to enhance student access to education and as a teaching tool can create a common platform for colleges and universities to build collaborative partnerships. Comrie
(2011) argues that edgeless universities offer more flexibility and efficiencies.
Borders and boundaries challenge the formation of partnerships, but when

colleges become more flexible and their systems more permeable, barriers to partnering dissolve. Comrie's (2011) research on the Edinburgh, Lothians, Fife and Borders Regional Articulation Hub (ELRAH) found that adaptive institutions that engage staff in collaborative curriculum development and have strong leadership had better outcomes for students. The ideal of adaptive approaches harkens to Heifetz's (1994) notion of leaders creating space to foster innovation and different approaches to problem solving.

Partnerships created in rural locations often are built on shared needs to create economies of scale and a shared ethos of rural living. Laferriere et al. (2010) reported on an initiative of the Ministry of Education in the province of Quebec, Canada, that funded a partnership of three universities and 50 rural schools in 13 sites. The purpose of the initiative was to strengthen the village schools that were struggling with low enrollment and closures.

The partnership was initiated by a university faculty member who presented the idea of rural networked schools to a knowledge transfer firm that already had connections with the Ministry of Education (Laferriere et al., 2010). The proposed partnership aligned with the Ministry of Education's vision for an innovative approach to the problem of equal opportunity facing the rural schools in the province and the project commenced with government funds. The partnership progressed over four phases. The success of phase one led to increased funding and expansion of the initiative. One significant development was that teachers from different schools who had previously been working in isolation started using technology to form teams and establish collaborative links. Reflection on action was undertaken in pairs, and in some cases databases for reflection were created. Research results were compiled primarily at the classroom level, and organizational change was studied at the school and school district levels (Laferriere et al., 2010).

Technology can bring together a wider range of options for selection of partners and can help build trust due to increased electronic communication venues.

The three-way school-university-government partnership in Canada was effective because each partner played a role in helping the others and contributed to a knowledge-building community. In addition, the alignment of the visions of the schools and university fit into the Ministry of Education's goals. The government was responsible for providing the resources and direction, and the university participants conducted teaching and research activities both on-site and online. Communication among partners was enhanced using technology for both synchronous and asynchronous connections. The multiple phases of the project allowed for feedback to occur that improved processes and created opportunities for organizational learning within the partnership. A shared vision of knowledge building for students and creating support for rural school districts was critical for partnership buy-in.

Central to value alignment as a motivating force to partner is discovering overlapping areas of common ground among potential partners. A visualization of this concept is a Venn diagram, which can show the areas of common interests among multiple stakeholders. Support and improvement of local communities provides one motivation for partners that builds on shared values. Even though value alignment provides a shared starting point for each organization, it does not mean that success is automatic. Attention to cultural differences and individualized administrative operations becomes critical to smooth operations. Conflict is inevitable when working with others, thus making early conversations about governance for the newly created partnership important (Eckel & Hartley, 2008). Protocols are needed to address differences and to create a partnership identity that helps to ameliorate situations when the demands of the individual institutions compete with the partnership ambitions (Amey et al., 2010).

Partners motivated to work with others based on shared values and program desires begin from a point of strength, yet this feature alone does not assure long-term success. Questions that emerge for partners who feel they are starting from a place of value alignment include:

- How do we *know* that our values really align with those of a potential partner?
- What evidence or history of working together supports our feeling of value alignment?
- Despite agreement regarding overarching goals for the partnership, do our institutional cultures and frameworks align as well?
- What type of partnership governance is required to support the new collaboration? How does this structure align with the protocols and operational procedures of each partner's organization?
- How can technology help identify partners with shared interests? How can technology support future communication venues?
- How does each partner define its shared values? For example, if our institution states that it values social justice, how does our meaning of social justice align with those of our potential partner?

Strategic Leadership

Organizational leaders may seek to form partnerships to advance the institution's mission and to retain or enhance competitive advantage. Strategic leadership can be the motivating force behind a partnership in that individual institutional leaders encourage matches. Partnerships aid in creating organizational change, and change may result from presidential vision, internal pressures, or external dictates (Astin & Astin, 2000). Presidential vision may provide the motivation to link institutional strategic plans with particular types of partnering opportunities.

Leaders can use the institution's strategic plan as a means to determine which partnerships best help meet the goals.

Links to the institution's strategic plan may start with top-level leaders, but others in the institution may act on this strategy as well. College faculty members prove to be natural collaborators given their role in knowledge building and connections within institutions. For instance, Burriss (2010) describes a partnership that created a curricular joint venture that "connects disciplines and creates collaborations important to academia, industry, and knowledge-driven economic development" (p. v). In this case, the connections drew on curriculum as a source of similar values (Eckel & Hartley, 2008), but the motivations moved beyond this to become strategic as the partnership helped the individual players accomplish institutional strategic goals and build on shared values. The teaming was strategic in that neither institution could do this alone.

Partnerships add synergy as individual organizations cannot reach their goals alone.

Increasingly, international initiatives are becoming embedded in the strategic direction of colleges and universities (e.g., Kalamazoo College, Beloit College, University of Maryland). These initiatives can vary from a desire for all graduates to have an international experience to internationalization of the curriculum to offering joint degrees with institutions in other countries.

The awareness that it is critical to increase global competency in college graduates (Koprucu, 2009) provides one venue to operationalize strategic leadership. The options for partnering may coalesce around travel via study abroad to partnering with international colleges to hosting visiting faculty to developing joint degrees. Here, the central element is that the partnership develops given the strategic direction of the college.

Like international initiatives, concerns over environmental issues address global challenges. The Illinois Council of Community College Presidents built on the early success of some of its campuses with programs focusing on environmental sustainability. Early small-scale collaborations among three founding community colleges have grown to include all 48 community colleges in the state and are coordinated through the Illinois Green Economy Network (IGEN). Four areas of focus include green campuses, green communities, green curricula, and green workforce development. The strategic leadership of the council recognized an area of potential growth and an opportunity to partner not just among the community colleges in the state, but also with community, industry, and workforce development. Forming a network creates a neutral organization to coordinate efforts of all partners and helps provide structural support for activities and an entity with no affiliation with any one college.

Partners may create an auxiliary organization and structure to fulfill the ambitions of the partnership, and this new entity creates a neutral space that better supports change.

Individual college presidents may lead the efforts to support partnerships to advance strategic goals, or institutional members may recognize that their work can support overall institutional objectives by their pursuing particular partnership options (Astin & Astin, 2000). The difference inherent in strategic leadership providing the motivation to partner is that the partnership has a built-in connection to mission and planning to achieve goals and has upper-level leadership buy-in.

When strategic leadership provides the motivation to partner, a particular set of guiding questions proves useful. Questions that emerge include:

- How does this partnership help us obtain our strategic objectives?
- What type of environmental scanning and vetting needs to occur to assess potential partners?
- How do we assess which partners hold the greatest option for long-term success?

- If I am a mid-level leader, how do I advocate for a partnership with upper-level leaders that highlights the links to our strategic objectives?
- How are judgments on whether to partner evaluated based on strategic leadership?
- What assures that strategic leadership guiding the decision to partner really meets the needs of the organization, not just the needs of the leader?

Summary

Each of the motivating factors outlined in this section provides a different impetus to form partnerships, but each has a different starting point and consideration of short- or long-term viability. Moreover, *who* is making the decision to partner matters in terms of access to decision-making power, control of resources, and ability to obtain institutional buy-in. Taking time to ask questions in the formation stage becomes critical.

Roles Within Partnerships

Regardless of the reasons behind forming partnerships, a number of different roles emerge during the process. First, individuals hold distinct roles within their home institutions and these positions are located all along the hierarchical reporting chain. Associated with the responsibilities of their "day job" are a set of job functions, responsibilities, and obligations. When joining a new group of partners, individuals negotiate and juggle their places. Second, roles within partnerships create a set of duties that, while complementing those done in the home institution, are new. Depending on the motivation behind the initial group formation, the home institution may be more or less supportive of committing individuals to the partnership.

Individuals must juggle job responsibilities at their home institution and the tasks of their partnership roles. Depending on the motives for creating the partnership, individuals may have more or less buy-in to their new partnership roles.

The traditional phases in team development of forming, storming, norming, and performing (Tuckman, 1965) begin to set the stage for how partnership roles emerge and evolve. For instance, individuals may become involved in a partnership due to personal desires and become champions for the group, or they may be assigned to the partnership and find themselves involved because of their home institutional roles that serve as a particular cog in the collaboration. Dualities of roles create tensions in partnerships due to individual loyalty to the home institution versus responsibility to the new partnership.

Bensimon and Neumann (1993) explore the notion of complex teams as a means to integrate leadership to "adapt to technologically complex and information-rich environments" (Kanter, 1983, p. ix). The advantage of team leadership is the creativity of solutions that emerge from diverse perspectives, facilitation of cognitive complexity, peer support, and increased account-ability (Bensimon & Neumann, 1993, pp. 5–8). Bensimon and Neumann (1993) posit three functions of presidential teams:

1. utilitarian function—getting the work done
2. expressive function—framing problems
3. cognitive function—thinking collaboratively to find solutions

In practice, the leadership teams Bensimon and Neumann (1993) studied were either actually used or illusory. These same patterns work in partner-ships, particularly regarding the notion of working together in reality or in name only. Within these teams emerge a number of different roles that con-tribute to team thinking. A critical component of team leadership involves team thinking, which "requires individuals to work their minds and express their thinking publicly" (Bensimon & Neumann, 1993, p. 57). Central to this position is an assumption that team members bring diverse perspectives to the issues at hand. Bensimon and Neumann (1993) go on to define eight thinking roles for presidential teams that may also apply to partnership roles. Their list included the following five core roles:

1. definer—frames issues and defines reality
2. analyst—explores and assesses the issues at hand
3. interpreter—translates how others may view decisions outside the group
4. critic—takes on the role of critic and devil's advocate
5. synthesizer—looks broadly at the issues and brings together a summary (1993, p. 59)

Supporting roles include disparity monitor, task monitor, and emotional monitor. Newly formed partnerships could benefit from reflecting on how these important team roles might be addressed within the partnership. The combination of these roles helps create the thinking team and allows a move from an illusory team to a real one. Negotiating partner roles at the inception of the newly formed collaboration can establish a stronger foundation for the group. Up-front conversations about who is responsible for what can reveal whether any core roles are missing.

Individuals come to the partnership with a set of skills, professional expertise, and both personal and institutional motivations. The roles filled in the new group may contribute to how motivated individuals support partnership success. Role theory contends that individuals have various roles in life, including those that emerge from position and those created from social roles (Mead, 1934). Role conflict occurs when individuals attempt to balance competing roles that act in contradiction to one another (Macionis, 2006). There is built-in role conflict inherent in partnership work as individuals involved have roles associated with their home institutions and with the newly formed group. The following section reviews the roles within partnerships based on levels of individual responsibility and links to home institutions and the role of leadership, again within both the partnership and the home institution.

Individuals and leaders are faced with a series of questions at the beginning of partnering. Questions that emerge include:

- How does this partnership affect me individually?

    o Will I have to report to two supervisors?
    o What happens when there is a conflict about prioritizing my work deadlines?
    o What role do I see myself playing in the new partnership?
    o Do I believe in the goals of the partnership?

- As a leader, what is my role in the partnership?

    o How do I decide how to allocate resources?
    o Who are the right people to involve based on partnership needs?
    o What happens when there is conflict that pits my institution's needs against those of the partnership?
    o How will decisions be made?

Levels

Differences emerge in roles in a strategic partnership that are unlike those in a traditional partnership. In a traditional partnership, primary roles are linked to the home institution and those created in the partnership are viewed as temporal in nature. Strategic partnership roles, on the other hand, result in less role conflict (Macionis, 2006) because the partnership supports the strategic objectives and mission of the home institution, and thus, more

consistency in roles is apparent. Individuals participating in the partnership are rewarded at the home institution for their partnership involvement
because of how the partnership helps fulfill strategic goals. The involvement
of individuals from various organizational levels provides the opportunity to
create the team roles advocated by Bensimon and Neumann (1993) that can
best support burgeoning partnerships.

Roles differ depending on the type of partnership in effect. Strategic
partnership roles result in less role conflict.

The complexity of partnerships is based in part on the roles found at
various levels of the partnership. Individuals may be involved in the governing structure of the newly formed group, may be the person or persons who
are the face of the partnership and working with stakeholders, may be the
behind-the-scenes administrative staff that support the bureaucracy of keeping the partnership working, or may be a central leader in forming plans
for the collaboration (Bensimon & Neumann, 1993). Associated with this
notion of levels is the power each person brings to the table, both individual
power and power linked with institutional roles (Morgan, 2006). These roles
contribute to the ways in which relationships of the partnership are operationalized; we explore the role of relationships more fully in the next chapter. What is critical to understand is that there are several moving parts to
the partnership, multiple levels of operation and understanding, and often a
mismatch of intentions or motivations. The dynamic nature of partnerships
brings with it the promise of accomplishing more together, but also the conflict of loyalty to the home institution.

Multiple levels of operation and roles exist within partnerships. Individuals at different levels bring varying types of power and access to
resources to the partnership.

For example, the Pathways to College Network (a project of the Institute for Higher Education Policy [IHEP]) has a central mission to improve
access and success for underserved students to higher education. One of its
principles advocates for the involvement of "leaders at all levels in establishing policies, programs, and practices that facilitate student transitions

toward postsecondary attainment" (Pathways to College Network, 2004, p. 1). IHEP's objectives are met when leaders at multiple levels are working toward the same goals. The ideal of multiple points of leadership and decision making remains core to the potential of collaborative leadership (Hickman, 2010). Individuals bring different levels of social capital to the partnership, some of which is linked to their position within their home institutions. University and community partnerships often highlight the unevenness of power based on institutional affiliation with universities wielding more power than the lower socioeconomic communities located nearby (Liu, Elliott, Loggins, & Nayve, 2006).

Another way of thinking of the levels involved in partnerships is to consider the concept of boundaries. Traditionally, boundary theory applies to the ease of movement between home and work responsibilities (Nippert-Eng, 1996), whereas border theory (Clark, 2000) focuses on the psychological and physical borders between the two domains. Approaches to navigating these border transitions range from separation of the spheres of work and home to integration of competing elements. Individuals within partnerships face similar boundary transitions. Here, the strength of the boundaries operates both within the partnership and between the institutions involved (Daniels, 2011). The permeability of the borders between partnering institutions may depend on the roles of the individuals in question (see Figure 2.1). Individuals representing each of the partners illustrated in the following figure have more or less difficulty in fulfilling their partnership roles based on how easy it is to cross boundaries. Partner #1 in this example will have the easiest time given the permeable boundaries this partner has relative to the others, whereas partner #2 will face more difficulties given less open boundaries

Figure 2.1 Partnership boundaries

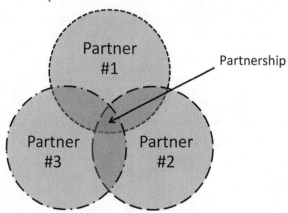

than the other partners. As trust among the partners builds, these boundaries become more permeable.

Those who are involved at the periphery of either their home institution or new partnership core mission, or at lower levels within the hierarchy of responsibility, have more difficulty in dedicating time and energy to the new partnership work and this makes border crossing more difficult. Simultaneously, those on the periphery or at the bottom may have greater latitude to opt out or be less involved, thereby causing less friction with boundary transitions than those who are seen as more central and who then actually have more navigating to do. Because multiple boundaries have to be negotiated, it is helpful to consider the levels of partnership involvement and the roles individuals play at these junctures. Questions to ask regarding levels of involvement include both individual-level questions and questions for leaders:

- How does this partnership influence my work role at my home institution?
- What is my role in the new partnership, and how does this tie in to my role at my home institution? Is it rewarded?
- If I am initiating the new partnership, what resources can I tap at my home institution given my role?
- As a top level leader, what role do I have in supporting the partnership? Do I see this as a real team effort or one in name only?
- What in-house process may support or challenge the ability to cross partnership boundaries?

Leadership

Leadership is central when developing new partnerships (Astin & Astin, 2000). In researching elements that contributed to successful public-private pairings involving the business sector, local governments, and public community colleges, Young (2010) found that a champion was central to success. Here the leader plays a role in the formation and implementation of the partnership by providing the central force needed to make the partnership happen.

The role of a champion and top-level leader buy-in are central to models of change (Fullan, 2006; Kotter & Cohen, 2002). Organizational change may emerge from presidential vision, internal pressures, or external dictates (Astin & Astin, 2000). Strategic leadership may guide change initiatives, including the drive to partner with others. As noted earlier, change may be pushed from outside due to policy mandates or from internal needs and goals.

Internal pressures may include the need to address economic challenges, but champions may also come from grassroots levels and non-top-level roles (Watson, 2007).

Leadership is critical to partnership success. Partnership champions may come from different levels of the organization—from top-level to grassroots leaders.

IHEP's Pathways to College Network (previously outlined) argues that strong leadership is required to meet their goal for college access (Pathways to College Network, 2004). Here, policy leaders must mandate rigorous, aligned curricula; school leaders should require college preparation curricula for all students; college leaders should be clear about what is required for college readiness; and finally, community leaders should reinforce beliefs that education is necessary and valued (Pathways to College Network, 2004). Partnerships and change require top-level buy-in to the process (Kotter & Cohen, 2002). Yet, beyond this is a need to communicate the change throughout the organization and the partnering institutions to ensure that a common mission guides the process. Table 2.1 highlights leadership roles in traditional and strategic partnerships relative to the various sources of partnership motivations.

TABLE 2.1
Leadership Roles Relative to Source of Motivation

Source of Motivation	Traditional Partnerships	Strategic Partnerships
Economic	• Promote partnerships that help alleviate resource constraints. • Mid-level leaders pursue alliances to support unit-level work and to take advantage of grant-writing opportunities. • Tap existing relationships that correspond to requirements for grants, to share space, or to coordinate on joint programming.	• Promote partnerships that align with the college's strategic plan and address resource issues. • Mid-level leaders seek economic benefits only if they also support institutional goals. • Conduct environmental scans to find partners best suited to meeting strategic resource objectives.

(Continues)

TABLE 2.1

Leadership Roles Relative to Source of Motivation (Continued)

Source of Motivation	Traditional Partnerships	Strategic Partnerships
Policy	• Seek partners based on policy requirements or mandates. • Mid-level leaders seek partners that help meet immediate needs for following the rules. • Compliance versus strategic change guides actions. • Leadership occurs via a series of transactions.	• Seek partners based on dual fit of policy requirements and strategic objectives. • All levels of leaders look for fit with overarching organizational goals. • Leadership seeks transformation of current systems, using policy as a lever.
Value alignment	• Individuals throughout the institution may be motivated to work with others based on similar interests and desires. • Value alignment is individually oriented versus aligned to organizational goals.	• Environmental scanning points to partners that align with organizational values and strategic goals. • Leaders throughout the organization judge potential partnerships on value alignment with strategic objectives.

Organizational Alignment

Despite perceptions of the natural alliances among various partners, particularly when two or more educational institutions are involved, inherent cultural and organizational differences exist. Differences in cultures and institutional mission highlight the balancing act between being competitors and collaborators (Flora & Hirt, 2010). Kitagawa (2005) researched university entrepreneurship activities and regional engagement and found that in order to have better partnership interactions, "the various internal and external governance features have to be studied, as sometimes conflicting forces are at work" (p. 65). Creating a common and shared process helps avoid potential conflicts.

Scanning for potential partners translates to locating partners with a similar scope of activities and compatible administrative structures and motivations to participate. In analyzing critical requirements for strategic international partnerships to occur, Barnes (2011a, pp. 2–4) concludes there are five key criteria to address: (a) breadth of impact, (b) depth of impact, (c) strong faculty support, (d) demonstrable mutual benefit, and (e) sustainability. Being intentional in seeking partners can support organizational alignment and forestall some of the biggest barriers to partnering. Building on existing relationships, both on individual and institutional levels, creates a bridge to building trust and creating a space to negotiate partnership details. The development of a partnership governing structure can help in navigating the type of issues that emerge due to different organizational expectations (Radwan, 2011).

Partnerships built on a shared understanding of goals, motivations, and organizational processes are poised for sustainability.

The shared meaning of terms, conceptual ideas, and ultimate goals of the partnership influences ultimate success. When partnerships are a result of happenstance, organizations may find alignment between organizational motivations and priorities occurring due to luck or the ability to meet short-term objectives. Strategic partnerships, on the other hand, have more intentional alignment among partners as leaders and organizations seek out partners based on the ability of other institutions and individual partners to help obtain institutional goals. Doing an environmental scan for potential partners allows leaders to determine those institutions that best support the directions sought.

Considering the various types of motivations outlined in this chapter, it is apparent that the starting points of partnerships dictate how organizational alignment is even considered. When economic motivations are behind the desire to join forces, once the objectives are obtained or, at a minimum when the immediate crisis is circumvented, there is little reason to maintain the partnership. As well, policy often serves as the impetus for collaborating, either in the quest for capacity building or to obtain particular objectives. The ability to provide incentives or repercussions to follow through on mandates influences compliance with stated policies. Partnerships that are formed based on value alignment build on a foundation of shared understanding and a desire to obtain particular outcomes. In this case, as long as values stay aligned, there is an intrinsic desire to see the partnership succeed. Finally, when partnerships are formed due to strategic leadership, environmental scanning allows for partners to join forces to fulfill organizational strategic plans.

Summary Points

- The initial source of motivation or rationale to partner influences ultimate outcomes.
- Partnerships based on shared beliefs and values have a greater chance of long-term success.
- Traditional partnerships may shift to strategic partnerships when leaders recognize the alignment of institutional goals with the potential emerging from the partnering relationship.
- The roles of the partners in both their home institutions and within the partnership affect what type of power individuals use in the newly formed partnership and what type of power or influence they have in their home institution.
- Complex cognitive teams provide more flexibility and tap into a wider range of expertise and experience.
- Organizational culture influences alignment for partners—challenges may emerge when partners lack shared understandings of ideas, processes, or structures.

CASE #2: THE PROPOSAL: GETTING TO YES

Partner history has implications for both the formation of the collaboration and long-term sustainability. This case involves two four-year universities in a midwestern state. Entrepreneurial College (EC) has a long history of outreach programming and alternative delivery of courses and programs. Outreach programming first emerged from delivery of college courses on military campuses and programming at off-campus sites throughout the state and country. The decline in the state's traditional, residential college student base has placed additional pressures on these off-campus entrepreneurial activities to bring in funding for the college. Additionally, for-profit online programming has begun making inroads in the higher education market in the state. In this context, EC was focused on increasing programming through a variety of means.

In the 1990s, several university centers were created on community college campuses in the state. These centers provided a location for some of the four-year universities to offer the final two years of programming to community college graduates and for the creation of 2 + 2 programming in which the first two years are offered at the community college and the last two years are provided by the university.

The centers were popular with residents as they meant students could live at home, work, and not have to move to a new city to finish their degree. EC offered programming at the four university centers in the state, and was motivated to offer this programming to expand its reach within the state, and to augment revenues via the tuition generated in these university centers.

Rural Comprehensive University (RCU) faced many of the same economic challenges found at EC. Additionally, RCU sought to increase its academic prestige and stature within the state. As with many colleges, RCU was looking at initiating some doctoral programs to aid in its desire to become a more prominent research university. The current economic climate and the university's rural location, however, were impediments to this goal. As with other regional universities, one of the first doctoral programs RCU contemplated was a doctorate in education. EdD programs historically emerged from comprehensive and teaching colleges to meet regional needs. Over time, these programs often expanded to offer programming in higher education or counseling and often provided the basis for ultimate creation of PhD degree programs. A needs assessment showed that the region could support a doctoral program, but the RCU administration was nervous about the cost for starting such a program.

The educational leadership department at EC recently offered an off-campus doctoral cohort program at a community college 50 miles away from RCU. Cohort programs deliver coursework and degrees from start to finish in lockstep progress to a group of students. The cohort of students registers each semester for a series of classes, thus guaranteeing a revenue stream for Entrepreneurial College and assurances for students that they will get the classes they need to obtain their degree. Additionally, research indicated that students in doctoral cohorts receive more support and are more likely to persist to degree completion.

Rural Comprehensive University hired two of the doctoral graduates of EC's cohort program as new assistant professors in its educational leadership program. Conversations between these two graduates and their EC faculty planted the seeds for a partnership between EC and RCU. The first informal conversation began at a dinner at the American Educational Research Association conference with the two graduates and two EC faculty members. The dinner conversation about how to offer a shared degree sparked a series of subsequent meetings, which resulted in a proposal in which RCU would offer several classes that would transfer to the EC doctoral degree program. Upon completion of these courses, EC faculty would travel to the RCU campus to deliver an on-site doctoral cohort program.

Two pathways were proposed. One involved a degree ladder program option in which RCU graduates with an educational specialist degree (EdS) would only need to take core doctoral and research courses with EC—their coursework from the EdS would transfer to the program to complete degree requirements. Alternatively, area residents with a master's degree could apply directly to the doctoral program. These students would take core doctoral courses provided by EC faculty and concentration and similar courses provided by RCU faculty. The four individuals involved saw this proposal as a win-win for both institutions.

Problems emerged, however, in getting the proposal approved on both campuses. At EC, the graduate school dean questioned the precedent that would be set by transferring in more credits than university policy allowed. An exemption would be required for approval through the graduate council. A different problem emerged at RCU. The graduate dean had experience with EC when she worked in a different state, and the experience was contentious and unpleasant. She raised questions about motivations of EC faculty members and concerns over RCU "losing" out in the deal. The RCU dean was skeptical that the stated intentions of the EC faculty members to help student access were genuine, and thought instead EC was trying to cut into RCU college territory.

Case Questions

- What type of motivations guided this partnership?
- How might this proposal have been framed differently to allay institutional fears?
- What potential difficulties might occur with this partnership?
- Is student learning and support the real motivation, or does empire building also emerge?
- How might the original partners have foreseen some of the ultimate problems?
- What information would be required of leaders in deciding to pursue the partnership? How might this differ by leadership level in the organization?
- How might EU and RCU use this model to develop other partnerships?

3

RELATIONSHIPS AND PARTNERS

Partnerships by their nature involve developing and sustaining relationships. Relationship building occurs within and among various levels of the involved institutions and includes individuals in a range of positions of responsibility. How and why partners are chosen affects how relationships develop and the impact they have on the partnership itself, both in how it works and whether it lasts (Parmigiani & Rivera-Santos, 2011). Individual relationships shift over the life of the partnership, with different ebbs and flows of partner involvement. Sometimes individuals play prominent roles, both on a personal level and through their institutional roles; at other times, their contributions and roles recede. The start of the partnership proves to be a critical and sensitive time. In particular, people involved in establishing and maintaining the partnerships possess different levels of social capital (Coleman, 1988)—for example, close ties with others, trusting relationships, and levels of responsibility and power within the home organization.

At the crux of relationships are varying levels of individuals' social capital and connections with others. Here, social capital refers to the strength of relationships, reputation of individuals, and the intensity of social networks. Social capital often is a basis for why certain relationships become relevant within partnerships. Connections made based on the use of an individual's social capital support and make available different opportunities for cultivating relationships that contribute to the start of partnerships and, perhaps more important, to how partnerships are sustained. But, in some cases, burgeoning relationships fail to accomplish much for the partnership. Likewise, over time changes occur in the strategic objectives and goals for institutions, influencing the motivating factors for the individual partnering organizations and straining the social capital of those involved, ultimately resulting in challenges to sustainability. When organizational goals change, how the partnership helps fulfill the new objectives is questioned. International partnerships add a complicating layer to the situation, with relationships taking on a nuanced role due to cross-cultural contexts (Tubbeh & Williams, 2010); yet, as with all collaborations, these relationships require sufficient time to develop the social capital and trust necessary for sustaining interactions. This chapter outlines the role of relationships throughout the partnership with case examples highlighting the various stages.

Relationships are a cornerstone of partnerships. People involved in establishing and maintaining partnerships possess different levels of social capital—for example, close ties with others, trusting relationships, and levels of responsibility and power within the home organizations.

Traditional partnerships often emerge due to relationships that are loosely coupled to the organization (Weick, 1976). Loosely coupled institutional units create a location in the organizational hierarchy that is not central to operations but is responsive to environmental changes. Because these areas are peripheral, more risk and experimentation may take place to nurture innovation without the specter of failure affecting the core functions of the institution. The social networks created through relationships among loosely coupled areas allow for testing innovations in settings not tied directly to the core enterprise, so they are less risky. Thus, on the one hand, new ideas that fail do not take down the rest of the organization. On the other hand, when innovations succeed, they, too, are not tied into the organizational structure or institutionalized. Therefore, even when collaborations are successful, it is harder to see long-term success or to have the ability to replicate innovations throughout the institution because they are loosely coupled to the college.

Strategic partnerships build instead on the dense and central networks of the organization. Many collaborative activities that start as a joint project at the individual level through loose affiliations with the institution may change over time and evolve into a partnership that supports the strategic goals of the institution (Amey, 2010). Here, there is not only deeper trust among those involved in strategic partnerships, but also an awareness of how the partnership helps achieve institutional goals. Social capital increases for those involved in the strategic partnership as their work is recognized as central to operations, and the outcomes of the partnership contribute to overall institutional objectives. In this case, what may have started as an initial loose coupling of the partnership to the institution becomes tighter (Weick, 1976) and more processes become institutionalized.

Traditional partnerships often build on individual relationships that are loosely coupled to the central mission of the organization, whereas strategic partnerships emerge from singling out the relationships that provide central leveraging to meet organizational strategic objectives.

Questions that can help guide understanding of the relationships involved in partnership building and sustainability include:

- What is the genesis of the relationship?
    - Are we "friends" who want to work together?
    - Do we share common goals for the partnership?
    - Were we sought out because of how our area/organization can help meet strategic objectives?
- What level of resources/skills/expertise do we bring to the partnership?
- What level of resources/skills/expertise do others bring to the partnership?
- How has the relationship changed over time?

The group process involved in strategic partnerships mimics the underlying premises of thought communities (John-Steiner, 2000) or long-term partnerships (Creamer, 2004). According to John-Steiner (2000), thought community refers to "experienced thinkers who collaborate with an intensity that can lead to a change in their domain's dominant paradigm" (p. 196). The essence of a thought community is how relationships evolve over time based on a similar commitment to an area of inquiry and how the time spent together allows for deeper questioning of long-held assumptions or ways of operation (Eddy & Garza Mitchell, 2012). Simplistically, this might be conceived as questioning old practices and establishing new patterns of work. The formation of new partnerships tests traditional forms of operations. New relationships create different patterns for interacting and involve a new cast of individuals with whom to engage. Each partner brings to the table a preference for how to work as well as a range of areas of expertise and access to resources. Creamer's (2004) study of long-term collaborations found that the groups were able to create efficiencies, adjust their thinking, and obtain a more holistic, global perspective of the issues at hand. Finally, these long-term groups were able to challenge current practices, given their time together and the trust built among members. In the end, long-term collaboration results in accomplishing more together as a group than the individuals could have done on their own.

Long-term relationships create efficiencies, adjust individuals' thinking, and create a more holistic, global perspective to apply to problems.

Change is at the heart of partnerships. Not only does change occur in what the partnership can accomplish by having individuals working together, but change also happens on an individual level. Individual learning occurs based on interactions within the partnership. As adult learners, individuals approach learning based on six tenets: adults (a) want to know why they need to learn something new; (b) draw from their experience to begin to understand new learning; (c) desire self-direction in their learning; (d) link learning to immediate application in their work; (e) focus best on application of learning versus the content; and (f) draw from internal motivations rather than external motivations (Knowles, Holton, & Swanson, 2011). Considering the role of individuals in forming relationships as a building block for partnerships, it is helpful to understand more about how individuals learn and what motivates them to change their behavior.

Individuals come to new situations with a mental map of expectations (Senge, 1990), so it is important to consider how reactions to partnering are based on an individual's experience working with others. If a previous situation resulted in a bad experience, an individual will be reluctant to want to partner again (e.g., see the case at the end of the previous chapter). If, however, the relationship was positive, an individual may see all opportunities to partner as equally attractive even when they might not all be as advantageous. These initial relationships also contribute to the social capital of those involved (Coleman, 1988). Understanding more about how experience guides current decision making and how individuals approach change will help in knowing why some partnerships built on the efforts of a few individuals succeed while others fail.

Individuals bring mental models to their partnership work, remembering both the good and the bad of previous collaborations. Recognizing the role of these modes of thinking can aid in knowing why some partnerships succeed and others fail.

Not all partnerships are seen as good ventures to pursue. Harris (2005) argues that "the dominant model of partnership is primarily concerned with promoting the modernizing agenda, and is instrumentalist and economically driven" (p. 71). She further advocates for conceptualizing partnerships as learning partnerships. Holding the concept of learning central helps illustrate what motivates individuals and how the partnership may implement ideas of organizational learning (Kezar, 2005).

Understanding that the past influences the present creates a set of questions to consider for partnering:

- Based on experience, how do I feel about partnering with others?
  - o What are my assumptions about how the partnership process works?
  - o Do I have experience with the particular partner in question that jades my view of the current partnership opportunity?
- What did I learn from my experiences in past partnerships?
- What is different about this current partnership?
- What leads me to believe that this partnership will be different from any in the past?

This chapter first explores the role of social capital (Coleman, 1988) in building and sustaining partnerships. How social capital is used differs for traditional partnerships and strategic partnerships, and social capital also changes over time. Access to institutional resources measures one aspect of a person's social capital. Thus, the resources individuals and groups can access in their home institutions contribute to the success of the partnerships, and their absence can hinder progress. Decision making within partnerships also occurs on multiple levels. First, decision making occurs within the group of partners, those typically on the ground, and, second, decision making happens within each of the partnering organizations. On both levels of decision making, traditional and strategic partnerships operate differently. These differences appear throughout the various stages of partnership formation and implementation. Finally, changes manifest within the partnerships over time, in which, for instance, a relationship that was crucial to the formation of the partnership may wane or may become more crucial as time passes. Typically, sustainability develops with the passage of time and continued commitment by the partners to the partnership goals.

Social Capital

Bourdieu (1986) defined the concept of *social capital* as "the aggregate of the actual or potential resources which are linked to the possession of a durable network of more or less institutionalized relationships of mutual acquaintance or recognition" (p. 248). In essence, this means that friendships and acquaintanceships of individuals allow them access to the resources of others in the group, yet the social capital among individuals varies based on the amount and quality of the resources available (Portes, 2000). Whom you know matters. The level and type of social capital, hence, can provide individuals with access to others with expertise or connections that allow access to institutional resources that normally would be beyond their own power to get. Social capital emerges not so much from the power or knowledge one personally possesses, but rather through an individual's links to the power and resources of others. The strength of relationships and the social network provides more leverage than possible on an individual level (Coleman, 1988).

Information, centrality to key operations, density, and trust are the key aspects of social capital that are important to partnerships. Whom you know matters.

Previous research pointed out the role of social capital in partnerships (Amey et al., 2010; Dhillon, 2009). In a study of post-16 learning partnerships in England, Dhillon (2009) found multiple layers of collaboration among the partnership networks and high levels of trust, shared norms, and values among the partners. The success of the partnerships occurred due to individuals' access to the larger network of resources and connections. As relationships are at the root of building social capital for and among individuals, it is important to understand more about partner selection. Pidduck and Carey (2006) sought to uncover the criteria for choosing partners and found four sources of influence in picking partners: requirements, resource availability, social network, and reputation.

Weighing these four criteria for partnership selection helps shed light on the differences between traditional and strategic partnerships, too. Traditional partners might be selected based on meeting immediate institutional requirements or fulfilling personal agendas of loosely coupled entities. Additionally, the availability of and access to resources may provide motivation to partner; however, partnerships based solely on resources are more prone to failure and are more temporal in nature (Eddy, 2007, 2010b). Once the initial obligation of the exchange is met or the resources expended, the partnership often dissolves.

Existing relationships can provide a connection in social networks to what individuals know is currently important for their organizations. Strategic partnerships seek out partners using a social network that aligns reputation of the institution with strategic planning objectives. Here, resource availability may play a part in choosing the best partner as well, but the basis for partnering goes beyond mere finances. How partners are selected or emerge in strategic partnerships differs based on the objectives or desired goals of the potential collaboration. Even though both traditional and strategic partnerships consider similar criteria for partnering, the weight given to factors, such as requirements and reputation, differs.

How social capital is accessed and used varies for partnerships. Key components of social capital are the use of information, centrality of individuals to operations, density of relationships, and trust (Coleman, 1988). Individuals possess varying amounts of social capital depending on each of these factors. The adage that information is power proves true in building social capital (Morgan, 2006). Just as personal knowledge and expertise are factors of influence, so is access to information—be it knowledge about something or about operations and plans. Thus, the more central individuals are to key decision-making opportunities in the organization, the more social capital they acquire based on what they know of operations and how they can influence decisions. Individuals who are involved in setting the direction for the organization also have influence over the direction of strategic planning and insider knowledge of the direction of future plans. Maletzke (2009) found that the relationships of university researchers and USAID staff helped in forming partnerships to strengthen food industries in developing countries. Yet, the social capital of the researchers could not overcome institutional barriers inherent in the system as the faculty members were too far removed from the central decision-making process to influence change.

Social capital emerges not so much from the power or knowledge one personally possesses, but rather through an individual's links to the power and resources of others.

Associated with the concept of centrality to operations and decisions is the density of relationships. Here, density refers to the number of ties that individuals have to one another and their scope of influence. Close ties and relationships create greater density of relationships. One factor influencing density is location. We know that an individual's position within the organization provides access to resources, information, and decision making. But location also is literally *where* the partner organizations are located. Institutions located in rural or remote regions are physically removed from population hubs. Proximity to potential partners affects not only the choice of partners available but also the opportunity to meet potential partners. Rural schools, for instance, suffer from a loss of social capital over time (Jolly & Deloney, 1996) as population exodus occurs and existing education providers must merge or close. Increased use of technology, however, provides a glimmer of hope for increased connectivity and social capital as opportunities to collaborate move beyond physical boundaries (Jolly & Deloney, 1996). Assessing the type of density available within a partnership requires considering not only the critical mass of partners, but also the ties that bind them by proximity or commitment to the relationship.

Granovetter (1983) expounded on the strength of weak ties among individuals. Weak ties create connections between networks that provide contacts not normally available within a dense network. You might think of this as links among acquaintances versus someone you know very well. The loose coupling (Weick, 1976) between organizations created by these weak ties to networks provides increased access to potential partners. A weak tie might emerge when a partner *knows someone who knows someone* who ultimately turns into a great collaborator. Individuals who create weak ties often have cognitive flexibility that allows them to span boundaries that link networks together. Critical to fostering these types of relationships is trust.

Trust builds as a result of social actors committing to and repaying obligations (Coleman, 1990). Thus, similar to an IOU, the more outstanding obligations owed to individuals, the greater their social capital. Le Ber and Branzei (2010a) found that relational attachment was a key factor in sustaining partnerships and that "relational attachment grows with good partners—through specific investments the exchange partners make in the relationship over time" (p. 163). The level of trust created over time can sustain both traditional and strategic partnerships. It is the addition of fulfilling organizational strategy in the case of the strategic partnerships, however, that can create sustainability. As Ferman and Hill (2004) point out, the challenges inherent in traditional university-community research partnerships include "complications relating to conflicting agendas, differing capacities, and context" (Kajner, Fletcher, & Makokis, 2011, p. 4). A shared agenda helps build trust and relationships over time.

Trust builds as a result of social actors committing to and repaying obligations, and this builds over time.

How partnerships begin sets the stage for future interactions and sets expectations for communication and information sharing. At this stage the social capital of individuals provides a platform for connecting. For example, in 2007, the state of Illinois passed the College and Career Readiness (CCR) Act (Khan, Castro, Bragg, Barrientos, & Baber, 2009) with the central aim of addressing rising remediation rates in community colleges. Under the CCR Act, the state of Illinois funded pilot projects in which community colleges partnered with high schools to implement the objectives of the act, to ascertain the effectiveness of these partnerships in enhancing students' college readiness. The goals common to the pilot site projects included promoting partnerships between schools and colleges, providing students with the skills to perform better on placement tests, and facilitating their transition from high school to college (Khan et al., 2009). The beginning of this partnership rested on past relationships.

The pilot colleges built on existing communication networks in place with their school partners. Colleges tended to partner with schools with which they already had links, and the level of the partner's social capital contributed to the type of connections possible. During the pilot's implementation phase, colleges experimented with mechanisms to foster relationship building. A majority of the community colleges held meetings with the school administrators to ensure alignment between the high schools and colleges of the goals and strategies to promote student success. Some experimented with semester-long programs, offering courses in reading, mathematics, and college study skills to prepare students for college work. Others offered workshops and orientations to allow the students the opportunity to familiarize themselves with what they could expect in college. Many schools used a combination of these activities (Khan et al., 2009). An Office of Community College Research and Leadership (OCCRL) study of the pilot project at the end of the second year reported that preliminary test results suggested improvement in students' skills across several sites as a result of the partnership (Baber, Castro, & Bragg, 2010). Strategic leadership by the heads of the partner institutions helped support and advocate for the collaborations through allocation of resources, and leadership proved critical in nurturing budding relationships.

Social network analysis (Carrington, Scott, & Wasserman, 2005) provides a mechanism for measuring and tracking relationships over time. Increased understanding of the ties that bind together individuals and groups begins to take the mystery out of why people work together (Honeycutt, 2009). A research study investigating the creation and maintenance of a community college–university transfer partnership found that previous relationships between institutions and presidential support for partnership practices were critical to success, as were sustained funding and a university presence on the two-year campuses (Kisker, 2005). It is often presidential support that ensures availability of the resources necessary to make partnerships work. Position confers access to resources and provides enhanced social capital. Tracking the beginning sources of relationships helps in understanding better what contributes to sustainability, and tracing the money trail to sources of power illuminates factors of social capital.

> Social network analysis provides increased understanding of the ties that bind together individuals and groups and begins to take the mystery out of why people work together.

Resource dependency theory, as well, provides a useful way for exploring social capital and how access to resources occurs via an individual's position and centrality to decision making. "The basic argument of resource dependency theory is that an analysis of the inter-organizational network can help an organization's managers understand the power/dependence relationships that exist between their organization and other network actors" (Hatch & Cunliffe, 2006, p. 80). Awareness of the organization's dependence on the resources of others provides a way to identify what is important to the effectiveness of an organization and to finding ways to offset some of this influence by creating countervailing dependence. Heightened dependence on the resources of others creates vulnerability unless it is matched by something else required in the partnerships—for instance, information. At its root, power rests with those who can control access to resources (Morgan, 2006). Yet, seeking shared goals can shift institutions from competitors to collaborators (Flores & Claeys, 2011; Watt-Malcolm, 2011). For example, Le Ber and Branzei (2010b) researched cross-sector partnerships (i.e., for-profit and not-for-profit collaborations) from the point of view of the beneficiaries, in particular looking at value creation. They problematized the concept of a resource-based view (RBV) in which "firms with superior resources (i.e., valuable, rare, inimitable and organized to exploit) create and appropriate or capture more value than their competitors" (p. 600). Instead, Le Ber and Branzei (2010b) used critical theory to showcase asymmetric levels of contributions and mismatches of power. Central to these concepts are the role of voice—with the focus on the beneficiaries. "Critical theories articulate the role the marginalized could play in value creation (principles), the conditions that may enable or hinder their contribution to value creation (relations) and the interactions that reify power asymmetries or dependencies (relational processes)" (p. 608). Le Ber and Branzei (2010b) focus on moments of tension in cross-sector partnerships, arguing that breaches within the relationships undergirding the joint venture might signal failure, but also noting that "relational processes are inherently flexible and, we suggest, may create opportunities for reassessing the role of different parties in value creation" (p. 617). The notion of "generative tension" (p. 617) allows for a variety of outcomes. The voice of the beneficiary, which is often students in educational partnerships, influences how partnership goals are met. Applying critical theory to analyzing partnerships thus challenges us to understand how the voices of those we believe we are serving with educational partnerships are in fact contributing to the process or understanding the value of what is created via the partnership. Student involvement can prove critical when they are the intended beneficiary of the partnership.

Applying critical theory to analyzing partnerships thus challenges us to understand how the voices of those we believe we are serving with educational partnerships are in fact contributing to the process or understanding the value of what is created via the partnership.

The concept of social capital is complex and often difficult to understand with all its nuances and applications. Figure 3.1 visualizes how social capital contributes to the formation of partnerships. The level of individuals' social capital (step 1) contributes to the creation of social networks (step 2). The dense or weak ties of the relationships within networks forecast the scope of connections possible. Those with weak ties to a variety of networks (Granovetter, 1983) are able to increase the range and number of relationships possible when a host of networks is accessed. Likewise, the level and type of social capital of those involved contributes to potential outcomes as each individual's level of capital, and resulting access to resources, varies. Partnerships emerge from social networks and the complementary use of resources available, including the reputation of the organizations (step 3). Inherent in the ideal of reputation is an assumption of how much trust exists or is presumed to exist based on experiences and past involvement. The building blocks for social capital and the formation of partnerships are similar for both traditional and strategic partnerships. The main differences are in the interpretation of requirements and the role of institutional reputation. The notion of the requirements for partnering harks back to the motivations for partnering. Here, strategic partnerships are built on each of the partners meeting strategic objectives. For traditional partnerships, however, the requirement may be more time-bound and short-term, or localized in a noncentral area of the organization. Once the immediate need is met, the traditional partnership has little reason to continue.

The levels of social capital of the initial partners may vary, too. For instance, in strategic partnerships, individual partners seek to meet institutional objectives and inherently have support of top-level leaders as a result. The links to meeting strategic goals can provide different levels of access to resources and make the partnership more central to operations. Nowell (2010) found that partners that have a very different philosophical stance in the partnership negatively influence the effectiveness of the overall collaborative. Relationships formed within collaborations suffer when values do not align. Thus, sustainability is more likely when values and objectives align among partners (Eddy, 2010b). The reputation of the organization also is a clue to what is valued in the strategic plan, and the reputation of individuals involved in the partnership illustrates the level of social capital they possess.

As partners are considered, the following questions focusing on social capital should be asked:

- Who in my network would be the best partner?

  o How well do I know this person?
  o Is this a weak tie or a strong tie?

- What influences my partner selection: requirements, resource availability, social network, and/or reputation?
- What type of resources can a potential partner access? How dependent is my organization on these resources?
- How would I rate the trust I feel with this potential partner?

Figure 3.1 The role of social capital in partnership formation

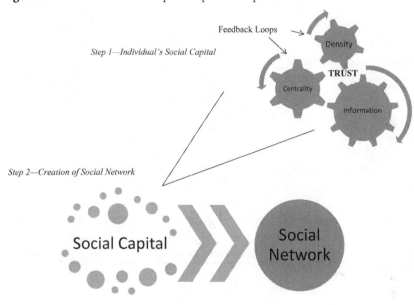

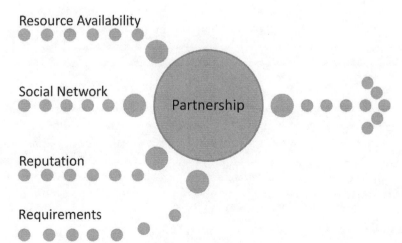

Role of Relationships in Decision Making

Decisions are made throughout the partnership process, starting with whom to partner and ending with whether to continue the partnership. Understanding more about the decision-making process can highlight critical points in the partnership-building process and underscore where influence could occur to help support and foster partnerships. Central to the decision-making process are the relationships of the people involved. This section reviews samples of decision-making models and shows how they operate within partnerships.

Decision making involves choice, process, and change (Chaffee, 1983). Within partnerships, the first choice is whether to partner. As we said in chapter 2, various motivations lead groups to partner and various relationships either support or impede this process. In traditional partnerships, the relationships most often tapped when making the choice to partner are on the individual level and the choice often occurs when there is a pressing, immediate need, which is often bound to a particular problem to solve or mandate to address. Relationships at this stage of the traditional partnership rely most on individuals' levels of connection and social capital. Strategic partnerships, however, may tap relationships more deeply embedded in the organization. The individuals involved in strategic partnerships are making the choice to partner based not so much on their individual needs, but rather on the needs of the organization and the ability of the partnership to help meet strategic goals of the organization.

Decision making involves choice, process, and change. Here, the choice in traditional partnerships focuses on picking a partner to help address a pressing immediate need, whereas in strategic partnerships the choice of partner links to strategic organizational goals.

The next stage of decision making involves implementing the initial choice. The implementation phase may follow one of several different types of decision-making models, each of which builds on relationships differently. Five models of decision making are presented: rational, collegial, political, bureaucratic, and organized anarchy (Chaffee, 1983). Finally, feedback loops provide information on what is required to change or adjust as a result of the original decision. The type of relationships in place for the partnership influences the decision-making process.

A rational model of decision making relies on making a choice between known alternatives and seeks a means to an end in which trade-offs are weighed to find the best solution to a problem (Chaffee, 1983; Hammond, Keeney, & Raiffa, 2001). In this case, the partners agree on the final goal, be it creating a program to address literacy in the community or working together to meet a state mandate for back-to-work programs. This common set of objectives helps the group seek out ways to fulfill its objectives. In this model of decision making, alternative options are well known and can be assessed to allow analysis of the possible outcomes. The process occurs sequentially, one step after another, rather than simultaneously. In a perfect world, this type of decision making allows for maximizing choice with predictable outcomes. When strong relationships exist among the partners, there is less variability regarding values and more rationality is possible. Yet, Eisenhardt and Zbaracki (1992) report "that goals can be inconsistent across people and time, search behavior is often local, and standard operating procedures guide much of organizational behavior" (p. 18). Individual preference often influences the choice of alternatives, particularly when there are power differences in the group, and not all alternatives are given equal consideration. "The complexity of the problem and the conflict among the decision makers often influence the shape of the decision path" (Eisenhardt & Zbaracki, 1992, p. 22). In partnerships in which the individuals know one another well, and when the outcomes are clearly defined and of a smaller scope, a rational decision-making model may work. As problems become more complex, are more central to operational plans, and involve more people and relationships, a rational model of decision making breaks down.

A collegial model of decision making is often assumed to exist in colleges. This model rests on faculty acting together in seeking a common goal. When applied to decisions within partnerships, however, this basic premise may not apply as those involved may not be peers and may not share common goals. In addition, the typical time involved in reaching consensus in a collegial model often exceeds reasonable expectations, especially when partnering with those in business who are accustomed to a very different and quicker pace for getting things done. This conflict in organizational cultural values (Bolman & Deal, 2008) is often at the root of problems within partnerships. Some of this conflict is avoided if the partnership is small and the relationships among the partners are strong.

A political model of decision making assumes instead that conflicting values and objectives exist and that individual interests guide behavior (Chaffee, 1983). Conflicts are resolved through negotiation and influenced by the amount of power each person brings to the situation. The type of power available to individuals connects to their social capital. Individuals may form coalitions, with the dominant coalition wielding the most power (Morgan, 2006; Scott, 2008). The fluid nature of these relationships is based on the goals and values of the various individuals regarding the current issue. Changes in the context, outcomes, and values can create odd bedfellows (Eddy, 2007).

Political decision making often appears in traditional partnerships as individual partners look to garner the most benefit from the collaboration. Here, relationships may create opportunities for certain partnerships to form, but the benefits of participation are rooted more in seeking advancement for an individual partner than necessarily looking at the larger goal of moving the partnership forward as a unit. Strategic partnerships, instead, may be viewed with relationships at the institutional level rather than at the individual level. In this case, the links to decision making based on advancement of the institution's goals and objectives closely tie into core mission. Yet, even these partnerships are based in power and relationships. As Watt-Malcolm (2011) argued, "However, with partnerships, tensions exist because stakeholders compete to gain and maintain control of their institutional territories and established standards" (p. 256). Seeking gain on an individual or single institutional level pulls away from collective goals of the partnership as individual advantage is sought.

We argue, however, that strategic partnerships have greater potential longevity given the ties to institutional goals with relationships based on more than individual power and advancement. As such, strategic partnerships may use political decision making to provide a platform for addressing conflicts. Through the feedback loop in this process, the partnership can change and address issues rather than having the conflict result in the collaboration falling apart. "A collaborative partnership entails mutual respect and acknowledgement of others [*sic*] voices, strengths, values, and assets. Moreover, to guarantee the sustainability of project goals, the collaborative partnership should lead to changes in policies within the partner institutions and these policies must be examined periodically to determine the impact of these changes" (Flores & Claeys, 2011, p. 335). What becomes assumed in this case is that the individuals involved in the strategic partnership begin to move away from seeing this as individually rooted and instead the partnership, as an entity, begins to accrue social capital.

Many colleges and organizations are based on bureaucratic forms of structure. Existing hierarchy and standard operating procedures create a situation for bureaucratic decision making that may be unquestioned (Chaffee, 1983). Instead of weighing options, as in the rational decision-making model, or creating a platform to resolve conflict, as in the political decision-making model, routine policies and structures build on past practices and policies. In this case, the past guides how decision making occurs in the future. An example that highlights this scenario is budgeting—last year's budget is the basis for making incremental changes for the current year. An established partnership might use this form of decision making; relationships formed over time are predictable, programs are in place, and the level of decisions required is rooted in day-to-day operations instead of planning for the future.

Forms of decision making affect partnerships. Central to this process are individual roles, power, and context.

Today's colleges and organizations face a chaotic environment in which change is happening rapidly and the future is unpredictable. Cohen and March (1986) first introduced the notion of ambiguity and garbage-can decision making in leading colleges (Cohen, March, & Olsen, 1972). Here, the ideal of an organized anarchy builds on "diversity of goals, ill-understood technology, and scarcity of time and resources" (Chaffee, 1983, p. 24). Links between cause and effect become tenuous. The idea that decisions occur as a result of a mix of problems, solutions, and actors thrown into a garbage can makes predicting outcomes impossible. Individuals in this instance base their solutions and possibilities for partnering on limited information and unpredictable outcomes. In the case of traditional partnering, the root of the decision often may be the circumstantial timing of issues, funding, and individuals with a previous relationship intact. Even though strategic partnering may be based on some level of serendipity, the link to mission and goals guides the choice among the options available. Staying true to this center helps guide decision making in this instance.

The role of relationships in practice varies depending on the type of decision-making model in place. It is helpful to understand the variety of ways in which decisions are made as recognition of the process can aid in the decisions individuals make. For instance, if a partner realizes that a bureaucratic decision-making model is in place in an institution it is seeking to partner with, decisions can be linked to process and procedures to make the partnership look more attractive. Taking a balcony view (Heifetz, 1994) of the process within the organizations in question helps stakeholders understand the actions unfolding and provides the potential for guiding how decisions are made. The level of social capital of the individuals involved creates one lever of influence and understanding the process creates another. Over time, however, relationships change as the partnership progresses. The next section explores this change more fully.

Decision making is central to all partnerships and begins with picking partners and may end with the decision to disband the partnerships. Thus, reflecting on the decision-making process is critical. The following questions can guide this reflective process:

- What type of information is known?
  - o Can a rational decision-making process occur?
  - o Does the amount of information that is unknown jeopardize the use of a rational decision-making model?
- How much conflict is anticipated in the partnership?
  - o How much power do I possess to leverage in this process?
  - o How much power or influence do others possess?
  - o How can we create a forum in which conflicts are resolved?
- What type of feedback loops exist to help inform decision making?

Relationship Changes Over Time

Relationships are not static. Individuals gain and use their social capital in making decisions, negotiating for resources, and seeking support for the partnership over time. In addition, new relationships form depending on changing needs of the partners, and old relationships may wither as social capital is expended. Le Ber and Branzei (2010a) explored the relational processes involved in strategic cross-sector partnership in the Canadian health care industry. The researchers found three factors involved in relational recalibrations: relational attachment, partner complacency, and partner disillusionment. They determined that partnerships based on strategic value resulted in more resiliency and more resourcefulness in tackling problems that emerged over time given the competing role conflict due to institutional loyalties. It is through the constant negotiation of roles and conflict over time that relationships must be continuously managed. This section first reviews the elements involved in the beginning stages of relationships and then moves on to discuss changing relationships. Changes may involve different roles for partners or may entail dissolution of the relationship.

Building Relationships

A relationship may begin for a number of reasons. Informal, personal relationships provide a starting point for what may emerge as a connection that develops into a formal partnership (Amey, Eddy, & Ozaki, 2007), this is especially the case in traditional partnerships. These informal connections can form when individuals meet at the gym or in another community venue and may spill over into more formal settings for work. Serving on organizational committees, advisory boards, and public school committees results in contexts that mix stakeholders together in ways that formal positions may not afford. A critical element in this early stage is building trust. A study of research partnerships with aboriginal people in Canada and university researchers found that "working with community partners to establish trust began very early in the project" (Kajner, Fletcher, & Makokis, 2011, p. 4). This early trust building can occur when the relationships are more informal and less is at stake.

In the beginning stages of strategic partnerships, identification of shared goals and needs helps determine which relationships should be nurtured. For example, Flores and Claeys (2011) advocated for community colleges to play a larger role in promoting access for Latina/o students to teacher education programs and that these partnerships should move beyond mere articulation agreements. Their research included a case study on the Academy for Teaching Excellence in a Hispanic Serving Institution in Texas, a program to promote college access for Latino students to teaching programs. When the partners were asked to reflect on how stakeholders were identified, they commented on the creation of a Partnership Advisory Leadership Stakeholders (PALS) group. According to Flores and Claeys (2011), one participant noted, "Our PALS meetings provided participants the venue for increased interaction and ownership in identifying agenda and action items" (p. 329). In this instance, the start of the relationship included dialogue among the partners that strengthened shared understanding of goals and the creation of trust.

A distinction can be made early on in the partnership formation stage regarding the type of joint venture desired—one of collaboration to obtain jointly designed goals or one of cooperative arrangement based on coordination of efforts (Center for Higher Education Policy Analysis [CHEPA], 2005). CHEPA identified several practices to improve partnership success; notable among their listing was the creation of mutual relationships and trust. Assumed in this idea is the role of open and ongoing communication. The experiences and practices of those involved early on in building relationships set the stage for future patterns of behavior and expectations among partners. Thus, if ground rules are established about processes, shared goals created, and some accomplishments obtained as relationships grow, there is more chance for longer-term success.

> How relationships form and develop affects partnerships.
> Strategic partnerships build on collaborative efforts to obtain jointly
> designed goals, whereas traditional partnerships are based more on
> coordination of efforts.

Flora and Hirt (2010) reviewed partnerships among higher education institutions that sought to share space in which multiple institutions can offer degree programs. They found that the stakeholders (communities, institutions, students) were motivated by different reasons to participate or take advantage of the institutional collaboration. Using St. George's (2006) system model, they sorted rationales into state-centric models or neoliberal models. State-centric approaches view education as an investment in human capital and align with education's public good arguments. Neoliberal approaches, however, advocate for decentralization of higher education oversight and more institutional autonomy in which funding is linked to outputs. Cooperative relationships emerged based on shared values of the state-centric model that focused on the benefits of the relationships. Further, Flora and Hirt (2010) investigated the organizational forces driving the partnerships and found motivations to include collaboration, competition, and equilibrium, concluding, "the tug between these high collaboration and high competition times is offset through the independent center administration, resulting in a state of equilibrium" (p. 585). The ways relationships were formed initially set up the situation for competition versus collaboration, but these initial associations occurred within the organization's influencing context.

On one level, it is important to recognize the influence of organizational operations on initial relationship building. DiMaggio and Powell (1983) argue that "organizations compete not just for resources and customers, but for political power and institutional legitimacy, for social as well as economic fitness" (p. 150). Thus, many initial relationships form based on the ability of another partner to help acquire or leverage resources for institutional gain. The calculating appearance of judging with whom to form relationships may not always be superficially apparent, but an underlying tug of power and control is always at work in making the choice among potential partners and projects.

In addition to the influence of the institutional context in building relationships, the role of policy also creates a stage for action (Gomez & de los Santos, 1993). State policy can support burgeoning relationships in partnerships by reviewing interagency collaboration and funding formulas and considering policy levers such as incentives to foster multi-agency cooperation, coordination with federal programs, and expansion of existing partnership. Browne-Ferrigno (2011) reviewed partnership relationships in Kentucky when new policy requirements redesigned principal preparation programs. Instead of emerging organically based on mutual need, regional proximity, or perceived advantage, the author questioned whether "university-district partnerships can emerge simply through legislative mandate" (Browne-Ferrigno, 2011, p. 737). The mandate created requirements that differed markedly from previous program structures. University professors were queried on their perspective of the changes, and the findings concluded there were high levels of concern with the new process. In particular, concern was noted regarding interpersonal relationships and the shift from personal trust built up over time among partners versus partners thrust together without this critical element. The unfunded mandate was viewed with suspicion. Browne-Ferrigno (2011) suggested that "Kentucky policymakers mandated that second-order changes (Fullan, 2005) be instituted by a specific date but without consideration for the myriad impediments to institutional collaboration or the economic and geographic conditions within the commonwealth" (p. 753). The ways in which partnerships emerge based on budding relationships establishes a foundation upon which the future is built for the collaboration. These points of initiation may share some similarities between traditional and strategic partnerships, but differences soon become apparent.

The questions to consider at the beginning of a partnership include:

- What is motivating this partnership?
  - o What's in it for me?
  - o Do I envision this partnership fulfilling a short-term or long-term need?
- What do I know about my potential partners?
- How does this partnership fit with my organization's strategic goals?
- What is the context for this partnership?

Changing Relationships

Over time, partners reevaluate their participation in the partnership. Individuals involved in the partnership may move on from the home organization and no longer be involved in the partnership; the goals and vision of the partners may no longer align; objectives may have been accomplished and no need remains to stay involved; or the external context may change, making the partnership irrelevant. Le Ber and Branzei (2010a) note how role (re)calibration for partners occurs over time as "expectations form and reform cumulating forward toward the shared purpose of the relationship" (p. 152).

Role changes may occur due to trigger events, both positive and negative, and result in shifts in relationships. In addition, complacency in relationships may occur over time (Le Ber & Branzei, 2010a), and this complacency erodes the relational attachment. Over time, the ongoing nurturing of partnership relationships is critical for sustainability and achieving goals. Le Ber and Branzei (2010a) pointed out the following in their research conclusions: "Taken together, our propositions suggest that dyad success (or failure) hinges on partners' motivation to iteratively realign their roles" (p. 166). In order for relationships to be long-standing, engagement and attention to feedback about the partnership and relationships along the way becomes critical.

For the past 60 years, Dunbar High School (pseudonym), an urban Massachusetts school, has partnered with various entities, including UMass Boston, the Trefler Foundation, youth advocacy groups, the neighborhood health center, and the Northeast and Islands Regional Educational Laboratory at Brown University (LAB) as well as various businesses such as the New England Telephone Company and the consortium of Boston businesses called the Private Industry Council (PIC) (Leonard, 2011). Dunbar drew so much community interest and investment because it was a troubled school plagued with a high dropout rate, low test scores, and instances of school violence. Some of the school's partnerships were more effective over time than others. For instance, one successful and enduring partnership involved Dunbar and UMass Boston (Leonard, 2011). The relationship between the two entities formally started in 1968 when, as part of the Upward Bound program, the university began to invite promising students to UMass Boston for after-school academic support. This partnership was very effective in promoting student development. Dunbar's partnership with UMass strengthened over time. In 1997, UMass Boston undertook to turn around the whole school. With funding from the Trefler Foundation, college faculty members were placed inside the school to work on school reform with teachers, administrators, and students. Over three years, various innovations such as structuring of learning communities and placement of UMass faculty in internship positions in the school's classrooms were introduced (Leonard, 2011). These measures resulted in a lower student-teacher ratio and a steady supply of teachers for future teaching positions.

A partnership that proved to be ineffective, however, was between Dunbar and LAB (Leonard, 2011). The partnership was started in the late 1990s with an impressive budget and elaborate planning. It failed, however, largely because the LAB team did not attempt to form relationships with the school's administrator, and most of the students and teachers were not even aware of the partnership. As we argue in this chapter, relationships differ in scope and intensity within and between organizations, and relationship building is critical to long-term partnership success. Without relationships, well-intentioned and structurally well-planned partnership efforts can flop.

Over two decades, from the 1970s to the late 1990s, Dunbar worked more closely with UMass Boston and shored up many relationships. The school district ultimately showed increases in graduation rates and average daily student attendance during this time (Leonard, 2011). These gains coincided with the school's partnerships that evolved over time. Relationships were nurtured and communication routes opened that helped contribute to shared understanding of objectives. For a long-term partnership to succeed, the partners have to form strong relationships at the individual level. Here, relationships were the central resource of importance, even more than money.

Relationships differ in scope and intensity within and between organizations and change over time. Relationship building is critical to long-term partnership success. Without relationships, well-intentioned and structurally well-planned partnership efforts can flop.

In traditional partnerships, the social network created may be focused too narrowly on a specific task or be closely tied to particular champions. Thus, even though change occurs, it is limited in nature. For strategic partnerships, the social network is tied to the larger entity of the partnership and moves beyond strict individual interests to encompass the larger needs of the partnership and the institutional strategic plan. In this case, relationships may change based on changes in needs, people, or goals. It is via strong feedback loops that alterations occur.

Questions to pose over time include:

- Are the reasons to stay in the partnership still valid?
- Does the partnership fulfill a different purpose than originally intended? Is still useful?
- How have the changes in our internal/external context influenced how we look at the existing partnership?
- Have changes in personnel among the partners changed the effectiveness/utility of the partnership?

Over time, the weak ties (Granovetter, 1983) that help foster creation of initial relationships develop into strong ties for established relationships. Contributing to the strength of these ties are clear and strong communication

TABLE 3.1

Relationships Over Time

Beginning Relationships	*Changing Relationships*
• Institutional context and policy requirements set the stage • Informal to formal • Motivations—public good versus individual gain • Linked to social capital	• Creation of trust • Changes in organization/partnership needs recast relationships • Stability of actors/partners leads to sustainability • Strategic goal alignment and recalibration

networks, development of trust, and creation of shared consensus on standard operating procedures for the partnership. The success of the partnership provides increased cohesion among partners and a position of strength in looking to extend the partnership and involve new partners (Gregersen, Sowa, & Flynn, 2011).

The basis of interorganizational relationships (IORs) includes a broad array of configurations. Parmigiani and Rivera-Santos (2011) reviewed those relationships based on co-exploration and co-exploitation. For comparison, relationships based on co-exploitation center more fully on exchange of resources and fall in line with our notion of traditional partnerships that are built on the ideal of transactions. Co-exploration, instead, aligns with our concept of strategic partnerships that build on shared goal attainment. Knowing more about the relationships undergirding the models of partnerships helps in providing support to ensure optimal success or to understand why some partnerships fail. Table 3.1 outlines some of the central points for building and changing relationships over time.

Summary Points

- Relationships provide a critical building block in the formation of partnerships.
- An individual's level of social capital influences who is asked to partner, the level of resources available, centrality to decision making, and the type of knowledge accessible to partners.
- Traditional partnerships are coupled more loosely to an organization's core mission and planning efforts.
- Relationships change over the course of the partnerships, either expanding the social capital of those involved or spending this capital.

- Relationships influence the decision-making process within partnerships and within the home institution.
- Institutional operations and policy influence relationships within organizations and among partners.

CASE #3: THE POWER OF ONE

The role of the champion provides a critical element to partnership formation and sustainability. First, a champion can pull together disparate partners to form a collaborative venture. This ability may be due to the champion's high level of social capital, skill at framing the argument, or the perfect storm of good timing. Second, the champion can help hold the partnership together during times of strain and conflict. The leadership of the champion during times of distress can help partners come to a compromise.

In a small European country, available grant funding that required collaborations motivated a variety of partners to come together in response to a national request for proposals (RFP). One group, Technological Infrastructure (TI), had a champion who was well known and well respected in the country. Bill Reagan started his career as an academic and then branched out to the private sector to work in technology. Reagan worked with a variety of individuals over the course of his work life, including those in formal research roles and those on the ground in the field implementing technology.

When the RFP was posted, Reagan was the likely candidate to pull together a range of partners given his years in the field and his reputation. Others turned to him as the natural leader for the proposal effort, a call he gladly accepted. Reagan was able to tap into university partners, business partners, and individual academic scholars to help craft an ultimately successful proposal. He brought together members to the group that did not know each other before the partnership—he was the only person in common for everyone. When partners were asked how things went so well, the typical response was, "Because Bill was involved, he made things happen."

The RFP was successful and TI gained funding to create a new partnership to address technological needs in the country that would be used as a platform upon which future growth and collaboration could occur. As a group, TI created a new governing board for its activities and established a unique mission and strategic plan. This separate entity ultimately spawned two new enterprises from its initial grant work. Throughout this process, even when an executive director was hired, Reagan still helped guide actions. Reagan's power and influence was particularly notable when individual partners began to squabble over ownership of partner products. As one participant noted, "When there were disagreements, Bill put his foot down and took charge. He got the troublemakers to fall in line with the goals of the larger group."

Recently, another RFP call was announced. As the group discussed options for a proposal, the conversations provided a moment for reflection over accomplishments and next steps. As a group, TI operated separately from the organizations of the main partners, but it was integrally tied to the home institutions' strategic plans. These close ties created continued institutional support. However, some of the partner institutions were beginning to revise their organizational goals and plans, and as a result, their future involvement with TI was coming into question. In addition, the Great Recession meant that a number of individuals were laid off and the loss of their involvement in TI was beginning to strain the infrastructure of the collaboration.

All eyes turned to Bill as these changes were unfolding. He was able to address many of the initial fears, but fissures were beginning to appear. He cajoled and argued with partners and to date has been able to keep things moving forward. Also, because of Bill's clout, the partners were nervous about the day he would step down and retire. As of now, there was no likely candidate with the same level of influence to step into the champion role. The question left unanswered was: What would happen to TI when Bill wasn't there?

Case Questions

- What is the influence of context in this case (e.g., organizational size, budget, number of partners)?
- What are the advantages of a champion with weak ties to others?
- What would help institutionalize this partnership to sustain the loss of the central champion?
- How might individuals accrue more social capital to acquire the type of power needed to hold together a partnership?
- What types of relationships are required for successful partnerships?
- How might this case analysis differ if the partnership were traditional instead of strategic?

4

COMMUNICATION AND FRAMING

Communication is central to leadership (Bolman & Deal, 2008; Morgan, 2006) and to advancing change on campus (Hickman, 2010; Kotter & Cohen, 2002). Likewise, the role of communication and information sharing in partnerships is critical. How information is shared or presented to others can make a difference in how individuals react to new situations or requests (Fairhurst, 2011; Fairhurst & Sarr, 1996; Neumann, 1995). Study of organizational communication began in the 1930s and 1940s (Tompkins & Wanca-Thibault, 2001), around the same time as the increased focus on how to improve efficiencies and effectiveness in business occurred. A review of early research on organizational communication (Tompkins, 1967) categorized the focus of study into two areas, that dealing with formal and informal routes of communication and that dealing with superior-subordinate relations. This research mirrored the emphasis on top-down management styles in vogue at the time. By the mid-1980s, research on organizational communication viewed communication as occurring at multiple levels and influenced by interdisciplinary intersections (Jablin, Putnam, Roberts, & Porter, 1987). More recent inquiry regarding communication concerns the use of metaphors (Morgan, 2006), voice and discourse (Putnam, Philips, & Chapman, 1996), and networks (Taylor, 1993). Further, social network analysis (Carrington et al., 2005) embeds the routes of communication into a social context with an emphasis on relationships, thus highlighting how some individuals serve as key linchpins in sharing information. Popular literature might reference these individuals as "champions" of a project (Brinkerhoff, 2005); as we noted in the previous chapter, the success of these champions often depends on the type and extent of relationship linkages they possess.

At the heart of partnerships are interactions and relationships that build on strong interpersonal exchanges and communication networks. Some leaders or champions for change have an intuitive sense of the importance of communication in relationship building or an ability to use communication persuasively (Morgan, 2006). For others, the time it takes to prepare messages or to work on fostering better relations may be more difficult personally or not seen as critical institutionally (Bolman & Deal, 2008). Yet, fostering strategic partnerships requires well-developed communication networks and shared meaning among partners. This chapter highlights some types of communicating that might be used in building partnerships. Critical to communication networks is the art of framing (Fairhurst & Sarr, 1996).

At the heart of partnerships are interactions and relationships that build on strong interpersonal exchanges and communication networks. Framing by partners and leaders influences how the partnership is interpreted by others.

Framing applies on the individual level when people are faced with situations and interpret the event based on their own underlying schemata (Goffman, 1974), or when leaders present a particular set of meanings over another to help guide organizational members in interpreting events (Fairhurst, 2011; Fairhurst & Sarr, 1996). The two-way operation of framing presents an opportunity for individual partners to understand the new collaboration, but also to shape how both those in the inner circle of the partnership and within their home organizations understand the partnership. Leaders can frame events based on the concept of seeing the glass as half-empty or half-full; how leaders call attention to this interpretation begins to address how framing influences others. For example, Neumann (1995) reviews how two different presidents faced resource challenges—one president conveyed a sense of optimism and forward-looking potential; the other president called more attention to the challenges facing the campus, and as a result, campus members worried about the position of the college.

The two directions of framing are important to consider, especially at the points of intersection and influence. First, individuals can view events from their vantage point and based on their experiences. The concept of keying (Goffman, 1974) showcases how individuals ascribe meaning to new situations based on experiences (Senge, 1990) and how they use this grounding to begin to understand anomalies to expectations. Keying is the process by which new information is transposed onto existing understandings. Today, we might think of this as individuals having a place to "hook" new information based on experiences that are similar. Rekeying can occur when events are understood differently but are still connected to the primary base of understanding (Goffman, 1974). The context for opportunities to rekey highlights the important role of framing for leaders. How leaders frame actions influences others' interpretations (Fairhurst & Sarr, 1996). Framing by leaders sets the stage for creating a particular reality for the group. The social construction of ambiguous situations allows for many different interpretations, thus how the leader defines or makes sense of the events guides institutional members' understanding.

How leaders frame actions influences the interpretations of others. Framing by leaders sets the stage for creating a particular reality for the group.

Framing by leaders involves three components: language, thought, and forethought (Fairhurst & Sarr, 1996). Language helps focus attention on the core issues of concern, categorize information, and create meaning by using metaphors. The thought process for leaders implies that they first must make meaning of the situation for themselves before framing for others. Once a leader has a sense of how he or she understands the situation, the leader can call upon this understanding when faced with situations requiring spontaneity. This advance priming provides grounding for leaders when they must speak off the cuff. According to Fairhurst and Sarr (1996), "They must know how to handle a wide range of people and situations in split-second moments of opportunity, when there is not time for carefully scripted speeches—only time to break into the conversation and frame" (p. 10). One can readily see how forethought, or the lack of it, plays out in media coverage of political candidates when they are stumping for election. The same holds true for educational leaders who face queries by their staff, trustees, and constituents. In the case of partnerships, how leaders frame the collaborative affects how key stakeholders understand the collaboration and can contribute to sustainability.

Communication and framing both center on concepts of influence and networks. Fairhurst (2001) argues that "individuals also select influence tactics based on their objectives and goals" (p. 391). She further outlines how pressure is used to change the behavior of others, rational persuasion and coalition tactics for peers and leaders, and, finally, how authoritarian leaders use hard influence tactics such as assertiveness when success is otherwise unlikely. The type of influence used depends on the audience and the person's leadership approach. Thus, understanding more about the communication process in partnerships means first identifying the leader and the role he or she holds regarding communicating and influencing. As with other elements of the partnership model, where the leader is located matters. For example, an individual leader in the partnership may exert influence over proximal partners, but may have more or less influence within the larger home institution. In the case of a traditional partnership, on the one hand, the scope of influence may be most critical at the partner level to achieve immediate success of partner goals versus situating the partnership within the larger goals of the home institution. In a strategic partnership, on the other hand, influence occurs at multiple levels. Influence in a strategic partnership begins at the institutional level in persuading stakeholders to buy in to the strategic plan and institutional goals. In this case, how the vision is communicated and understood helps to predict the level of buy-in by campus members.

According to Fairhurst (2001), two key components of the vision process include how the vision is articulated and how it is implemented or made routine. Articulation of a vision highlights why the current status quo falls short and how the vision helps mark the path for a better future. Fairhurst (2001) goes on to point out how leaders can use frame breaking to move change forward. Frame alignment and sensemaking aid in articulating the vision and include the following tactics as mechanisms to use by making reference to:

1. values and moral justifications
2. the collective and its identity
3. history
4. constituents' positive worth and efficacy as individuals and a collective
5. high expectations from collectives
6. distal over proximal goals (Fairhurst, 2001, p. 408)

Once the vision and goals are articulated, it is important to make them routine. Framing tactics can include use of jargon, positive spin, agenda setting, experienced predicaments, and possible futures. Of these, two show the most promise for change—experienced predicaments and possible futures (Fairhurst, 2001). The first option showcases differences between the vision and the current status, which points to how to make choices to accomplish the vision (Hosking & Morley, 1988). Second, possible futures are highlighted when choices are made to resolve the mismatches between current reality and the proposed vision. How leaders communicate the vision and possibilities for the future through framing influences how campus stakeholders react. The notion of a leader painting a picture of what the future *can be* helps to highlight what must change to achieve the vision.

Frame breaking can move change forward. Envisioning the possible future helps resolve the mismatch between current reality and the proposed vision.

In strategic partnerships, on the one hand, the vision or strategies are articulated so that campus members understand how to make choices between options. Thus, when the opportunity to partner presents itself, involved campus members will draw upon the larger institutional vision and goals as a metric for deciding whether they should become involved in the new collaboration. In traditional partnerships, on the other hand, the match of partnership goals and institutional goals is less critical. Instead, the partners' micro decisions are made on a more personal level and seek to achieve more immediate objectives.

The use of partners' influence depends on the communication networks in place. A number of theories help explain how communication networks emerge, maintain, and dissolve (Monge & Contractor, 2001). Central to these networks are the relationships between individuals involved. Brass (1995) outlines various types of strength or connection assigned to individual actors and provides definitions for these linkages. For example, the individuals involved may have indirect links because they have a colleague in common, or they may have frequent direct communication with one another. The stability and strength of the relationship contributes to how the communication network evolves. Brass (1995) identifies different roles individuals might play in the communication network; these include star (central role), liaison (links others to one another), bridge (member of both groups), gatekeeper (controls flow of information), or isolate (little to no links to the network) (p. 45). An individual's role in the network dictates how he or she might frame information for others and indicates other types of ties to resources, influence, and leadership.

As anyone working in an institution knows, there are both formal and informal networks of communication in operation. Formal structures usually align with organizational positions and job descriptions that dictate policy and processes for sharing information. Informal networks emerge based on personal connections, often known simply as the grapevine. Typically, traditional partnerships emerge through informal networks. Yet, these networks are also important in creating and maintaining strategic partnerships because informal networks help sustain information flow among partners.

Monge and Contractor (2001) outline a set of 10 theories that help explain the emergence of communication networks. Each of these theories illustrates how connections get started and, thus, highlights why some communication networks become sustainable while others dissolve. Emerging partnerships build on these communication networks. Monge and Contractor's (2001, pp. 450–451) theories include:

1. theories of self-interest (investments in opportunities)
2. theories of mutual-interest and collective action (joint value maximization)
3. exchange and dependency theories (exchange of valued resources)
4. contagion theories (exposure leads to influence)
5. cognitive theories (leads to shared meaning)
6. homophily theories (similar to others)
7. theories of physical and electronic proximity (influence of distance)
8. uncertainty reduction and contingency theories (close communication reduces uncertainty)
9. social support theories (gain or mobilize social resources)
10. theories of network evolution (selection and retention)

Within this list of theories, the evidence of intentional and happenstance connections being at the root of the created networks becomes obvious. For instance, mere proximity or continued exposure to individuals can allow a network to emerge, whereas, communication based on mutual interest or social support may be more evident in strategic partnerships given the ties to intentionality in these approaches. Closely linked to the forms of communication networks are the various levels of social capital individuals bring to the table and the connections these levels have to initial relationship development (Coleman, 1988). Ultimately, how individuals make sense of the partnership is what matters.

Sensemaking

Central to the framing process is sensemaking (Weick, 1995), which involves how leaders arrive at their own understanding of events and how they, in turn, help others understand the situation. The duality of sensemaking from

the individual and leader perspective means that framing is occurring simultaneously and on multiple levels, but with different intentions and outcomes
based on position. Whereas individuals try to make sense for themselves and
tie information to their own experiences, leaders must first make sense for
themselves and then frame this understanding for others. This two-step process for leaders creates opportunities for alternative outcomes as two leaders
might view the same situation and come up with two different courses of
action and ways of framing (Neumann, 1995). Weick's (1995) sensemaking
model provides a mechanism for seeing how leaders can frame partnerships
differently. Here, leadership in the partnership may also involve different levels. For example, change models point out how top-level leadership buy-in is
critical for success (Kotter & Cohen, 2002), but leadership in the partnership
itself is just as critical as positional leadership within the home institutions.

Central to the framing process is sensemaking, which involves how
leaders arrive at their own understanding of events and how they,
in turn, help others understand the situation.

How college presidents frame partnerships to the campus members,
however, can influence how the partnership operates within the institution
and beyond. In this case, it then matters whether the partnership is more
traditional or strategic. In a strategic partnership, upper-level leadership is
integral to the formation stage of defining direction and, as such, leaders
are in a particular position to be able to frame this partnership for others.
Whereas in traditional partnerships that may emerge at lower levels in the
institution due to individual alignment, upper-level leaders may have more
or less awareness of the partnership, and as a result, campus members have a
different understanding of how this form of partnership fits in with the larger
institutional mission.

In sensemaking, leaders draw on their own personal ways of interpreting and creating knowledge (Senge, 1990) as well as experiences and past
interactions with campus members. Kezar and Eckel (2002) assert that
sensemaking is central to transformational change. They note how the use
of persuasive and effective communication helps explain the change process
to staff, and they found that "through the intensified conversation and widespread involvement those leading the change efforts and others involved realized that different subgroups viewed the campus and its work differently"

(p. 307). Thus, how leaders communicate the change under way must account for the fact that different constituent groups have different views of the partnership, depending on their organizational location, their role in the partnership, and their involvement in forming the initiative. The central role for leaders in transformational change is "creating an environment where sensemaking activities [can] occur" (Kezar & Eckel, 2002, p. 314). The creation of a space and time to help campus members understand change is critical to success. The fact that sensemaking occurs at multiple levels helps ensure that all subgroups of the institution are reached, but intention must exist for this level of understanding to happen in the creation of a shared meaning.

As partnerships emerge, how the leaders have experienced partnerships in the past has bearing on how they approach new initiatives. In addition, how well defined and operationalized the strategic direction is for the institution can create a resource for leaders as they frame because they can have something to point to on campus that links the new partnerships to plans already under way and familiar to campus members. As we previously noted, a central tenet of strategic partnerships is the connection between the individual institutions' strategic plans and the objectives of the partnerships. Underlying strategic partnerships is a plan for how the collaboration helps advance institutional priorities.

As partnerships emerge, how the leaders have experienced partnerships in the past has bearing on how they approach new initiatives.

Weick's (1995) sensemaking framework is outlined in Table 4.1. The table illustrates the differences between how leaders might frame partnerships differently based on whether they are traditional or strategic. The perspective presented is that of the college president because of the critical nature of this role in partnerships. Yet, the application of the various steps applies to all types of leaders regardless of formal position. The model contains seven properties: identity construction, retrospective, enactment, social interaction, ongoing sensemaking, extracted cues, and plausible versus accurate (Weick, 1995). The first step in identity construction provides the location in which leaders first try to make sense of the situation and form an understanding of both the partnership itself and how the partnership fits with overarching institutional objectives; the latter is of particular importance in strategic partnerships. This initial step fills some of the function of priming (Goffman, 1974), the process by which leaders react spontaneously when needing to frame the situation for others because of the thinking they have done on the topic. Leaders as individuals, thus, tie in new information with experiences as they begin to come to new understandings. An assumption at this stage about leaders is that they come to their positions having

TABLE 4.1
Leader Sensemaking Framework—Traditional and Strategic

Sensemaking Properties	Traditional Partnerships	Strategic Partnerships
Pt. 1—Identity construction	• Sees the partnership as discrete from core operations • Values the partnership for what it currently offers the institution • Does not intentionally frame the partnership for campus members	• Sees connections between the partnership and the college's strategic plan • Values networks • Collaborative leadership influences understanding
Pt. 2—Retrospective	• Uses previous partnering experiences to guide negotiations for current partnership • Evaluates current collaborators without assessing other options • Applies a zero-sum perspective to determine continuing with partnership	• Assesses past collaborations to ascertain links with current strategic objectives • Builds on previous relationships • Looks for opportunities for synergy
Pt. 3—Enactment	• May have little awareness of the partnership and may not consider it vital to the home institution • If framing occurs, frames the partnership from the perspective of what it brings to the home institution • May provide only public press support for partnership, but no resources or real support	• Intentionally frames the partnership as critical to strategic objectives • Spends as much time promoting internally as externally • Provides concrete examples of how the partnership links to needs of the home institution

(Continues)

TABLE 4.1

Leader Sensemaking Framework—Traditional and Strategic (Continued)

Sensemaking Properties	Traditional Partnerships	Strategic Partnerships
Pt. 4—Social interaction	• Limited interaction of the leader with the partners • Highlights the partnership as a transaction for campus members • Those immediately involved in the partnership advocate for the collaboration • The champion of the partnership is prime advocate	• Uses opportunities for interactions to link the partnership with the overarching strategic plan • Promotes the partnership as a critical part of the institution • Uses other central leaders as proxy to highlight the partnership
Pt. 5—Ongoing sensemaking	• Project champion may or may not promote early successes to home institution leaders and campus members • Home campus leader may or may not continue calling attention to the partnership in wider campus events and media	• Highlights how partnership outcomes link to strategic plan • Continuously frames the partnership • Uses early successes to prompt further support for partnership
Pt. 6—Extracted cues	• Logo for the partnership is loosely linked to the home campus • Campus members do not connect the partnership symbols with their work • Rituals are infrequent and unpredictable	• Home institution promotes logo in media materials • Home campus members recognize symbol for the partnership • Partnership rituals are part of the home campus culture
Pt. 7—Plausible versus accurate	• Partner champions create and promote a positive internal story • Champion advocates for partnership to home institution leaders and campus members • Positive outcomes of the partnership happen to link to home institution goals	• Highlights how the partnership helps support institutional goals • Evaluation of goals and objectives seeks continued alignment of partner and home institution strategic goals

Adapted from Weick, 1995.

experienced a wide range of institutional events and problems. Of import then is how new leaders might frame situations differently from seasoned leaders and how a person's capacity for persuasive communication also influences the process and how this changes over time based on experience.

The second property of the model focuses on the retrospective nature of sensemaking (Weick, 1995). Here, experiences guide current understanding. If leaders were involved with successful collaborations in the past, they may view current opportunities to partner more favorably. However, previous partnerships that ended poorly create an experience that may be difficult to overcome. For example, when trying to broker a partnership between two institutions to provide coursework jointly for a degree program, one of the partners may view this opportunity as a win-win, while another may see this as a threat—that the other institution is trying to take over. This view of threat may be based on experiences either with the institution itself or with other failed partnerships. The shadow of experiences influences current understandings, particularly for leaders trying to frame the new project for others, but also for the various members of the institution involved in the partnership.

The third property, enactment (Weick, 1995), creates a critical point in the sensemaking process; this is the stage when leaders first begin to frame the partnership for others on campus. This first foray of communicating the partnership to the campus is important because it affects how campus members begin to understand the partnership, its place in the institution, and, perhaps most important, the individual's role in and obligation to the new collaboration. How the president frames at this stage is critical. Individuals may leave with an understanding of how the new collaboration helps support their work, or they may view the partnership as a threat that will take away resources from their units or projects.

Social interactions are at the heart of the fourth property of the model (Weick, 1995). Here, how information is shared among individuals shapes how they come to understand the issue at hand (Berger & Luckmann, 1966). In the telling and retelling, explaining and listening, and interactions with different individuals regarding the same topic, meaning is made at the individual and group level. As with other elements of partnerships, interactions occur on multiple levels and in diverse formats. First, those intimately involved in the partnership have interactions and exchanges that afford them an understanding of the project. Second, those involved in the partnership interact with others in their home institution, which affords an expanded sensemaking experience. Third, how institutional leaders frame the situation and the forms of social interaction in which they engage help to guide the sensemaking that occurs on campus (Eddy, 2003). For example, when campus leaders attend partnership meetings, they have an opportunity to engage with those most involved in the project, which can enhance the individual leader's understanding of how he or she might present the partnership to the larger campus community. Also, the presence of the positional leader at partnership meetings brings legitimacy to the process. How leaders then interact with other campus stakeholder groups and discuss the partnership influences how sensemaking occurs on an institutional level (Eddy, 2003). When leaders fail to present the partnership to the larger community or discuss the relative nature of the partnership to institutional priorities, this lack of discussion deemphasizes the importance of the project for others. However, when leaders outline how the project fits within the institution and give campus members an opportunity to communicate about the project, different interpretations evolve.

How information is shared among individuals shapes how they come to understand an issue. In the telling and retelling, explaining and listening, and interactions with different individuals about the same topic, meaning is made at the individual and group level.

Sensemaking is dynamic versus static, as individuals continue to make meaning of situations (Weick, 1995). As new information is presented, and as individuals continue to share views in various social interactions, changes occur in how one understands partnerships. Contributing to this ongoing sensemaking (the fifth property) are the outcomes of the partnership. Achievement of outlined goals and objectives helps reinforce the benefits of the partnership, while changes in personnel involved in the partnership or challenges to early stages of partner actions may derail the partnership. The notion of early successes for the partnership aligns with change theory (Kotter & Cohen, 2002). Positive outcomes provide momentum during the formation and development stage of partnerships, which generally means that some change is occurring.

The use of symbols and rituals forms the basis of the sixth property of Weick's (1995) model: extracted cues. Here, the symbols create a shorthand sign for what the partnership represents to both of the partners involved and the larger institutional audience. These cues are evidence that change is occurring and can represent how others should understand these changes (Harris, 1994). An example of a symbol might be a newly created logo for the partnership that may use the colors of the various institutions or build from the taglines of the institutions and highlight a blended, new approach. This representation can showcase visibly what is hoped for in the new partnership, but also tie it to the roots of the individual partners involved.

The seventh property in Weick's (1995) model highlights how in sense-making plausible explanations are as critical as accurate information. The ideal here is that those making sense of a situation must find their perspective believable. Black and Gregersen (2003) point out that individuals' mental maps create a set of brain barriers, including the failure to see. Individuals will "see" something when they believe it. Thus, if one creates a plausible set of rationales regarding how they make sense of a situation, they will believe this over information that, in fact, may be more accurate. For example, as Neumann (1995) found, when a leader presents a particular view of a situation on campus, be it hopeful or dire, this is the vision of reality that campus members believe instead of what may actually be happening. A president may highlight a vision of where the campus is moving and not point out the dire state of campus infrastructure, and this plausible future view overshadows the reality of peeling paint and leaky faucets. Even though it is often helpful for leaders to package future visions that are hopeful for stakeholders, a danger lurks in misleading the campus about real threats. Ethics (Gino & Margolis, 2011), therefore, play an important role in this last stage of sense-making. The role of leaders as "sense-*givers*" (Thayer, 1988, p. 250; italics in original) becomes central to understanding the role of partnerships within larger institutional operations.

Framing Change and Partnerships

Strategic institutional collaborations involve some form of second-order or substantive change (Bartunek & Moch, 1987), which requires individuals to make sense of new situations by questioning long-held assumptions, and leaders to frame these new ideas and relationships for institutional staff. This type of deep change occurs at different organizational levels and often happens simultaneously among various units. How change is communicated to the various actors involved in the partnership, how the change itself is framed, and how transitions are facilitated affect the success of the partnership. Framing thus involves reinterpretations throughout the organization and between partners. In addition, different types of framing and communication are required during various stages of the partnership. In particular, *who* frames the change and *how* this information is understood are critical elements to be reviewed. Times of uncertainty and change (Morgan, 2006) provide ripe opportunities for leaders to help campus members make sense of new events and to connect new information with experience (Senge, 1990; Weick, 1995).

> Framing involves leaders' providing reinterpretations about changes
> due to partnering. Times of uncertainty and change provide ripe
> opportunities for leaders to help others make sense of new events and
> to connect new information with experience.

The role of leaders in framing change is critical (Kezar & Eckel, 2002). How leaders talk about change and emerging partnerships on campus affects how others understand these new collaborations. When leaders recognize how framing can be used, they can approach communicating with campus members in particular ways. Also, when leaders understand their own preferences for communicating and framing, they can assess the best options for preparing their messages. Preparing in advance, or priming (Goffman, 1974), enables leaders to respond quickly and with some anticipation of how the message will be received. Different approaches to leadership result in corresponding differences in communicating (Fairhurst, 2001). When leaders take a transactional approach, they rely on connections with actions based on assurances of some form of payback. Here, campus members may be induced to support a partnership by promises of additional resources, more job responsibilities, or improved outcomes for constituency groups, including students. Leaders using a transformational style instead promote actions by staff based on collaborative dialogue and shared commitment to a particular outcome.

Eddy (2010c) outlines a series of framing options leaders may use as they communicate with campus members. Visionary framing seeks to focus campus attention on the future and on possibilities, relying heavily on Weick's (1995) stage of plausibility versus accuracy. Step-by-step framing, on the other hand, focuses campus attention on immediate actions, which emphasizes ongoing sensemaking for incremental advances. Finally, connective framing focuses on the joint construction of meaning of all institutional members and occurs iteratively through dialogue and social interactions (Berger & Luckmann, 1966).

Visionary Framing

Leaders who use visionary framing focus campus members' attention to the college's future and possibilities rather than the current state of the campus. Visionary framing relates to the final property of Weick's (1995) sensemaking model—namely, framing information in terms of plausible (as opposed to accurate or current) outcomes—and builds on Fairhurst's (2001) idea of possible futures. Leaders using this frame highlight potential that can emerge from partnerships and contrast what is possible through the collaboration versus what is currently in place. This type of comparison allows for intentional links with the strategic plan. Here, leaders can highlight how the partnership aligns with the strategic plan (or how it does not) and institutional members are then able to make sense of how the partnership can aid the institution in seeking its goals and fulfilling its mission. For traditional partnerships, visionary framing typically takes place more at the partnership level than at the institutional leadership level. Given their immediate involvement, the involved partners are able to articulate the future of the partnership. If the outcomes of the collaboration happen to align with the needs of campus leaders, the partnership will be incorporated into the larger framing the president does for campus members. But, because traditional partnerships do not necessarily begin based on the role they fill in achieving institutional strategic objectives, there is no guarantee that central administration will pay attention to the partnership or that it will be framed for the larger campus community.

> Leaders who use visionary framing focus campus members' attention on the college's future and possibilities rather than the current state of the home campus.

Framing information in a visionary way requires college leaders to operate on the cusp of uncertainty due to unpredictable outcomes (Morgan, 2006). Yet, in current times of turbulence and unknown futures, visionary framing by leaders is timely as it allows followers to focus on the college's possibilities rather than its realities. Leaders framing a future vision must provide a view of this potential for stakeholders to envision. Having more opportunity between creating the vision of the future and creating the reality of the projects allows time for grappling with these new ideas and can allow for enhanced sensemaking.

An example of visionary framing in Ireland emerged from national policy that focuses on the potential of Irish higher education and ambitious goal setting. In 2011, Ireland's Department of Education and Skills published the *National Strategy for Higher Education to 2030* (Higher Education Authority, 2011), which presents a vision of higher education in Ireland in accordance with the anticipated social, economic, and cultural challenges of the next two decades. The report is notable for its strong emphasis on collaborations and partnerships, both local and international. There is particular emphasis on "engagement" with community, enterprise, and other national and international education and training providers. In its vision of the future direction Irish higher education needs to take, the report recommends that smaller institutions should be encouraged to merge with others to pool resources and improve quality. Another recommendation is for greater inter-institutional collaboration and cooperation to achieve critical mass in highly specialized areas.

The 2011 report was published in the backdrop of existing partnerships that emerged as a result of the Higher Education Authority's 1998 Program for Research in Third Level Institutions (PRTLI), which provided funds for research collaborations. The Irish government's National Development Plan (NDP), 2007–2013, also emphasized the need for higher education collaborations to achieve the NDP strategic goals (Department of Education and Skills, Ireland, 2011). One example of these alliances is between University College Dublin (UCD) and Trinity College Dublin (TCD), which was a PRTLI-funded partnership to pool resources and to provide a platform for researchers to collaborate on molecular medicine research. From this initial collaboration emerged the decision to build a research partnership, dubbed the Innovation Alliance. The 2011 strategy group report highlights this partnership as an example of creating critical mass for change through collaboration. The vision created showcases an umbrella partnership that can foster joint projects between the universities and with additional partners.

Given the size of the country, the Irish Department of Education and Skills' (2011) vision places emphasis on collaborations between higher education institutions and seeks to create critical mass to accomplish more together. The *National Strategy* provides a forward-looking template for institutions in the country to use as a map for change. Further, the language in the document provides campus leaders and partners a context for framing partnership opportunities to campus members. How the collaborations are framed within the country and internally for each partner will contribute to the partnership's success. One motivation for creating a forward-looking plan is the threat of decreased funding. Partnering is viewed as a means to frame and create a new and different future for higher education in Ireland.

Visionary framing is represented by fluidity in processing information for campus members. Communication is adaptable and flexible. The leader has the flexibility to create the message needed for the varied stakeholder preferences. Here, communication is a two-way street in which campus input is anticipated and used to identify areas that require further explanation or focus. The greater the opportunities for interactions with stakeholders, the more opportunity the leader has to create a vision of the future (Berger &

Luckmann, 1966). More feedback loops also provide leaders with a chance to frame their visionary message based on the current campus mind-set.

Key Points of Visionary Framing

- Focus on future possibilities.
- Partners are critical in creating the picture of this future at their home organizations.
- College president has close awareness of the vision of the partnership and uses emissaries to carry and to repeat the message throughout the organization and the partnership.
- Campus members know how the partnership contributes to campus goals/objectives.

Step-by-Step Framing

Not all leaders are adept at framing information in a manner that is visionary, nor are all campuses in a place where this type of framing will succeed. Indeed, although most college presidents have ideas about what they would like their colleges to look like in the future, many find it easier to focus their own attention (and that of campus constituents) on the immediate next steps toward accomplishing longer-range goals. In this scenario, small, incremental steps present a road map for campus change. Although this framing method can be effective in moving the college along, especially for campuses that require healing due to past troubles with leadership or campus operations, leaders must still remind campus members why each step is required. Small changes are often more acceptable to campus members who may fear change (Black & Gregersen, 2003). Even though a final vision may not be readily apparent, seeing how the steps of change are achieving objectives will be important. It is important to note that step-by-step framing can lead to successful campus outcomes.

In step-by-step framing, leaders focus attention on immediate next steps to accomplish longer-range goals. Small, incremental steps present a road map for change to the campus. Small changes are often more acceptable to those who may fear change.

Using this approach to framing for partnerships allows leaders an opportunity to introduce the partnership slowly to the campus in a way that highlights how the new venture helps to achieve campus objectives. In strategic planning, objectives are identified and steps outlined to achieve outcomes (Rowley, Lujan, & Dolence, 1997). Leaders can incorporate into these stages of planning and implementation elements of the partnership, framing for campus members and college stakeholders how the partnership helps achieve the overall objectives of the plan. In traditional partnerships, step-by-step framing occurs with partnership leaders. This framing focuses first internally for the collaborative group and then externally with the individual partnering organizations involved.

With a long history of collaborations and government backing, higher education institutions (HEIs—university level) and further education institutions (FEIs—technical and vocational continuing education) in the United Kingdom form alliances to franchise degrees and collaborate on projects. One such endeavor was a partnership between a university and FEIs in Wales on an e-learning project that included an undergraduate degree, a foundation degree, and a master's program based mainly on online teaching and learning (Connolly et al., 2007). The project relied heavily on collaboration because the FEIs were located throughout Wales. Each institution entered the partnership because of its own interests, which included greater credibility with the Welsh Assembly, pooling of resources and expertise, and, for the FEIs, greater progress toward blurring the lines between HEIs and FEIs through introducing higher education courses and centers at FEIs.

One major advantage for the partners in the e-learning project was existing partnerships between the university and many of the participating FEIs (Connolly et al., 2007). However, each FEI was distinct in character, and this individuality meant that the university's collaboration with each FEI required a unique approach and presented its own set of challenges. The university initially led the project, but the role of the FEIs gradually became more central as FEI faculty's feedback was critical to the success of the courses in catering to the needs of the students (Connolly et al., 2007). In contrast to the franchising model already in place, this collaboration included a great deal of technical, customer service, and monitoring support from the university. Each FEI collaborated with the university, and in later stages of the project, the FEIs started to collaborate with each other as well.

With such a large project, staff management presented one of the greatest challenges. From the outset, the project manager played a key role in fostering a sense of purpose and unity in those involved (Connolly et al., 2007). However, as the project progressed, management needed to make adjustments in accordance with the changing needs of the collaboration. Also, as the project was a pilot, policies and procedures were not defined at the start and had to be developed along the way. Communication is key in any partnership, and this project was no exception. Those involved in the project pointed out that clear lines of communication, policies, and objectives are critical for the success of this kind of project.

Another challenge in this partnership was the difference in cultures of the participating institutions. One of the greatest achievements of the collaboration was bridging this cultural divide by acknowledging the differences and remaining focused on the common goals, mutual benefits, trust, and mutual respect (Connolly et al., 2007). The staff involved in the project agreed that it was a valuable professional development experience. The project was a learning experience for staff and students and such collaborations can greatly benefit FEIs, which are an important higher education resource.

The incremental change that occurred in the partnership outlined earlier built on existing relationships and organizational structures. There were clear mutual benefits for all partners, and staff brought both commitment and enthusiasm to the partnership. Yet, acknowledgment of differences in institutional cultures was needed. In this emerging partnership, challenges were addressed as they occurred and were handled in a linear fashion. There was no grand scheme guiding development of the partnership; rather, each step of the process emerged based on needs at the time.

Focusing on immediate needs and celebrating short-term successes can be enormously helpful in systematically moving a college campus toward a president's vision (Kotter & Cohen, 2002). However, campus leaders must continually work to help faculty and staff make sense of that forward progress and remind them how each step contributes to the overall vision, particularly for strategic partnerships that highlight links with institutional strategies. How messages are framed depends on how the partnership is linked to the home institution's strategic plan. Step-by-step framing will look different for new leaders from how it looks to seasoned leaders and will differ based on the type of partnership being developed. As individual leaders gain experience, they better understand how their messages will be received. Leaders in the partnerships themselves also play a role in framing, for both their partners and their home institutions.

Key Points of Step-by-Step Framing

- Focus on immediate next steps and actions.
- Partners may or may not have close links to and support of their home institutions.
- Campus leaders may have a future vision for the partnership, but campus members only see the current emphasis.
- Partners may use this type of framing initially within the partnership as it is developing and forming.

Connective Framing

Connective framing involves leaders bringing together campus members to create the campus story jointly (Fairhurst, 2001) and relies on continuous dialogue to update the framing of this story. In this type of framing, leaders work closely with campus members to create and communicate a vision for the institution. Connective framers often rely on connected ways of knowing (Belenky, Clinchy, Goldberger, & Tarule, 1997), and they emphasize understanding, empathy, acceptance, and collaboration. According to Birnbaum (1988), framing information in a connective way

> means providing forums for interaction in which the "negotiations" that determine reality can be carried out, making more explicit the assumptions behind present rules and ongoing processes so that they can be accepted or challenged, and giving prominence to certain activities that can serve as attention cues for others in the institution. (p. 78)

Campus leaders in this case create opportunities for dialogue that highlights how the partnership fits with the strategic plan and use information gleaned from these conversations to update plans. For leaders at the partnership level, dialogue provides an opportunity to create trust among partners and begin to establish common expectations.

Connective framing involves leaders bringing together campus members to jointly create the campus story, using continuous dialogue to revise and update the framing of this story.

Connective framers often are transformational leaders who prioritize dialogue. Connective framers work collaboratively with constituents across campus and frame issues from multiple perspectives so that campus members can see not only the next steps but also the future direction of the college. Ongoing sensemaking becomes a critical step in connective framing. The types of iterative dialogue occurring present opportunities to address assumptions about the partnership and about campus operations. Acknowledging assumptions and how they influence decisions provides a step toward making second-order change (Bartunek & Moch, 1987); in particular, investigating the assumptions about the partnership and how it fits with institutional goals and objectives creates an open platform for dialogue and change. According to Duffy (2008), strategic communication connects elements of the institution's vision, mission, and strategic goals to larger community needs. This understanding of the work gives purpose to campus members and helps motivate them to participate in the partnership.

An example of connective framing occurred in Kentucky (Browne-Ferrigno, 2011). In 2005 the federal government mandated a statewide school leadership preparation program redesign in Kentucky through grant awards to Kentucky-based organizations (HJR 14, 2006). The U.S. Department of Education listed partnerships as one of 10 components of innovative leadership preparation. Additionally, the Wallace Foundation, a New York–based private national philanthropic organization, has been actively involved and heavily invested in school leadership preparation programs, and its research and funding has influenced programming. A third source of influence on leadership preparation in Kentucky is the Southern Regional Education Board (SREB), which has been involved in redesign and training initiatives in the state. In 2008, to expedite compliance with the national mandate, the Kentucky General Assembly changed its policy to align it with the redesigned programs (16 KAR 3:050, 2008).

The Wallace Foundation set the precedent and indirectly shaped state policy through its funding of Kentucky entities to create and conduct school leadership development programs (Browne-Ferrigno, 2011). Foundation funding encouraged Kentucky shareholders to form advocacy groups that supported the development of state policy (Fowler, 2012), including specific guidelines for colleges and universities for redesigning their leadership preparation programs. What remains unknown in this case is how mandated transformational change becomes sustainable.

The Jefferson County Public Schools' (JCPS) model for school leadership preparation has been held up as the epitome of what the initiative is meant to achieve (Browne-Ferrigno, 2011). Prior connections within the district laid the foundation for the ultimate success of the partnership, and its urban location and existing collaboration with the university created opportunities to advance the strategic plans of the institutions via the new policy mandates. The JCPS example reinforces the important role of monetary and technical support in the success of such collaborative initiatives. Thus, the grant only enabled an already successful partnership to expand its collaboration. The school leadership preparation initiative was spearheaded by the private philanthropic organization with support from local residents. These two forces combined to shape state policy regarding principal preparation policies. Campus and school leaders were able to collaborate most effectively given their proximity and previous relationships. The holistic management of the collaboration afforded a different view and framing for the individual partners and for the collective.

Connective framing is marked by adaptable communication that relies on feedback to change plans. Here adaptability and flexibility are different from those two characteristics in visionary framing. Instead of a focus on reporting out the leaders' vision to best match that of campus stakeholders, campus members are intricately tied to formation of the framing message and can readily identify their contributions. Only through joint creation of plans using dialogue is a final approach formed. Yet, as with other types of decisions on campus, final responsibility still resides with the president, who is accountable to overseeing boards of trustees and campus stakeholders. Thus, while multiple perspectives are used to connect the message on campus, how the campus leaders present the platform for dialogue and how they operationalize the jointly created plans makes a difference. Leaders operating from a connective perspective use input from a variety of sources, adjusting actions based on these interactions because connective leaders don't simply rely on their own thoughts and orientations; instead, they take into consideration a wide array of perspectives. Thus, their framing occurs in many ways through the facilitation of dialogue on campus.

Key Points of Connective Framing

- Collaboration and dialogue are cornerstones for connective framing.
- Feedback loops allow for constant adjustment for framing.
- The partnership is well connected to and emerges from organizational planning.
- Transformational leadership fosters and encourages dialogue.

Summary

Regardless of how information is communicated on campus, framing meaning for campus members is a central component of how others understand developing and ongoing partnerships. Communication is the linchpin to other actions on campus, reinforcing planning efforts, decisions, and actions. How leaders communicate is based on their own preferences, but adeptness at multiple forms of getting the message out to campus members assures that more stakeholders hear the message and make sense out of campus priorities. Leaders at multiple levels have great power in managing meaning on campus and can use the various communication venues to their advantage in moving their campuses forward.

In traditional partnerships, communication is rooted in more technical forms of information sharing and contains the norms and language of the partnering organizations. Here, on the one hand, communication involves exchanges about the process, tactics, and deliverables of the collaboration.

The goal is not to arrive at any new language or shared understanding; rather, the assumption is that members need to hear information using terms with which they are familiar and within existing communication routes. Communication and framing for strategic partnerships, on the other hand, involves the need to create shared language that reflects a distinct new understanding of the partnership and framing that considers the bigger scope of the resulting outcomes of the partnership. Framing in this instance will likely include some new terminology that still highlights ties to the institution's goals. The notion of multidisciplinary curricular programming helps to illustrate this concept. When distinct disciplines collaborate to form a new course offering or program, each discipline brings to the venture a distinct vocabulary and conceptual foundation. In creating a multidisciplinary approach to a topic, terms need to be defined so that all the collaborators understand their meaning and use.

Communication and framing for strategic partnerships involves the need to create shared language and framing that considers the bigger scope of the outcomes of the partnership.

Who does the framing may also differ between traditional and strategic partnerships. In traditional partnerships, framing occurs most often among those immediately involved in the new venture. For instance, if a partnership occurs between a faculty member and a community agency, those doing the majority of the framing will be the faculty member and those leading the community agency. Strategic partnerships, however, assume a higher level of leadership involved in the framing because top-level positional leaders will frame for campus stakeholders how the partnership aligns with the institution's strategic plan. An overarching message is constructed, and those at various levels throughout the organization may participate in framing at their level and fill the role of becoming a communication link or emissary for the overarching message. In this case, shared meaning and understanding of the message is critical. Questions that emerge when considering framing include:

- Is my partnership a traditional or strategic one?
- How do I determine what frame is in use?
  - What would the key features be if the frame was visionary? Step-by-step? Connective?
  - How might it look different if I am at a top- or mid-level position?

- After determining what frame is in use, how do I communicate about it to others?

  o To whom should I communicate?
  o Will I communicate the same way to each stakeholder?

Boundaries

Boundaries exist among partners because of different organizational contexts and forms of operation. Inherent in these boundaries are sources of power, which may be emphasized or leveraged by the framing that occurs within each partnering institution. Daniels (2011) found in his research with interagency participants in England that "different organizational configurations directed participants' attention to different forms of action and the development of different forms of professional identity as each site moved towards multi-agency work" (p. 44). Framing focused attention in a way that either supported or challenged the burgeoning partnership. Daniels (2011) concluded that those institutions with the weakest boundaries allowed for more transformation to occur, whereas those with strong boundaries exerted more power and control and resistance to change. Leaders can influence boundaries by working on creating stronger boundaries to restrict collaboration and instead promote acquisition of other units in subservient roles, or on opening up the boundaries to enhance opportunities for collaboration. Here, approaches to leadership contribute to how boundaries are perceived.

Weak institutional boundaries allow for more transformation to occur. Through framing, leaders can fortify boundaries either to restrict collaboration or to open them to enhance collaboration.

According to Warmington et al. (2004), boundary-crossing among partners results in creation of new professional practices and forms of interacting. These individuals are able to walk between both "worlds and translate the cultural models of one group for another" (Hora & Millar, 2011, p. 92). Often, these boundary-crossers have high levels of social capital and strong social networks. The process of partnering changes the context and thus creates new dynamics and pathways for communicating. The partnership ultimately creates new spaces in which individual partners and institutions may recast how they relate information among the various stakeholders and involves a jockeying for power. The loose coupling (Weick, 1976) of institutional areas and departments provides a context for weaker boundaries, within the institution and among organizations. This setting creates uncertainty and, as a result, an opportunity for leaders, within the partnership and institutional leaders, to frame the new joint venture. The level of power and influence the leader possesses can sway the reach of the framing that occurs, not to mention the access to resources to help support the partnership. Bernstein (2000) reviewed the notion of power and control in pedagogy within schools. He looked at two levels, the macro-level of institutional structure and the micro-level of personal interactions. In this case, the interactional level occurred between teachers and their approaches to pedagogy. Framing exerts a type of control of the boundaries and in the priority given to meaning making (Bernstein, 2000).

Leaders play a critical role in boundary management of partnerships and how stakeholders perceive these boundaries. Traditional partnerships often retain strong boundaries, with the partnership only loosely coupled to the home organization's core operations. Here, the lack of framing of the partnership by top-level leaders actually keeps these boundaries strong and organizations resistant to change. Because leaders do not acknowledge the role of the traditional partnership within the institution, campus members may be unaware of the work of the partners and will assume correctly that the partnership is not deemed central to the college. Strategic partnerships instead have weaker boundaries. Leaders seek out partners that will help meet their institutions' goals and objectives. As a result, these leaders are intentional about framing the work of the partnership to campus members.

Summary Points

- How leaders communicate and frame change influences how change is interpreted by campus members.
- Sensemaking must occur for leaders before they can help frame meaning for others.
- Leaders frame traditional partnerships and strategic partnerships differently.
- How partnerships are understood on campus affects sustainability of the partnership.
- Links exist between approaches to leadership and approaches to framing.
- Communication in traditional partnerships has a more technical orientation, with the focus on processes, tactics, and existing terminology.

- Framing in strategic partnerships involves the creation of shared terms and language and takes on a multidisciplinary orientation.
- The types of boundaries that exist among organizations either create barriers to partnering or foster collaboration.

CASE #4: THE WIZARD BEHIND THE CURTAIN

Leaders play a central role in telling the campus story; they help embellish traditional strengths, signal new directions, and tie together various initiatives seamlessly. When a good saga is created and the outgoing message is well received, partnerships obtain greater buy-in from stakeholders. At Notebook Community College, the president, Douglas Rain, was particularly adept at captivating his audience as he spun different stories during a conversation. The college was small, located in a rural area of the state about two hours from the "big city." The president recalled how his first impression of the campus was of a hopeful future. He stated, "Many of the senior faculty would be retiring in five years or fewer and this gave me the opportunity to develop some perspectives on campus, to develop not only new programs, but new views within the traditional programs." Rain felt that he could cast old ways of doing things in a different way. Campus members were ripe for change, and this created a context in which to create a new institutional saga and partner with an expanded number of collaborators.

One of the first initiatives Rain undertook was to start a program in which all incoming freshmen received a laptop. He put out internal campus RFPs to allow departments some additional funding if they were willing to be early adopters of intentionally integrating the use of laptops within classroom settings. Pretty soon, programs began to expand, the college was receiving accolades for its work regarding integration of technology, and faculty and staff turned into believers. As Rain recounts campus members' reactions he remembers that the comment was, "Wow, he's not just talking about things!" Putting words and actions together helped to sell the new vision of the college as a critical collaborator for new ideas and projects.

Yet, concerns were raised about how much change the college could sustain. As President Rain tried to focus on the positive aspects of the college, rather than its deteriorating infrastructure, lower pay scales, and student dropout, he seemed to be casting an even wider net in seeking external funding via partnerships and making the college more entrepreneurial. Despite a central strategic planning document, new projects and initiatives were often undertaken. In the past year alone, the college had started a student garden project that provided fresh produce for the campus dining halls, opened an on-campus dairy and cheese store, created the Equine Institute, started an animal identification program for thoroughbred horses, built a cogeneration plant for electricity generation, and started work on a methane program to generate electricity. Most of these initiatives involved working with outside businesses or researchers at other colleges. The president identified himself as a visionary leader who was excited about the possibilities on campus. He used every communication vehicle on campus at his disposal to promote the story of the college as a place of innovation. Rain walked around campus and engaged people in conversations, sent out campus e-mails, held town-hall-style meetings, and met with community leaders; and in all these venues he kept weaving in stories of campus growth, optimism, and success.

The focus of growing businesses on campus and in the community helped contribute to shoring up economically an area in which the family farm was becoming a relic of the past and area kids were moving out of the region to seek better opportunities. But as President Rain noted, campus members will often complain, "Douglas, we have more ideas than we have money or time to deal with, so slow down." Making some of the business-oriented decisions meant that Rain often acted unilaterally and without campus consultation as he created new partnerships with external organizations.

Case Questions

- As President Rain framed change on campus, how critical was it to connect the message to the college's strategic vision?
- How did the president first understand the campus saga himself before framing it for others?
- What might be key differences in framing for a small, rural college leader versus a big, urban college leader?
- Can a campus engage in too many partnerships?

- In this case, innovation was the thread that was woven throughout all the campus partnerships. How can a college or a college leader come up with a centralized message like this that ties together a wide range of partnerships?
- How would you categorize the partnerships on this campus—traditional or strategic?

5

ORGANIZING PARTNERSHIPS
The Role of Structure and Resources

J ust as individual relationships play a role in partnerships, so do the structures and cultures of the institutions involved. Each partnering organization has its own way of operating, which affects how it deals with its partners and what type of resources it can contribute to the project (Pfeffer & Salancik, 1978); it may even affect partner choice (Pidduck & Carey, 2006). As we know, partnering institutions are motivated by different factors and, as a result, devote more or fewer of their resources to partnership development and ongoing operations. Over time, institutions may also find the importance of the partnership shifting. Changes in priorities, resources, or leadership affect traditional partnerships in particular, but strategic partnerships are also subject to shifting strategic objectives that may enhance existing partnerships or make them less relevant to institutional goals. Two central organizational features influencing partnership development and sustainability are organizational structures and the use of organizational capital in various forms (e.g., time, human capital, funding, space, etc.).

There are several ways to look at organizational structures. Institutional theory builds on a symbolic-interpretive environmental approach to viewing organizations (Hatch & Cunliffe, 2006). From this perspective, individuals see knowledge as relative and believe that organizations are socially constructed realities that are mediated by individuals. Selznick (1957) first opened the door to considering organizations as fluid when he introduced the concept of institutional theory based on his observations that organizations

101

adapt and react to a range of influencing factors, including both internal desires for change and external public demands (Astin & Astin, 2000). The structures that may be affected in partnerships include new uses of space, time, and human resources, which may lead to changes in workplace norms (Gardner, 2011). Internal changes may mean that a collective or shared approach is taken for activities that previously occurred in isolation. New norms that emerge due to change take time to be incorporated into the culture, into the fabric of the institution, and into partnership structure (Schein, 2010).

Institutional theory highlights how organizations are fluid—they adapt and react to a range of internal and external influencing factors.

We have argued that there are many embedded assumptions in mandates and calls to partner that require working across sectors. One assumption is that education organizations will not have trouble partnering because there is a meta-goal of learning and teaching that crosses public education and higher education, and they all fall within the same organizational market domain of educational institutions (Fullan, 2005; Gross, 1988). On a conceptual level, this may be accurate, but across organizational levels—and therefore, across any partnership—educational organizations are not uniform in goals, structures, norms, cultures, and processes. Perceived and real differences confound partnerships, even within the most similar organizations, such as between a high-performing and low-performing elementary school, or between two similarly sized public universities. The differences in structure, culture, and resources can be even more problematic and dramatic when the collaboration is between an educational institution and a for-profit organization (Casion & Gewolb, 2013; Googins & Rochlin, 2000).

We approach organizational structures and resources from two main perspectives. The first looks at how these critical features of partnerships are identified and understood through different organizational frameworks (Bolman & Deal, 2008; Hatch & Cunliffe, 2006). At a basic level, how one identifies structures that work or do not work, what resources can be brought to the partnership and at what cost, and so on, are a function of the perspective used to look at both the partnership itself and the organizations used to form it (Bess & Dee, 2008a). The second perspective focuses on similarities and differences in how we view structures and resources when examining traditional and strategic partnerships. We argue that, even while the inventory of resources and structures may not change, their meaning, use, and importance do change when viewed from different partnership perspectives. Overarching these two aspects of organizational perspectives is the policy context. Reactions to policies and the demands of accountability create an environment of reaction within organizations and sectors.

Policy Context

Implementation strategies, goals, and standards for accountability differ quite a bit across sectors, which makes the mandate approach to traditional partnering problematic for those required to do the actual work (Andrews & Entwistle, 2010). It is especially important early on in the partnership formation process to discuss and agree on expectations and partnership goals (Hora & Millar, 2011). We argue that in traditional partnerships, certain priorities are assumed to matter more than operational structures and cultures, such as external mandates and obtaining funding. For example, calls for proposals for Race to the Top funding set in motion radical changes in school processes, and the requirement to have in place unified data systems that crossed educational institutions resulted in states passing legislation and putting structures into place to meet the proposal requirements. These changes were required for grant submission, which, if you did not get an award, became an unfunded mandate of partnering without the prerequisite understandings, common purpose, institutional and systemic changes, and personnel to support the initiative (Rabe, 2007). The proposal mandates for Race to the Top funding would translate differently within strategic partnerships because partners would be aligned better to meet strategic objectives, thus making the shelf life of any preceding requirements an investment that can endure beyond the single activity of a grant application.

Differences across sectors make policy mandates problematic for those required to do the actual work because of mismatches in cultures, operations, and motivations.

Capacity building, while often thought to require financial inducements, also takes into account human capacity, skill development, increased collaboration, and longer-term developmental objectives rather than just short-term compliance (McDonnell & Elmore, 1987). The investments here of time, support, and possible funding help sow the seeds for development of partnership capital built on shared norms, meanings, and trust (Amey et al., 2010). The policy expectation here is for future returns. In the case of partnerships, bargaining focuses on the capacity of the partnership to create a win-win outcome that is the result of mutually beneficial bargaining rather than positional bargaining that focuses on individual payouts. McDonnell and Elmore (1987) argue that there can be intermediate returns from capacity-building investments, which might help explain why one would continue to invest beyond the first phase of partnership development. What this form of policy instrument also suggests from a leadership perspective is the need to publicly recognize the accomplishment of short-term goals so that members see why the partnership is important (Kotter & Cohen, 2002), or as McDonnell and Elmore state: "policymakers use immediate measures as proxies for longer-term effects" (p. 139). This longer-term outlook speaks to an organization's culture of tolerance for ambiguity and a willingness not to have fully matured returns immediately, which might be a challenge in this age of immediate accountability.

System changing requires a break from past practices and operations as a result of a shift in authority (McDonnell & Elmore, 1987). The underlying assumption here is that the current form of operations is not working and something must change. In the case of partnerships, the work of change agents throughout the organization is evidence of a change in authority. In addition, the development of partnership capital results in the creation of a new and different type of authority from before. "Altering the distribution of authority among institutions, by broadening or narrowing the type of institutions that participate in the production of things of public value, will significantly change the nature of what is produced or the efficiency with which it is produced" (McDonnell & Elmore, 1987, p. 143). Partnerships, as a result, hold great promise and potential in their ability to result in system changes and new ways of addressing problems together.

Depending on the dominant frame of organizational structure in place within the organizations that are partnering and within the partnership itself, leaders-champions-implementers will see and potentially select different policy instruments to achieve their objectives (McDonnell & Elmore, 1987) or means of creating change (Bolman & Deal, 2008). In a highly structured or bureaucratic organization, a rational approach to partnering may occur that attempts to identify assumptions and underlying reasons to partner and what would be involved, including weighing costs and benefits, in a very logical fashion (Chaffee, 1983). Top-down mandates, whether internal or external to the institution, often err on the side of assuming extreme rationality between partners, with the notion that structures and processes can readily align within market niches. With compliance with the mandate as a goal, the assumption is that system rationality (rules, regulations, norms and compliance, etc.) overcomes distinctions among partners; that there is a best plan that can be discerned and then followed; and that issues of power, culture, individual identity, and values succumb to logical implementation of directives or coercion.

The type of organizational structure in place influences the way partnerships are viewed and how champions can best promote these burgeoning collaborations.

From a more political perspective, a leader might look at the partnering arrangement from a win/loss bargaining perspective, tallying up what the organization might hope to gain or lose. Often, at its root is a "What's in it for me?" mentality. While this perspective might be most realistic for resource-constrained organizations (Pfeffer & Salancik, 1978), how conflicting interests are resolved can use varying forms of negotiation. According to Baldridge (1971), first, what receives attention in a political approach targets what gets decided. Various interests may be represented by partners, with those most prominent receiving the most attention. Second, who gets to make the decision matters. When decisions are made by those on the ground in the partnership, particular interests are represented, as opposed to when decisions are made by leaders more removed from the work of the actual partnership. Third, the range of options considered depends on the prominence of particular information in the decision making. Comparatively, a rational model assumes all options are considered. The advantage of the political perspective is that conflicts can result in airing a wider range of considerations, whereas the disadvantage is the abuse of power by those in more dominant positions (Morgan, 2006). The inequities of resource bases can create tensions in partnerships if they are not dealt with in a forthright matter.

When policies and perspectives emerge from a collegial vantage point, partners are viewed as colleagues and decisions are made collectively. Educational institutions consist in the main of faculty professionals, and the collegial process of governance and decision making is strong (Baldridge, Curtis, Ecker, & Riley, 1977). Yet, this model often proves cumbersome due to the time required to reach consensus and an inability to address conflicts satisfactorily. Further, recent shifts to a neoliberal orientation of operation forces thinking and decision making based increasingly on business norms (Slaughter & Rhoades, 2004). What may occur within partnerships is a focus on collegial approaches in the day-to-day operations of the partnership or in initiation of the partnership and a move to other forms of more complex decision making as the partnership becomes larger and more embedded into the fabric of home institutions and as an entity distinct from the individual partners. Understanding more about the frameworks of organizations that partner can help participants understand the partnership process more fully.

Partners and campus leaders should consider the following questions relative to the policy context:

- What type of policy instrument is in place?

  o A mandate that we are required to follow?
  o An inducement that might provide some benefits for following?
  o A change in capacity that expands our ability to address the policy goals?
  o A system change that alters authority?

- How are the policy goals interpreted in my organization?

  o Do we assume a rational mode of application of the policy based on a bureaucratic model?
  o Does a political organizational setting exist in which policies supporting partnering are viewed as win/lose?
  o Do we have a collegial model of operations in place that builds on consensus?

Identifying Frameworks

Partners differ in their perspectives due to their orienting paradigms and operating frames (Bolman & Deal, 2008); thus, how individuals view reality contributes to the paradigms that guide their worldviews. Burrell and Morgan (1979) presented four paradigms based on objective versus subjective views of reality and approaches to change:

1. The functionalist paradigm relies on an objective view of reality and a preference for regulation and control.
2. The interpretivist paradigm views reality as a set of subjective interpretations and demonstrates a preference for stability.
3. The radical humanist paradigm builds on a subjectivist view of reality and is oriented toward change.
4. The radical structuralist paradigm conceptualizes an objective reality and prefers change. (Bess & Dee, 2008a, p. 44)

Because these approaches are so distinctive, individuals operating from differing paradigms are at odds with one another. Thus, partners need to determine the paradigms they hold to ensure that they align within the partnership. Next they should consider the organizational structures that emerge based on these underlying paradigms. When partnerships develop, better alignment of these philosophical orientations creates better supports for success.

Structure

Bess and Dee (2008a, 2008b) discuss the complexity of higher education and review a number of operating frames of reference that function slightly differently depending on the viewer's philosophical orientation. Within each frame are assorted assumptions about organizational design—how work is assigned, how reporting lines flow, how functional areas interact, and how communication occurs. Organizations may be oriented within structural, human resource, political, or symbolic frameworks (Bolman & Deal, 2008), and as a result roles may look different within each. Yet, this typology often belies the interactive influence of the frames (Bensimon, 1989) and the need to view organizations more organically and adaptively. Viewing partnerships from a systems perspective highlights the connections between partners and the environment. The influence of the proximate environment (Hatch & Cunliffe, 2006) is particularly relevant when dealing with partnerships, especially when the external environment is complex and volatile.

Organizational structure adapts to external stimuli and includes work assignments, reporting lines, functional area interactions, and how communication occurs.

While we immediately tend to think of organizational charts and physical plant when considering organizational structures, it is important to recognize that decision-making processes, communication and information flow, and working relationships between units are also part of structure (Hatch & Cunliffe, 2006). Although culture is harder to discern, it, too, contributes to how things really get done and how partnerships evolve and become institutionalized or how they create second-order change (Schein, 2010). All of these facets of institutions help define the boundaries of an organization at any level, foster its identity, and facilitate or inhibit its ability to align resources, goals, and values (Kuk, Banning, & Amey, 2010).

Galbraith (2002) proposed that organizational design is key to institutional effectiveness, and we would argue also to strategic partnerships specifically. His theory emphasizes five components:

1. strategy
2. structure
3. process
4. rewards
5. people

Each of these components of organizations can contribute to establishing strategic partnerships. Just as the actual structures are important for the design, so are implementation and process. Included in these steps for partnerships are setting up joint processes regarding planning, decision making, implementation, and evaluation (Galbraith, 2002, p. 66).

Forming partnerships draws from the research on organizational structure design, but with the added complexity of multiple partner involvement and potential differences in underlying operating organizational frameworks. As we argue throughout this volume, the planning process is critical because it brings partners together to assess needs, set goals, plan evaluation, inventory resources/assets, design implementations, and so on. This initial planning process should allow for identification of shared goals as well as developing policy coherence, negotiating resource allocation, and determining sustained commitment to the partnership (Rowley et al., 1997). These activities occur at multiple levels and need to be connected sufficiently or risk the partnership falling apart. Gardner (2011) argues that executive leaders may state the vision but project directors handle the day-to-day and have to continually reinforce goals, create joint understanding, and evaluate process. Those involved in the partnership on the ground are boundary spanners with their home institutions (Bess & Dee, 2008b). These border-crossers may change with time as the positions tend to be more informal rather than maintaining a particular role in the structure (Clark, 2000).

Gardner (2011) offers three types of structures for partnerships based on Mintzberg's (1979) categories that were present to one degree or another. Mintzberg outlines five parts of organizing structures: the operating core, the middle line, the strategic apex, support staff, and the technostructure. The first type of partnership organization outlined by Gardner (2011) was the single-tier partnership. "This form is straightforward with the technostructure (internal expertise of the partnership), leadership and support aspects missing" (p. 69). Because of these missing links, the single-tier partnership may not be well known to others in the organization and not integrated into the organizational design, which results in less access to organizational resources and capital. Alternatively, multi-tier partnerships include the full range of features of Mintzberg's (1979) model. The final type of partnership structure Gardner (2011) outlines is a complex-brokered model in which the technostructure originates from outside the partnership. As we have argued, sustainability results in partnerships that are able to continue once initial funding or mandates disappear. The partnership network that emerges in multi-tier or complex-brokered models of partnerships enables first-order change to emerge, but deeper second-order change might still be elusive if underlying assumptions about partnership motivations, operations, and alignment remain unexamined.

Based on the Mintzberg (1979) model, mid-level managers may not always realize the strategic value of some partnership initiatives. This short-coming underscores the need for communication and framing at all levels. Gardner (2011) posits that the design of funded projects undermines sustainability. Yet, someone needs to pay attention to sustainability and determine how to insert the role of the partnership and its objectives into the ongoing work of the organization so that the appropriate structural processes adapt to the point that the partnership becomes part of the fabric of the institution. Differences between traditional and strategic partnerships may revolve around the type of structural model in place—either simple and single-tier or complex-brokered. In the complex-brokered model, Gardner (2011) argues that aspects of structure and support are borrowed or brokered from existing structures rather than developed for or embedded in the projects themselves. For example, grants

---

Executive leaders may state the partnership vision, but project directors handle the day-to-day business and have to continually reinforce goals, create joint understanding, and evaluate processes. Boundary spanners prove critical to this framing.

---

administration is done by a central grants office rather than anyone in the partnership taking the time to understand this part of the process. This type of brokering may occur along the range of elements in Mintzberg's (1979) model, such that the content expertise, technical expertise, or management relies on a range of consultants rather than training those within the partnership or home institution to do the work. This process creates an elaborate network instead of a strategic partnership and may not be sustainable.

Other aspects of structure and processes that may become critical within the partnership include work structures and reward structures. For example, the assignment of teaching, work hours, or contract stipulations, where they exist, sets the framework for how work will be done within the partnership. Who assigns the work and how closely the project is tied to job performance evaluation sets the stage for how partnership work is enacted and what motivates individuals to continue the work and have it embedded long term. Seemingly simple issues such as accounting systems and permission to use work resources like computers for efforts not tied to your job description may dictate how the partnership's goals are accomplished. Moreover, there are also the larger institutional versions of the same set of considerations. On an individual level, staff might be concerned about their own investment of time and resources into a partnership. Likewise, the institution may consider its own interests over those of the partnership.

Another element of structure concerns credit for the partnership's work. Who gets named first in the partnership may imply a certain level of credit and may assume a certain level of power. Who gets monetary credit or how student credit hours are awarded further contributes to the structural elements of the partnership organization. The internal governance of the partnership might be dictated by partner structure; leaders from the business partners may be accustomed to top-down decision-making authority, whereas in educational organizations, faculty prerogative may influence curricular-related decisions. Meshing structural reward systems thus plays a role in the partnership design and can set the stage for long-term viability of the partnership. Because each partner has its own reporting hierarchy, discussions about organizational design are critical during partnership development.

The range of questions that emerges when partners consider organizational structure include:

- What type of paradigm does our institution use? What type among our potential partners?

  o How might the paradigms partners use create challenges?
  o How might the paradigms partners use leverage deep change?

- What structure of partnership would provide the best outcomes for our goals (single-tier; multi-tier; complex-brokered)?
- Who in our organization is a boundary spanner? How can we foster more border crossing by our staff?

Frames

Viewing organizations using different frames can provide insights into actions and help explain why particular events or reactions unfold the way they do. "A frame is a mental model—a set of ideas and assumptions—that you carry in your head to help you understand and negotiate a particular 'territory'" (Bolman & Deal, 2008, p. 11). The ability to "see" and comprehend organizational operations quickly and unconsciously creates a fast process in which individuals come to conclusions or assessments of their understanding quickly, and these judgments influence how they interact with others. Gladwell (2005) describes this process in *Blink* and the metaphor serves well, as in a "blink of the eye," individuals take in information and draw conclusions about partners, the partnership, and individuals' roles.

Complementing one's paradigm, individuals use frames to make sense of organizations and these frames hold assumptions about roles and structures.

The four-frame model put forth by Bolman and Deal (2008) offers a means to compartmentalize organizational operations, with the conclusion that those able to operate from multiple frameworks see a greater view of what is really going on. The frames include structural, human resource, political, and symbolic, and each of the frames has a set of underlying assumptions that help in understanding how those operating from these perspectives see the world and help illustrate the mental maps they use.

The structural frame builds on the notion of rationality, rules, and formal roles and responsibilities. Several key assumptions are held. The overarching reason for organizations to exist is to achieve established goals and objectives, which are achieved through specialization and division of labor (Weber, 1948). Coordination and control guide staff and employees. Decisions are made rationally and from the perspective of what will benefit the organization first and foremost rather than following individual agendas. Structures are designed based on current circumstances, and when things go awry, careful analysis and restructuring can resolve the problems (Bolman & Deal, 2008). The metaphors applied to the structural frame are a factory or machine (Morgan, 2006). In partnerships, a structural orientation would result in rules and processes that need to be addressed and aligned for the greatest success. The danger is that longer-term sustainability might be jeopardized when there is misalignment among the home institutions of the partners regarding processes and procedures.

The tight boundaries between parts of the organization operating in a structural frame create little expectation for working outside the specialized functions of the defined job description. Partnerships in this kind of organization most likely would be established in one of two ways. One way is top-down by presidents and CEOs using formal agreements; stipulating with other senior leaders how the partnership would unfold, or at least its goals and timetable; and then sending directives down the line to be enacted. Various state and federal mandates mirror this approach, where the decisions to partner are made at the highest levels with an assumption that, having been decreed, the partnership will move forward and succeed (McDonnell & Elmore, 1987). Another way in which partnerships may be established in a functional bureaucracy is at the other organizational extreme—at the grassroots (Kezar & Lester, 2009). In these instances, partners are often those with personal relationships (those not directed by their job description) who want to work together or see a need they can address by working together. These arrangements typically are connected to recognized job function but the institutions where partners are employed do not necessarily recognize or sanction them. Here, "I like working with you so let's do this together" or "If you and I just put our heads together, we can figure this out" characterizes the rationale.

The extent to which partnerships initiated this way at this level take hold is spurious, though it can be done. Typically, these collaborations become highly associated only with the individuals involved and constitute ways of working around the intact system rather than trying to change it (Bartunek & Moch, 1987). Tight bureaucracies may inhibit rather than promote effective partnerships, because they are designed for routine and less-questioned practices. At the same time, they are efficient and rational. Flexible, organic organizational structures may be more amenable to strategic partnerships, or at least those that are bringing perceived newness and capacity building to the table (Argyris & Schön, 1978). Organic structures allow for more creative, critical thinking and focus less on how to put new ideas into old structures. In the end, successful partnerships need both structure and flexibility. Leaders throughout the organization must understand the difference created by the nature of organizational structures on partnering.

Organic structures allow for more creative, critical thinking and focus less on how to put new ideas into old structures.

The human resource frame evolved when assumptions were questioned regarding the role of employees and what motivates staff to work. A core assumption in this frame is that organizations exist to serve human needs rather than the reverse. The relationship between individuals and organizations is symbiotic—they need each other—and when the fit is poor, both suffer (Bolman & Deal, 2008). When the fit is good, benefits accrue to individuals and the organization. The metaphor associated with the human resource frame is family. At phase two of partnership development, a focus on the human element can begin to establish rapport among partners and may be the driving force to initiate the partnership.

Like the individual relationships that might initially drive partnerships in a structural frame, these links are a source of partnership development from a human resource perspective. In professional organizations, personal expertise is a source of value and influence. Alliances emerge because the focus of the organization is on supporting individuals. Consider an example of faculty working across institutions based on common interests in research. They may find that this work aligns with the call for funding proposals that require partnerships among institutions. The alignment of the partners in this case occurs organically and from the ground up (Kezar & Lester, 2009). The relationships here tend to be person-centric, however, and may not last beyond the participation of the individuals involved. In this case, how the partnership is institutionalized will matter for sustainability when the initial champions are gone.

The political frame views organizations as the scene of competing interests and conflicts. Assumptions central to this perspective are that organizations are filled with differing coalitions and that these groups have fundamentally different core operating values and worldviews. Decisions are made based on the allocation of scarce resources, building on the notion of resource dependence theory (Pfeffer & Salancik, 1978). Battling over scarce resources results in conflict in everyday operations. It is through negotiation and brokering that goals and objectives are determined (Bolman & Deal, 2008). Because so much of partnership work is interacting among different organizations, conflicts are bound to emerge. Differing power bases influence how decisions might be made, and the desire to pool resources and talents together reinforces the role of these resources in decision making. An apt metaphor for the political frame is a jungle (Bolman & Deal, 2008).

In the political frame, power contributes to how conflicts are resolved. The role of power is so central to partnerships that we dedicate a section to this topic. The power of influence is particularly salient in partnerships because how the agenda is established and objectives are determined create the guiding framework for the partnership. Jockeying for position occurs throughout the partnership, especially when it is first established. Relationships continue to evolve over the duration of the partnership as power shifts and trust builds.

> The battle over scarce resources creates conflicts within partnerships,
> with those in control of resources wielding more power.

The symbolic frame focuses on the meanings individuals take from situations versus reality. As a result, multiple meanings might emerge depending on viewpoint. The use of symbols helps create meaning and lessen ambiguity. Often in newly created partnerships a first order of business is to create a logo that represents the new entity. Ceremonies and rituals help reinforce the stories of the organizations, with newcomers inculcated with these stories of origin. Consider how pervasive the story remains of the origins of Apple or Hewett-Packard and the infamous garages that served as their starting sites. Partnerships build on similar stories of origin, and ultimately, the culture created holds the group together. Metaphors associated with the symbolic frame include theater, carnival, and temple (Bolman & Deal, 2008).

The type of culture in place influences how partnerships start and develop. When the culture is more structural in nature, individuals may be less willing to change their work roles and functions when new partnerships are formed. More collegial cultures, on the other hand, may provide a more welcoming environment for new partners. Moreover, a culture will emerge in the newly formed partnership that may or may not affect the organizational design of the new collaboration and set the stage for how trust is built (Bergquist & Pawlak, 2008).

As partners consider the types of frames their home institutions use, it becomes evident that mismatches in frame orientation among partners may create conflict. Emerging questions include:

- What type of organizational frame and orientation does our institution use? What type(s) do our potential partners use?
- How much can the leader influence the predominant frame throughout the institution relative to how the historic culture of operations guides actions? How does this influence the partnership?
- Research shows that leaders able to use multiple frames have greater success. How can leaders learn to operate outside their comfort zone? How can leaders manage the intersection of multiple frames throughout the partnership?

Resources

The amount of social or organizational capital that individuals have influences how relationships are negotiated, including educational partnerships.

Factors contributing to the level of influence one brings to the table incorporate the type of support individuals have in their own institutions, the level of tension and willingness to negotiate among partners, and the formality of the partnership arrangement—ranging from informal to formal (Gray, 1989). Resource dependency theory (Pfeffer & Salancik, 1978) underscores the power associated with possession of key resources among partners. On the one hand, organizations are vulnerable when they are too dependent on others for resources central to their operations. On the other hand, partnerships provide a means for pooling resources and working together that allows institutions more protection from the vagaries of the environment. The negotiation that takes place among partners, however, still retains various levers of power that often favor one partner's position over another's. Over time, as trust builds, resource and power differentials may become mediated. Yet, a danger exists in institutions that enter external partnerships for the wrong reasons or when these partnerships result in mission drift for the home organization (Bess & Dee, 2008a). Adaptive organizations are able to change their internal operations to address environmental challenges and thus provide a better fit (Heifetz, 1994).

Organizational capital emerges from a number of sources and may look different depending on the frame in operation. Organizational capital includes resources—both physical and human capital, structure, influencing power, network connections, patterns of interaction and decision making, culture, and longevity of personnel, to name a few. The recent focus on academic capitalism points to the growing levels of organizational capital vested in academic administrators relative to faculty (Slaughter & Rhoades, 2004) and the push for market-driven decision making, including the desire to partner for efficiencies.

An assumption about organizational resources among partners is that they are not distributed evenly within a given unit or across units, and that organizational capital related to the partnership is also not stable over time (Gardner, 2011; Kotter & Cohen, 2002; Morgan, 2006). Organizational capital may accrue or be tied to formal positions or may be a function of other less tangible aspects of the organization, such as years of institutional experience, expertise, control of resources, and networks (Morgan, 2006). How individuals in the partnership can draw upon organizational capital and use organizational structures to benefit the partnership varies—sometimes based on position, sometimes based on sources of power and proximity to decision making, and sometimes based on personal desires (Foucault, 2001). Individual decision making regarding the desire or ability to access organizational capital may rest on the choice of how much a person wants to invest his or her own social capital into the program, how much trust exists that the other partners will follow through or invest, and how much competition there is for the scarce organizational resources available. For example, a superintendent and community college president may be able to access resources that create an articulation agreement between the schools, but the teachers or faculty in the classroom have to negotiate differently based on their access to resources and decision making about curriculum and how they spend their time. The choice to engage in a partnership and to use a portion of organizational resources happens by default in other projects receiving fewer resources or none at all.

Organizational resources are not distributed evenly among partners and individuals have varying levels of access to organizational capital within their home institutions. Thus, organizational capital within partnerships is not stable over time.

The desire to partner may be based on the fact that other similar types of colleges are opting to partner. Institutional isomorphism influences how resources are deployed as universities continually compare their work to others'. DiMaggio and Powell (1983) posited three forms of institutional isomorphism: coercive, mimetic, and normative. Coercive pressures occur via legislative mandates or in the presence of power differentials among institutions, with those with more power influencing those with less. Mimetic isomorphism results in institutions copying the behavior of others, whereas normative isomorphism occurs based on the norms in the field. Thus, for partnerships, multiple factors influence behavior. Who has the power to commit organizational resources matters. Because there are few, if any, overarching norms for partnering, policy mandates or the behavior of bigger, more powerful partners has great impact on other organizations. Seeking to replicate successful partnerships is also a motivator, but one that must be viewed with caution as environmental and situational factors will differ. What works in one location may not work in another.

When contemplating organizational resources, several questions emerge for partners, and these questions change over the evolution of the partnership:

- What type of resources do I have control over and can commit to a partnership? How might this change over time?
- What type of resources does my potential partner bring to the relationship? How might this change over time?
- How central are the resources of others to my core operations?

- How does the presence of other successful/failed partnerships influence the formation of my current partnership?

Power

Power is not only the ability to get others to do something but the potential ability to do so through influencing relationships (Bess & Dee, 2008a). All members of the organization have power and the ability to effect change (Kezar & Lester, 2009; Morgan, 2006). Power exists in multiple forms. Morgan (2006) categorizes 14 different sources of power (see Table 5.1); because the power of gender management is less central to our conversation on partnerships, this power element is not included in the table.

According to Foucault (2001), *practices of the self* inherently consider relations of power, and when individuals speak the truth (parrhesiastic), it proves dangerous to their work roles, reputation, and social capital. Thus, those with less power are wary of engaging with others and may question motivations. Shaping faculty members' and institutions' choices about partnership participation involves a range of self-choices, which include deciding to act based on rewards, travel, prestige, and recognition. Partners bring varying degrees of power to the partnership and the intersection of all these variables creates a high level of uncertainty.

Power held by individuals and by organizations might change over time within the partnership. Roles predict some power sources, with formalized positions affording a level of legitimacy and access to resources (Bess & Dee, 2008a). Other power emerges due to what individuals know and their involvement in informal networks (Morgan, 2006). Role conflict occurs when there are incongruities about role expectations (Gross, Mason, & McEachern, 1958). This problem crops up in partnerships when roles at the home institution and within the partnership differ and require competing actions by individuals.

Individuals make choices based on a number of factors. As Foucault (1982) argues, two key components undergird the reconstitution of identity: technologies of power and practices of self.

> Technologies of power are external to self, and exert pressure from the outside, while practices of self are operated by individuals themselves, who have the agency to utilize strategies of power to manage and affect their constitution as subjects through recognition of the possible subject positions available. (p. 208)

The pressure to partner based on economics of scale, stakeholder demand, or policymaker mandates all work to influence individuals about partnering choices.

TABLE 5.1
Power Differences in Traditional and Strategic Partnerships

Sources of Power	Traditional Partnerships	Strategic Partnerships
Formal authority	• Reliance on formal roles and hierarchy • Partnership leaders may have more authority in the partnership than their home institution	• Leaders use authority to frame partnership • Leaders use authority to engage in organizational learning
Control of scarce resources	• Level of access to institutional resources depends on position • Certain partners may have access to particular resources that are critical to the partnership	• Positional leaders have greater range of access to resources • Strategic objectives guide use of scarce resources
Use of organizational structure, rules, and regulations	• Policy mandates and inducements guide partner selection and partnership formation • Creation of standard operating procedures in partnership typically based on hierarchy	• Policy for capacity building and system changing guides partnership formation • Strategic plan guides partner selection
Control of decision processes	• Partnership decision making loosely coupled with home institution process • Localized within the partnership	• Partnership decision making tightly coupled with home institution goals • Linked to home institutions
Control of knowledge and information	• Partners hold close to information and only share as trust develops • Information localized • Informal leaders hold specialized knowledge	• Partners share information to obtain overall objectives • Open systems of communication
Control of boundaries	• Champions serve as individual border-crossers • Vested in individuals versus institution	• Leaders conduct environmental scanning to identify potential partners • Collaborative leadership creates more porous boundaries

(Continues)

TABLE 5.1
Power Differences in Traditional and Strategic Partnerships (Continued)

Sources of Power	Traditional Partnerships	Strategic Partnerships
Ability to cope with uncertainty	• Initial champions tend to be early adaptors of change and higher risk takers • Resistance to change given existing mental maps	• Adaptive leadership provides neutral space for work • Organizational learning creates feedback loops to deal with uncertainty
Control of technology	• Partnership technology may be distinct and separate from home institution • Social media focused on partnership versus links to home institution	• Partnership technology may link more closely to home institution • Social media used to disseminate and frame partnership
Interpersonal alliances, networks, and control of "informal organization"	• Social capital of partnership champion critical • Social networking often based on informal relationships	• Leaders throughout the institution use their networks • More social network hubs exist due to collaborative leadership
Control of counterorganizations	• Loose coupling allows partnership to have weak links to home institution • Framing by partnership leaders	• Transparent communication and focus on strategic objectives provide platform for conflict resolution
Symbolism and the management of meaning	• Partnership identity is created via logos and public relations • Framing of the partnership on home campus depends on level of coupling—tight or loose	• Leaders frame the critical role of the partnership to achieve strategic objectives • Framing occurs on multiple levels
Structural factors that define the stage of action	• Creation of partnership structure creates culture for new group • Pull of home institution roles may constrain new partner roles	• Partnership roles are identified and embedded in home institutions • Partnership structure organic
The power one already has	• Social capital of individuals is high and contributes to network development • Individual social capital increases due to partnership work	• Both formal and informal leaders have power and use this to leverage strategic objectives • Power increases due to ongoing organizational learning

Adapted from Morgan, 2006.

Technologies of power (Foucault, 1986), which are built on power structures within the organization, determine how individuals act and view organizational members as mere objects of transactions. Technologies of power have increased in institutions of higher education as colleges seek to meet the demands of the marketplace, resulting in greater pressure for faculty to perform more. Tensions evolve when institutions constantly react to external pressures (using the postmodern idea of fluidity; Bauman, 2001), and these pressures affect organizational and personal choices. As individuals struggle to position themselves and to create their professional identity, they must navigate their own agency and sense of self relative to the norms of the profession and institutional environment. A delicate balancing act results.

By their nature partnerships create a negotiated environment. How individuals and institutions come to agreement is based on a number of factors, including motivations, resource dependency, external demands, leader charisma and influence, and choices on how best to use assets and resources. These decisions are influenced not only by the frames in practice, but also by the type and amount of power the various actors hold. Creating a neutral space (Amey & Brown, 2004) can provide a place in which power and role conflicts can be worked out and negotiated. How partners determine boundaries is an important consideration to long-term sustainability (Hora & Millar, 2011).

A number of questions emerge when considering the role of power in partnerships:

- What type of power do I have?
  - How does external power (technologies of power) influence my actions?
  - How do practices of self interact with the power of other actors?
- What type of power will work best to support the partnership?
- What type of power do potential partners possess? How will this best support the partnership?
- What are the outcomes of interactions of the various power factors among partners? Counteracting versus leveraging?

Organizing Traditional and Strategic Partnerships

Strategy provides organizations with direction and focus and can help eliminate uncertainty (Mintzberg, 1987). Chaffee (1985) underscores the multidimensional and situational elements of strategy and offers three models of strategy: Model I-Linear Strategy; Model II-Adaptive Strategy; Model

III-Interpretive Strategy. Merely thinking about strategic partnerships as monolithic is simplistic and ignores the complexity of the strategic process. As noted in the earlier review of the various frameworks and paradigms used in organizations, the *how* and *what* of organizations matters. Thus, *how* strategic plans are formed and for *what* reasons will also influence partnerships. Further, Gourville (2004) distinguishes between the structural and psychological aspects of strategy. In the case of the former, a plan is in place with steps to achieve objectives, but this logical progression must also account for individuals' readiness to follow the plan as they weigh the pros and cons. Fear of the unknown and the mental maps of current practice create barriers to change (Black & Gregersen, 2003).

How strategic plans are formed and for *what* reasons will influence partnerships. All partnerships involve change, which often results in initial resistance.

Strategic partnerships may be better at integrating the frames of organizations as they view work occurring less in silos and more in collaborations than those involved in traditional partnerships. In strategic partnerships, how resources start to be defined and used differently, or with different intentions, can influence how partnership capital emerges. When we think of educational organizations, including those involved in partnerships of any kind, obvious resources come to mind, including finances, political and bureaucratic power, and organizational size and "market share." From a strategic perspective, perhaps others come from blending resources across organizations to achieve shared goals. For example, building a partnership based on improving student learning is at the center of many large grant funder actions (e.g., Achieving the Dream, Lumina, Gates, Spencer) and involves pooling resources to achieve improvements for student learning. The alignment of the underlying ethos of improving educational opportunities provides easier access to resources for institutional leaders, ultimately creating a focus on campus change efforts that improve structures and supports for student learning. In traditional partnerships that rely instead more on a barter system, choices are based on transactions. For example, two organizations may decide to partner in a traditional partnership based on faculty or teacher interests in obtaining a grant that allows them both to accomplish a personal project. In this case, the grant provides a level of resources to supplement those available to the individual partners involved. The level of organizational resources may be limited by the location of the institutional partner in the organization and by other competing institutional projects.

Change and Partnerships

As we outlined in chapter 1, a number of change models can help inform our understanding of partnerships. Linear models typically include a series of steps to accomplish the desired change (Kotter & Cohen, 2002), whereas process models rely instead on a more dynamic system built on central foundational elements (Fullan, 2006). The application of any change model to partnerships, however, needs to consider the more complex relationships involved in partnering and how these social networks result in access to different forms of organizational resources (Granovetter, 1983). Further, the ties of organizational change to strategy distinguish between traditional and strategic partnerships. Adaptive change models allow for an encompassing look at the change process within partnerships (Heifetz, 1994; Kezar, 2013).

The type of change that occurs in partnerships depends on a variety of factors, all of which influence the type of organizational design created for the new partnership (Daft, 1995). Bess and Dee (2008a) created a matrix based on the work of Daft that highlights these relationships (see Table 5.2). The lower the levels of uncertainty and environmental complexity, the more structural or mechanistic the partnership design becomes. The higher the levels of environmental change and complexity, the more organic the type of structure created. In the latter case, partners are highly motivated to change current practices as they sense the urgency to do so (Kotter, 2008). Associated with the amount of change required is the type of change.

Incremental or first-order change builds on the status quo and is more associated with traditional partnerships. This level of change aligns with the low change categories in Table 5.2. Alternatively, strategic partnerships can result in deeper, more pervasive change that questions the status quo and the assumptions associated with current actions (Bartunek & Moch, 1987). This organic level of change takes into account feedback loops and changes in behaviors that are a result of input from the environment. Strategic change corresponds with the model in Table 5.2 at these higher levels of change.

First-order change is associated with the policy instruments of mandates and inducements (McDonnell & Elmore, 1987). Second-order change assesses the goals and processes in practice to determine whether they are the most appropriate and effective, and then changes the system to better meet goals and objectives. Because underlying assumptions about goals and processes are examined and challenged, there is much greater opportunity to continually change and even change radically. Capacity building and system changing provide purposeful interaction among partners to do more than can be done independently.

TABLE 5.2
Links Between Organizational Design and Environmental Uncertainty

Amount of Environmental Change	Low (stable environment)	*Low Uncertainty* • Mechanistic structure; formal, centralized • Few departments • No integrating roles • Little imitation • Oriented toward current operations	*Low Moderate Uncertainty* • Mechanistic structure; formal, centralized • Many departments, some boundary spanning • Few integrating roles • Some imitation • Some planning
	High (unstable environment)	*Low Moderate Uncertainty* • Organic structure; teamwork, participatory, decentralized • Few departments, much boundary spanning • Quick to imitate • Oriented toward planning	*High Uncertainty* • Organic structure; teamwork, participatory, decentralized • Many departments, differentiated; extensive boundary spanning • Extensive imitation • Extensive planning and forecasting
		Simple	Complex
		Environmental Complexity	

From Bess & Dee, 2008a, p. 185.

Deeply held beliefs, relationships, patterns of behavior, standard operating procedures, and structures all are challenged on the way to second-order change. Leaders have to understand and facilitate the grieving process that goes with losing traditional ways of work, but also be willing to engage in this kind of more substantive change in meaningful ways (Bolman & Deal, 2008). Campus members must recognize and address the paradox of both trusting that change will be beneficial and acknowledging that they will have to be risk takers during the change process (Black & Gregersen, 2003). Embedded in the notion of risk taking is acceptance of failure. Changes to process can make long-term employees in particular wary of learning new systems, when they know and understand existing systems; Black and Gregersen (2003) refer to this as the failure to move.

First-order change builds on the status quo, whereas second-order change involves questioning underlying assumptions to achieve deep and transformative change.

A contributing factor to the type of change that occurs is the level of organizational learning in place (Argyris & Schön, 1974). First-order change (single-loop learning) uses feedback of existing systems and processes to correct performance errors. Second-order change assumes that double-loop learning occurs (Argyris & Schön, 1978). Evidence of generative learning (Senge, 1990) contributes to how we distinguish strategic partnerships from more traditional partnerships. In strategic partnerships, learning is embedded in the process for members throughout the organizations not just those directly responsible for or involved in the partnership.

The process of single-loop learning in traditional partnerships, on the one hand, may outline the joint agreement's specific roles and tasks, but not necessarily correspond with learning more about the point of any of these decisions or about the long-term impact of these choices. Double-loop learning in strategic partnerships, on the other hand, engages partners in conversations about learning goals, instructional strategies, academic/faculty expectations, shared strategic objectives, and so on, which allows both organizations to consider the types of changes required in their home institutions that will best accommodate and support the partnership. Yet, we should not assume that all organizations or partners are interested in second-order change or double-loop learning. Control, resistance to change, perceived power and status, and fear of failure all could contribute to lack of capacity to actually change to this extent (Black & Gregersen, 2003). If power in the partnership is located too centrally at the top, deep learning may become inhibited. The environment in which double-loop learning can flourish includes a culture of inquiry, risk taking, open communication, and decentralization (Argyris & Schön, 1978).

The emergence of international partnerships adds complexity to the partnership process. On the one hand, educational institutions desire to create global citizens in their institutions and to meet employer demands for more culturally savvy graduates (Slimbach, 2010). On the other hand, successful in-country partnerships are difficult to create and sustain, and the added layer of complexity due to working with organizations steeped in cultures that may differ significantly from that of the U.S. educational system creates an additional hurdle and potential stumbling block. The types of partnerships created internationally may emerge from individual faculty work or from institutional desires to enter new educational markets, which underscores how the motivation to partner may influence the type of systems required and the form of change needed. How individuals make sense of these forms of partnerships depends on the mental models they hold.

Change and partnerships result in a set of questions for partners, champions, and leaders, which include:

- Is the organizational environment stable or unstable? Simple or complex?
- What type of change results from the creation of the partnership— first-order or second-order?

  o How do institutional decision-making processes influence the type of change occurring?
  o What resistance exists to the change process brought about by the partnership?

- Does our institution engage in single-loop or double-loop learning? How does this influence the work of the partnership?
- How does the change process align with the policy climate?

Mental Models and Partnering

Mental models provide individuals and organizations with shortcuts in facing new situations as old practices and perspectives gleaned over time create a memory that is recalled when facing a similar situation. This quick point of mental access proves useful as individuals face myriad situations every day, but it also presents a challenge when these habitual mental maps become outdated (Black & Gregersen, 2003). Consider what occurs on the first day a construction roadblock is erected on your traditional route to work. You note the construction initially, but your pattern of driving to work is so ingrained that it may take you two, three, or more days of facing the roadblock to commit this information to memory before you remember to take the detour. Likewise, mental maps of organizational structure, operation, and goals are ingrained in the minds of workers in organizations. Changing these mental maps requires unlearning (Mezirow, 1990), in the case of individuals, and using double-loop learning, in the case of organizations. Shared mental models are present at the intersection of individual and organizational learning. Not all organizational members have the same mental maps, nor do all those operating in newly created partnerships. Over time, new mental models are built concerning the partnership.

Mental maps provide us with shortcuts as we face new situations, but they also may be limiting how we react to new events—both individually and organizationally.

Leaders of partnerships can use sensemaking to help shape the mental models of others. In this case, the partnership may provide a chance to learn new skills and rethink old patterns. It is easier to take risks in a trusting environment. Partnerships fall apart due to a lack of trust, an inability or unwillingness to relinquish control, complexity of the actual joint project, and differing abilities to learn new skills (Farrell & Seifert, 2007). In organizations with several partnerships, it may be confusing for institutional members to know at any given time who is a competitor and who is an ally (Gardner, 2011). Further, when the urgency to collaborate is framed as make-or-buy decisions, the decision becomes one of transaction costs versus a strategic alignment decision. Until partners create trust among themselves, various actors may be unwilling to share information or expertise because the mental map may still be one of competitor versus collaborator. It is ineffective and shortsighted to see partnerships as isolated sets of transaction or trade-offs. It is critical to consider partnerships holistically and to envision transferring what is learned within the partnership process as an influencing factor for operations.

Summary Points

- Institutions entering partnerships often have different underlying organizational frameworks.
- The type of paradigm and frameworks in place dictates how partnerships are formed and what elements receive priority.
- The level of organizational capital, in its wide variety of forms, can create power imbalances among partners.
- All partners bring different forms of resources and power to the collaboration.

- How power differentials are negotiated sets the stage for long-term sustainability or partnership failure.
- Individuals and organizations enter partnerships with different mental models, and these orientations may be based on role, network within the institution, and underlying philosophical orientation.

CASE #5: SHIFTING SANDS: WHAT REMAINS STANDING?

Time changes relationships and organizational needs. A partnership initiated 25 years ago in a small rural school district in the Midwest, Hill City, was meant to help the rural community build a new football stadium. After 10 years, the partnership generated millions of dollars in support for school athletics and created an endowment that benefited student programming. High school sports provided an opening to engage students in thinking about going on to college and advancing their education.

Hill City is a small community that formed when immigrants from Sweden, Italy, and French Canada moved to the region to work in the mining industry. There is little cultural diversity in the region. About a third of the population is under 18, with the area's largest population over 60. About 10% of families live below the poverty line. The largest employer in the region is the hospital, with increasing numbers of layoffs occurring in some of the few remaining manufacturing plants. These layoffs led to an exodus of population, resulting in a decrease in population over the past 20 years.

The public school is a hub of activity in the community and the strong commitment to education is reflected in the higher graduation rates and greater numbers of citizens with a high school diploma than the state average. This strong sense of support for education and tight-knit community led to the germination of the partnership. The high school operates with a staff of 24 teachers, but this group has worked to establish a range of community projects over time. The superintendent and athletic director were contemplating how they could fund new football uniforms for the school team and came up with the idea of a golf outing that would include two high school alumni who are nationally known coaches. The partnership tapped into relationships with two well-known alumni of Hill City School. Terry Ingersoll and Scott Morton graduated together in 1973 and have coached major sports teams at both the national and college level. One volunteer noted, "It's the small-town boy that makes good, and we have two of them. The uniqueness of this happening in a community is unreal, and their families have been instrumental in our community for years." This strong sense of community kept the partnership moving forward. The original golf classic committee was formed with a small group of six people and a meager goal of $40,000 to $50,000. The goal of the golf outing was to raise money solely for football stadium improvements. Eventually, the partnership evolved into a much larger undertaking that provided for both school and community needs.

The initial partnership was a golf outing fund-raiser that featured Ingersoll and Morton as special guests. Sponsors were invited to advertise on each golf hole and, for an additional fee, participate in the golf tournament. Over time this event expanded from one day to a weekend event with a Thursday night auction. As the golf classic grew each year, it boosted the local area's economy. Local businesses won contracts to provide needed services such as car rentals, hotels, trophies, golf shirts, and framed participant pictures. The money raised in the tournament endowed not only the Hill City School, but the surrounding community as well. Some local projects that were funded included remodeling the Little League fields, contributions to St. Vincent de Paul Society, a local housing remodeling project, and lights on the soccer field. The shared vision of community-school improvements guided the committee each year of the partnership.

What started as an event that yielded $65,000 for the school and community partners grew to one that now brought in close to $500,000 per year. The organizing team has been fairly constant over time, operating as a well-oiled machine. The result of leaders' hands-on involvement was an increase in the number and diversity of individuals who participated in each partnership. But these strong core supporters were aging. The success of the partnership's fund development also generated some strains over the distribution of funds. One city leader noted, "As we accumulated some money, we decided we better form a 501(c)(3) nonprofit entity. So we created the Hill City Charities Organization." Once the immediately needed infrastructure improvements were made, an endowment was established to provide for more lasting benefits. Yet, there was growing concern about sustaining the group's efforts. How would the work continue with Ingersoll and Morton's pending retirement from coaching? How do the shifting needs of the community change the partnership?

Case Questions

- What type of change needs to occur as a partnership changes over time?
- How does creating an adaptive space for discussing common issues help contribute to sustainability?
- What can long-standing partners do to help ensure the partnership's continuity?
- How do educational partners tap into community needs to help advance educational goals as well as community desires?
- What responsibility do "famous" partners have to ongoing partnerships?

6

LEADERSHIP AND PARTNERING

The role of a champion is key to a successful partnership. Champions jump-start partnerships by bringing individuals and organizations together; they broker details among partners; cajole and sell individuals on the collaboration; and help resolve the inevitable conflicts that emerge when working with others. Partnering represents a change in the status quo for those involved. Research documents that upper-level leaders are critical to successful change efforts (Kezar, 2013; Kotter & Cohen, 2002), including forming and sustaining partnerships (Amey et al., 2010). Even though upper-level leadership is central to establishing and maintaining collaborations, leadership may also be represented by central actors located at lower positions on the organizational hierarchy—the "doers" of the partnership.

Concepts of leading in the middle traditionally have received scant attention, but the push for collaborative leadership is beginning to change this perspective (Humphreys, 2013). The Association of American Colleges and Universities (AAC&U) launched an initiative in 2005 that focused on the role of Liberal Education and America's Promise (LEAP), and has conducted four national surveys under this program. An outcome of this work shows the need not only for students but also for higher education institutions to learn how to collaborate. Humphreys (2013), the vice president for policy and public engagement at AAC&U argues, "Just as in the business community, today's challenging environment in and for the higher education sector demands more collaborative leadership—especially put to use to bridge even more sectors and divides than in the past" (para. 3). Those engaged in the work of partnering are poised to fulfill this call and serve as examples for others.

According to Wergin (2007), accountability pressures and increased complexity in higher education are forcing a reevaluation of the long-standing tenets of collegial operations. Historically, faculty and administrators have negotiated how to deliver the core of college operations—namely, teaching and learning. Faculty members have long wielded a level of individual power given the professional bureaucracies in place that rely on the core function of faculty work in classrooms and research (Mintzberg, 1979). Wergin's (2007) concept of *leaders in place* builds on the notion that individuals throughout the institution have leadership abilities or the potential to lead. He contends that effective leaders recognize the potential for leadership throughout the organization and build on relationships to help "frame problems in ways that challenge traditional thinking while also acknowledging the need to work within the existing structure and culture" (p. 226). These leaders in positions of authority and in faculty roles are not afraid to take risks and give voice to the shared values of collaborations, realizing that the change process is adaptive (Heifetz, 1994).

Accountability pressures and increased complexity in higher education are forcing a reevaluation of the long-standing tenets of collegial operations. Collaborative leadership requires rethinking traditional leadership norms.

Central to successful outcomes in strategic partnerships is the creation of second-order change, which recognizes change at the institutional level, but acknowledges that change begins on an individual level (Kezar, 2013). Individuals are increasingly the building block level at which initial steps toward partnership development occur. Black and Gregersen (2008) argue that change occurs within organizations by changing individuals. Because resistance to change is endemic, it is important to better understand how to motivate individuals to want to change and to link this micro-level change to the organization's overarching strategic objectives. Often, the task of motivating is incumbent upon leaders. An analysis of the various levels of leadership evident in partnerships, and the role of leadership during the different stages of the partnership, showcases how leaders throughout the organization can help support the change efforts required to sustain partnerships and, ultimately, to transform higher education.

This chapter reviews the various roles of leadership in partnerships and highlights contributions of the various actors at different levels and stages of partnership development. Just as top-level leaders important, so are those without position who operate from a more informal level of leadership. Multilevel leadership becomes a lever for scaling the type of change required because of the complex relationships involved in partnerships. The leadership that boards of trustees provide can further advance the ideals of emerging partnerships. This chapter also explores the interaction of leaders using a collaborative leadership model and specifically identifies and discusses the role of the champion in partnerships. Finally, the role of leaders in adaptive change helps illustrate the symbiotic relationship of leading and change in both strategic and traditional partnerships.

Early in the development of the partnership, questions about leadership emerge. These include:

- Who is the champion for the partnership?
  - o Does this person have a formal leadership role?
  - o Is this champion an informal leader?

- How can the champion motivate others to buy in to the partnership?
- What will aid in shifting traditional modes of leadership into more collaborative forms?
- What questions must we ask to unearth long-held assumptions about leading that no longer work?

Leaders—Both Formal (Leaders) and Informal (leaders)

When addressing concepts of leadership, different images emerge for individuals based on their experiences, their conceptions of what it means to be a leader, and their desires regarding interactions with leaders. Thus, a brief review of the development of leadership theories helps frame how we situate leadership in partnerships. The "Great Man" views of leadership were based on the concept of leader as hero, and associated with a set of traits (Stogdill & Coons, 1957). Here, thinking about leadership meant focusing on a single top-level leader (Leader). Yet, time has shown that no universal set of traits was associated with being a great leader. Thus, a shift over time led to a view of leadership as situational.

Observing leadership based on what was required for a particular situation resulted in the emergence of contingency theories of leadership (Fielder, 1967), in which organizational needs dictated the appropriate type of leadership. Problems emanating from organizational conditions are addressed through a series of transactions with followers. In this case, clear lines of demarcation are set between Leaders and followers. How Leaders are able to influence followers emphasizes the authority and power vested in those in formal positions of leadership. Burns (1978) proposed that in transformational leadership, instead of the reliance on authority, Leaders focus on needs of followers and seeking overarching moral goals. Transformational leaders can be most effective in transforming higher education institutions in periods of crisis, in situations rife with adversity, or on small campuses (Leslie & Fretwell, 1996). In this case, power and influence are wielded to achieve desired changes.

Behavioral theories of leadership showcase how behaviors rather than traits provide a road map for effective leaders. Yet, like trait theory, this approach to leadership is based on an either/or dichotomy regarding behaviors instead of allowing for a full range of leadership characteristics. A move to cultural theories of leadership focuses on how leaders can help make meaning for organizational members and how leaders can frame a set of different interpretations for these members (Smircich & Morgan, 1982). Cognitive theories of leadership attempt to link more closely the roles of leaders and followers because through both individual leader and collective follower cognition, leadership occurs (Kuhnert & Lewis, 1989). Here, how Leaders think and learn influences how leadership occurs within the organization.

Early leadership theories relied on a list of particular traits or behaviors that leaders should possess. Over time, more complex thinking about leadership has highlighted the influence of culture on leadership and conceptions of leaders as learners. Current leadership theories emphasize collaboration and complexity.

This rich history of leadership theory development set the stage for more current thinking of collective forms of leadership. Known variously as shared leadership, distributed leadership, webs of inclusion, or collaborative/connected leadership, the underlying premise argues for actions by multiple organizational actors versus a single leader sitting atop the organizational chart. Multidimensional leadership (Eddy, 2010c) builds on the ideal of thinking broadly about leadership and argues for a fuller range of conceptions of leadership rather than historic two-dimensional models that implied there was a best way to lead. Instead, a multidimensional view of leadership recognizes that leadership attributes occur along a continuum, and there is no universal model for leadership. As leaders learn, their position within the multidimensional model changes, as does their thinking based on feedback. The ability to have more leadership flexibility is important in dynamic and changing partnerships. The following sections describe how the various levels of leadership interact within the partnership model and how the roles of leaders shift over the course of partnership development. Finally, we discuss collaborative leadership and its role in adaptive change.

Sitting and aspiring partnership leaders may contemplate the following questions, both at the beginning of the collaboration and as checkpoints throughout the partnership:

- What is my leadership approach?
  - How do I consider the role of followers in my organization? Partners?
  - What is the leadership approach of my potential/current partners?
- Given my organizational setting and pressing issues, what type of leadership approach works best?
- What is assumed about collaborative leadership within the partnership? How does this change with changes in personnel?

Levels of Leadership

We often equate the roles of positional leaders (Leaders) with vested authority (Weber, 1948). Yet, "having authority brings not only resources to bear but also serious constraints on the exercise of leadership" (Heifetz, 1994, p. 49). Pfeffer (1977) refers to the ambiguity of leadership and underscores the constraints on top-level leaders due to their position. For example, a leader of a college may agree with the purposes of a proposed partnership, but the faculty may think that the alignment diverts college resources that could be better spent on teaching and learning. In this case, the leader has limited authority and must use influence and argument framing to convince campus members of the value of partnering. College reporting structures also emphasize the role of faculty governance and the oversight and fiduciary responsibilities of a board of trustees.

Those operating in follower roles and without formal position enact leadership that may go beyond their ascribed roles and job expectations. "The adaptive demands of our societies require leadership that takes responsibility without waiting for revelation or request" (Heifetz, 1994, p. 276). Women and people of color historically have led without position or formal power but have been able to change systems. Evidence of the influence of this form of leadership abounds in community groups and social movements. Yet, those without authority must first recognize their ability to take action and next see how they might seize the opportunity to do so. These leaders must first *see* themselves as leaders before they take action to lead. Because leaders often serve as lightning rods in times of change, this level of informal leading requires individuals to deflect any pushback or resistance to change. Those operating without formal authority may not have the protection afforded to others or the privilege and resource base that allows them to weather conflict and attacks. The very real danger of losing one's job may be enough to prevent action by those who desire change but cannot afford to be swept up in the aftermath of resistance.

Providing a safe space in which to navigate the critical changes advocated is important, and those without authority have little or no control over this. Instead, informal leaders must be aware of how to time their actions based on the support of positional Leaders. For example, if an informal leader seeks to develop a partnership with a colleague in another organization based on shared interests, a traditional partnership that is not tightly connected to the college may provide a means to do this. The ability to be loosely coupled to the home organization (Weick, 1976) allows a degree of flexibility for leaders that those in position of authority do not always have. But the happenstance nature of these alliances means that partners are less connected to the infrastructure and resources of the home institution and may not be working on issues aligned with the strategic plan. Trade-offs may result.

Positional Leaders have authority and access to resources that informal leaders do not. Yet, authority does not ensure action and lack of position does not negate the ability to accomplish change. Trade-offs exist regardless of position.

Because of the ability to fly under the radar, Leaders may plant seeds of ideas with these informal leaders throughout the institution as a way to try out new initiatives without the risk of overcommitting the organization. Alternatively, leaders working under the auspices of a strategic partnership can use the alignment of their work with partners to link to the overarching goals of the organization, leveraging power and gaining resources in the process. Both levels of leadership bring assets and a range of supports to partnerships as well as their unique set of limitations (Kezar & Lester, 2011).

Leadership theories that support the broad range of individuals involved in partnerships, within the organization and with the partnership, require a focus on developing leaders as learners (Amey, 2005). Individual leaders often see only a limited view of the actions within the partnership, so it is critical that those leading at different levels understand that "others" might have different perspectives, depending on their location in the hierarchy, their role in the partnership, and their underlying schema or worldview (Kezar &

Lester, 2009). As highlighted in chapter 4, these differences in understanding require leaders to engage in framing and sensemaking to help create a cogent view of what is going on with the partnership.

Leaders at different levels within the organization may ask different questions at the start of a partnership, including:

- What can I do in my position to advocate for this partnership?
  - What resources can I access?
  - How tied is my role in the partnership to central activities of my home organization?
  - Can someone in a different position be a better advocate?
- How does this partnership help serve the functions of my role within my home institution?
- Is my approach to leadership the right one for this partnership?

Leaders and Partnership Development

Formal and informal leaders exert their influence in building partnerships in different ways, depending on the stage of development of the collaboration and their position in the hierarchy, both within their home institution and within the partnership. A central role for Leaders is obtaining buy-in to the partnership (Kotter, 2008). Positional leaders can obtain buy-in by increasing urgency regarding the changes needed in how the college operates. Gone are the days when colleges could stand alone without concern for the needs of the community or the luxury of sufficient resources to accomplish all that was hoped for in their strategic goals. As we discussed earlier in this volume, policymakers at the state and federal level, foundations and funders, and those involved with accreditation bodies increasingly see collaborations as a means to increase efficiencies and to build on the synergy emerging from alliances (Bastalich, 2010; Fowler, 2012).

It is important to understand the role of leadership in the antecedent phase of partnership development as these actions set the stage for ultimate outcomes. As reviewed in chapter 2, a number of motivations spur partnership development (economic, policy, value alignment, and strategic leadership). In the early phase of partnership formation, two central events occur. First, information is collected that helps paint a more complete picture of the current environment in which the potential partnership operates. Second, at the individual level, personal skills and desired goals are assessed. Whether this reflection is intentional links to the emergence of traditional or strategic partnerships.

Tapping into personal networks exposes individuals to opportunities to partner. The fact that someone is in your network, and interactions occur more frequently as a result, sets the stage for identifying this person as a potential partner. On a faculty level, two or more individuals may find themselves on state- or nationwide committees, and this proximity and shared interests and goals serve as the genesis of a partnership. Next, determining shared goals helps set the stage for mapping out partnership possibilities. An individual process of evaluating multiple partnering opportunities rather than merely joining others in more of a happenstance manner also drives the type of partnership that emerges. Strategic partnerships emerge when individuals are mindful of their organization's overarching strategic objectives and use these goals to determine which partnerships are more advantageous. In this case, partners may be sought intentionally based on alignment with institutional needs.

Personal networks provide an environment for locating and evaluating potential partners. When assessing partnerships with an eye toward supporting strategic goals rather than convenience, strategic partnerships emerge.

Positional Leaders evaluate the options for partnering from a different perch. Before looking for potential partnership opportunities, top-level leaders should investigate the reasons for partnering. Some partnerships emerge due to funders' requirements to find collaborators and partners. Other partnerships help meet strategic objectives of the institution. In order for better alignment to occur in partnering, it is necessary to know the institution's strategic objectives, which requires planning. A number of strategic planning approaches help institutions determine strategic goals (Barnes, 2011a; Eckel & Hartley, 2008). During the planning phase, it is important for positional Leaders to help members of their organization begin questioning underlying assumptions and long-held beliefs, because doing so leads to and supports organizational learning and change.

Kotter (2008) advocates increasing a sense of urgency to get organizations and stakeholders to act. As partnerships are being conceived, it is critical to determine which factors can support them, and for leaders to argue how and why the partnership helps address pressing needs. There is a distinction between a true and false sense of urgency. When true urgency is apparent, individuals see the need for action—*now!* "Urgent behavior is not driven by a belief that all is well or that everything is a mess but, instead, that the world contains great opportunities and great hazards" (Kotter, 2008, p. 8). As we argued earlier, it matters how leaders frame the partnership and the ultimate change that ensues. Policymakers sense urgency regarding economic development and educational reforms. They seek to guide changes by creating requirements for partnering in legislation and programs. For instance, the Trade Adjustment Assistance Community College and Career Training (TAACCCT) Grant Program targets preparing a better workforce and specifically requires collaboration to receive funding (see www.doleta.gov/taaccct).

Once partnerships are formed, positional leaders have access to human and capital resources that they can allocate to support development of the collaboration. At this stage, a commitment to building the collaborative context emerges (Kezar & Lester, 2009). A function of the collaborative context is to ensure that the internal structures support the needs of the partnership. Because of differences in culture and operations of the various partners involved, structural alignment might mean that the home institution has to make changes. For example, rewarding faculty members for contributions to collaborative efforts might involve revising the tenure and promotion process. As noted in chapter 4, another key role for positional leaders is how they frame the partnership to organizational members and key stakeholders. How individuals come to understand the partnership and its links to the home institution influences how they react to and support the work of the collective. Without this form of sensemaking, it is easy for campus members to view the partnership as a one-time event that does not concern them and can be ignored.

> Leaders must highlight the sense of urgency to partner and show institutional members why the partnership helps the strategic goals of the home organization.

Traditional partnerships often are seen as an activity that is removed from the central operations of the campus and from the institution's overarching goals. Members of the campus might see these forms of partnerships as temporary, particularly those partnerships in which collaboration was sought to obtain grant funding. Strategic partnerships, instead, are tightly linked to strategic objectives and provide an easier way for individuals to see connections—if they are framed by leaders. The urgency with which leaders present the partnership matters to how organizational members receive it (Kotter, 2008).

During the development process, positional leaders also play a role in getting campus members to question underlying assumptions about operations and how the partnership contributes to the organization. Kezar and Lester (2009) found in their study of successful collaborations that a number of types of learning were necessary. First, learning about the process of collaboration, looking to other partnerships to see what worked and what did not is important. Second, learning through the work of relationship building begins to create a sense of shared meaning. Third, learning how to be a good team member and about good group processing occurs. Bensimon and Neumann's (1993) notion of teams provides good support for this type of learning. Finally, learning about underlying assumptions within the organization and about how the organization operates is critical.

The leaders and collaborators who are the doers and champions play active roles during partnership development. They create the internal structures and rules of operation for the emerging partnership. Some of this structure may borrow from the home institution, but at a minimum will be influenced by individual history (Harris, 1994). Creating a governing structure and procedures may include joint meeting times that involve a leadership cabinet or governing board of the partnership. It is through this type of process that communication venues are established, norms are created, and trust emerges. Of particular importance is establishing mechanisms for dealing with conflict. Partnering by its nature involves dealing with individuals outside your own organization who may not share your perspectives on operations. The process of developing the vision and mission of the partnership helps create a shared goal.

Data collected by partners regarding progress and outcomes provide critical feedback to partners on what is working and what is not. The process can then be tweaked and improved to avoid failure.

Policymakers may have built in requirements to the initial policy that encourage collaboration and provide for various support mechanisms. For example, incubator space or funding for newly shared facilities may be part of the support provided. Requirements in the policy often include a timetable for evaluating the partnership with deadlines that create opportunities for data collection. Data can then be used to check on collaborative progress and serve as feedback loops to aid in partner learning and policy changes. This feedback helps craft new policy to support collaborations or revise current policies.

Sustaining partnerships is often an espoused goal of policy, but history shows that partnerships often fail once funding is gone (Eddy, 2007). To help keep collaborations going, top-level leaders can communicate the rationale and the importance of the partnership work to individuals in the organization. Creating a space in which the partnership is nurtured and can operate is also critical. Heifetz (1994) identifies three types of situations in which problems and associated solutions operate. Type I situations have clearly identifiable problems and associated solutions that are remedied by *technical* work (i.e., we have seen this problem before and know how to address it); Type II situations also have clearly evident problems, but the solution requires learning to address the problems, thus using both technical work and adaptive work (i.e., we can address part of the problem with what we know, but we must learn new behaviors and reactions); and Type III situations have problems that are not definable and technical or for which there are no known remedies (i.e., leaders must aid in learning, both to define the problem and to come up with a solution; Heifetz, 1994). Leaders are required to create the adaptive work required for sustainability of partnerships. How individuals and organizations learn becomes central to the long-term existence of the partnership.

Leaders of the partnership on the ground must document their work so the partnership has the ability to live beyond their work as the champion. Part of this process is engaging with leaders throughout their home institution so that other institutional members know about the work of the partnership and understand its links to the home institution's mission. How the leaders of the partnership tell the story of their work influences how those in the home institution understand it as well as addressing the need for sustaining the collaboration.

Board members represent another level of leadership within higher education institutions. Increasingly, boards of trustees at colleges are recasting their roles. "High performing boards in public-sector institutions don't wait for politicians to take the initiative" (Mactaggart, 2011, p. 17). Board members attempt to be proactive and anticipate needs in the state and country that might come down as mandates from policymakers. Yet, this leadership role for boards is complex. Not only do they work closely with the president to support change, the board also reviews the performance of the president. The balancing act of providing proactive board leadership and micromanaging the president is difficult. The very public resignation of Teresa Sullivan at the University of Virginia in 2012 due to her board's perception of the slow pace regarding online learning opportunities shows how micromanaging by a board can be detrimental (Hebel, Stripling, & Wilson, 2012). Ultimately, Sullivan was reinstated, but this case underscores that leading collaboratively is tough work and requires a great deal of communication, trust, and time.

Board members and presidents must understand the institutional context and associated needs. Shared understandings regarding the need to partner, the consequences of partner selection, and the planning for anticipated changes emerging from the partnership are important considerations for dialogue (Mactaggart, 2011). As with learning for individual leaders, shared learning is required to understand best how to make effective decisions. Once desired changes are identified, it is clearer which partnerships help fill the strategic objectives identified. Thus, early in the formation of partnerships, boards can help influence the partner selection process. "Collaboration in making change ranges from suggesting a few ideas to collectively arriving at a course of action" (Mactaggart, 2011, p. 44). The presence of a robust shared governance framework can prime a college for processing decisions regarding partnerships. As DePree (2004) aptly notes, "We cannot become what we need to be by remaining what we are" (p. 100).

Boards of trustees represent a key leadership roles for partnerships. Shared governance involves working together to make decisions and evaluate outcomes. Reactions to external issues spur partnering and change.

Leaders are found in a number of levels and roles, have varying levels of authority to guide change, and are able to leverage their influence differently depending on the assorted phases of the partnership. Table 6.1 highlights the various forms of intersection of leaders involved during the various partnership phases. In addition to the constructs of Leaders and leaders, we have included in this comparison the roles of leadership found with policymakers because policymakers ultimately influence change via partnering. As McDonnell and Elmore (1987) identify, capacity building and system changing that result from policy can yield more second-level change than policies that focus on mandates and inducements. Thus, instead of focusing on maintaining the status quo through transactions, deeper change occurs when systems are transformed.

Collaborative Leadership

According to Heifetz (1994), "By unhinging leadership from personality traits, we permit observations of the many different ways in which people exercise plenty of leadership every day without 'being leaders'" (p. 20). Acknowledging the contributions individuals make to leading alters how

TABLE 6.1
Levels of Leadership and Partnership Phases

Level of Leadership	Partnership Formation	Partnership Development	Sustaining Partnership
Leader	• Establish strategic priorities • Environmental scan for partner matching • Outreach to policymakers regarding state/ national agenda	• Resource allocation—both physical and human capital • Creating urgency for necessity of partnership • Guide questioning of underlying assumptions to create double-loop learning	• Creating adaptive space • Framing partnership for stakeholders— both internal and external • Use data to aid organizational learning
leader	• Self-assessment of skills, network connections, and goals • Evaluation of partnering options to assure alignment with personal and organizational objectives	• Creating partnership plan, including structure and governance • Establishing communication venues, which contribute to trust building and shared meaning	• Documentation of process to help institutionalization • Recognition of responsibility for collaborative leadership
Policy leader	• Policy creation via mandates; inducements; capacity building; system changing	• Creating data collection systems for feedback • Contribution of space or other supports to launch partnerships	• Evaluation of program data to determine match of intended outcomes • Revision of policy to best support programming that proves effective

we *see* the influence of their actions, in this case regarding the roles of both Leaders and leaders in partnerships. "Collaborative leadership is about taking risks to convince others of the merits of pursuing something new, appreciating varying points of view, and demonstrating acceptance and respect for others in pursuit of new ideas" (Wepner, 2011, p. 121). Leading from a collaborative perspective requires thinking differently about leadership and about the skills required when trying to work *with* people toward common goals. Wepner (2011) identifies eight essential characteristics of collaborative leaders:

1. knowledge
2. vision
3. interpersonal skills
4. entrepreneurial skills
5. negotiation skills
6. managerial skills
7. work ethic
8. confidence

Even though this listing is instructive, it harkens back to notions of trait theories and a checklist of requirements to become a better leader. Instead, an orientation to processes involved in connecting with others can be more instructive. Relationship building provides a critical foundation for collaborative leadership and for partnership building as noted in chapter 3.

> New leadership perspectives argue that leaders need to think more complexly and in more nuanced ways, scratching beneath surface observations to work from multiple perspectives, with multiple lenses, and questioning embedded assumptions and institutionalized practice to unearth the "why" of the college's practice not just the outputs that are tied to accountability and accrediting agencies. (Amey, 2012, p. 147)

Once the underlying reasons for partnering are revealed, collaborative leaders can begin to scan for potential partners that help complement the organization's strategic objectives. As we have noted throughout this volume, critical elements for partnership success include initial motivations for partnering, relationship building, and ongoing and reflective communication. Champions adept at these skills will find more success in the connections they make and the partnerships they help create.

Building from Bensimon and Neumann's (1993) team model and functions first presented in chapter 2 is a set of leadership capabilities that help support the development of team thinking. Included in this listing are: (a) the ability to understand the subjective experiences of particular others; (b) the ability to share and interact; (c) the ability to be critical; and (d) the ability to reflect and learn through reflection (Bensimon & Neumann, 1993, pp. 139–142). Recognizing that individuals hold particular perspectives, and associated with this view are limits of other perspectives, underscores the value gained by leading collectively. Individual and joint reflection can illuminate blind spots and critique positions.

> Teams that are more open and equalized in their conception of leadership, that view leadership as a shared process and a shared responsibility rather than as the property of just one person, are generally more effective at discerning the viewpoints, beliefs, and understandings of others. (Bensimon & Neumann, 1993, p. 145)

Creating team leadership within the organization and the partnership can provide leverage in achieving desired outcomes.

Once the underlying reasons for partnering are revealed, collaborative leaders can begin to scan for potential partners that help complement the organization's strategic objectives. Team leadership leverages better outcomes.

Connective leadership (Lipman-Blumen, 1996) develops behavioral theories that are direct, instrumental, and relational and includes nine leadership strategies that focus on mastering tasks, maximizing interactions, and contributing to others' tasks (the strategies include mentoring, helping, joining forces, empowering, networking, persuading, taking charge, outperforming, and excelling). The connective model builds on the needs to lead complex organizations and requires integration of formerly disparate and distinct actors, thus emphasizing that leaders need to be well versed in skills that help build this connection. Partnerships bring groups together with different experiences, operating cultures, and norms. Therefore, attention must be paid to bringing out shared understandings for all partners.

There are various models for collaborative leadership. We sought to build a model of collaborative leadership adept at supporting partnerships and one that recognizes the various levels of leadership involved. Figure 6.1 presents a view of collaborative leadership in partnerships. In this model, the circles represent the various phases of the partnerships: Phase One addresses the motivations for partnering and the antecedents in place that set the stage for the emerging partnership; Phase Two represents partnership formation, which includes the search for partners based on strategic or traditional objectives; and Phase Three

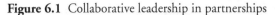
Figure 6.1 Collaborative leadership in partnerships

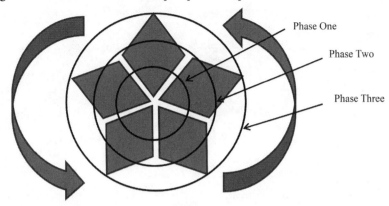

Phase One

Phase Two

Phase Three

includes the development of partnership capital that is based on how the partnership is framed, emergence of shared meaning and norms, building trust, and ongoing strategic alignment. The diamond shapes in the model represent the various forms of leadership within and among partnering organizations. Like a kaleidoscope, the dynamic nature of partnering illustrates leaders' different views depending on their location. The ability to think about multiple perspectives can allow leaders to see different alternatives and opportunities. The views from different positions underscore the importance of various levels of leadership involvement and provide a rationale for most effective collaborative leadership.

Heifetz (1994) observed that "each of us has blind spots that require the vision of others" (p. 268). Because of this, collaborative leadership helps fill the gaps created on an individual level. The concept of the Johari window points out the danger for leaders not knowing their own blind spots and provides a heuristic for leaders in partnerships to identify what others know about them and what they know about themselves (Luft & Ingham, 1955). By intersecting what others know about us and what we know about ourselves, our blind spots and what we do not know become more obvious. Using collaborative leadership helps highlight these shortcomings and can provide benefits within partnerships. For example, partner A may see how partner B's actions are perceived within the community, and partner B may not be aware of this view. In this case, partner A can point out this blind spot and partner B can address the perceptions by taking action. It is through feedback loops like this that collaborative leadership helps build stronger partnerships (see Figure 6.2).

Individuals interested in fostering collaborative leadership for partnering should reflect on the following questions:

Figure 6.2 Johari window and partnerships

	Known to Self	Unknown to Self
Known to Partners	*OPEN*	*BLIND*
Unknown to Partners	*HIDDEN*	*UNKNOWN*

- Which of the essential characteristics for collaborative leadership do I possess?
  - Which of these characteristics are present in leaders within my organization?
  - Which of these characteristics are present in leaders in the partnership?
- How can we build shared meaning and trust collaboratively?
- What does the present view of our kaleidoscope of collaborative leadership look like?
  - How does this view look depending on partnership stage?
  - What will move us from our current position?
  - Who has the best view of the various levels?

The Role of the Champion

The discussion about the role of leaders in partnerships up to this point revolves around historic ideas of leading and views of positional versus informal leaders. New ideals of collaborative leadership provide a more robust way to think about leadership within partnerships. We posit that considering instead of the label *leaders*, a more neutral term, *champion*, highlights the pivotal role of leadership, while at the same time making the level of leadership ambiguous. When leadership is not viewed as position, the playing field is leveled with respect to who can help support and sustain partnerships. Collaborative leadership supports the notion of champions and underscores the roles and responsibilities of leaders throughout partnerships and partner organizations. "A *champion* is defined as an individual who advocates for the development of a partnership and who brings together others to engage in the project" (Eddy, 2010a, pp. 28–29; italics added). The champion is a broker for the partnership, one who advocates the need and benefits of collaborating and helps persuade others to join in. This definition does not imply any requirements for a particular level of leadership or organizational position.

When the context in which partnering occurs is defined, by area of specialization or size of region, spotting champions is easier—much like the concept of seeing a big fish in a small pond. In these instances, champions with higher levels of social capital and social networking are able to leverage and negotiate both the creation and sustainability of partnerships (Eddy, 2010a). In research on campus-community partnerships, higher-developed partnerships contain three factors: (a) assigned staff as community organizers; (b) upper-level administrators as aggressive champions; and (c) community initiation for partnering (Zakocs, Tiwari, Vehige, & DeJong, 2008). Evident in this research are the roles of leaders throughout the organization and the partnership as well as the importance of a champion to trumpet the partnership. As Zakocs et al. (2008) found, highly placed leaders have a different perch from which to champion, given their access to both the pulpit to frame the partnership and to organizational (and personal) resources. Those with higher levels of social capital are able to influence others and can undertake more risks than can those with less social capital regardless of position.

More connections in the home organization and the partnership allow champions to cross borders and become boundary spanners, which heightens collaboration and adaptability (Wheatley, 1999). "When leadership is shared, a college has multiple ways of sensing environmental change, checking for problems, and monitoring campus performance" (Birnbaum, 1992, p. 187). Champions who recognize the importance of building partnership networks and the interactive nature of communication can leverage the collective energies and talents to achieve partnership goals. A champion who recognizes the role of reciprocal influence in building partnerships is central to ultimate success. In this case, the ability to appreciate the roles of the multiple actors in the partnership depends on the social capital of the champion (Coleman, 1988).

One way to view the role of champions is through agency and structure. Agency refers to the idea of individuals making choices. Serving as a counterbalance to these choices are structures and rules. Structuration theory (Giddens, 1984) brings this tension and dualism together. The dependent relationship of individuals and created structures emphasizes how "structures exist only in and through the activities of human agents" (p. 256). Likewise, structures influence individual actions. In creating partnerships, multiple levels of interactions occur and involve different organizational structures.

Champions access their own social capital and the resources at their disposal. They act as border-crossers in brokering partnerships.

Champions have agency within their home institution, and some of their power might be attributed to position, knowledge, or other aspects of social capital (Morgan, 2006). Because of their social networks, champions also have agency due to their boundary-spanning capabilities (Bess & Dee, 2008b). These abilities allow champions to advocate for and help create partnerships. Within the space of the newly formed partnership, the ability of individuals to make choices depends on the size of the partnership and the time spent on partnership development. For example, when two individual partners contemplate joining forces, most typically in a traditional partnership, they are able to make more choices among those possible than when the partnership is developed more fully and numerous others are involved. Likewise, the existence of structure within the partnership influences the amount of choice available. The formation of a new partnership structure builds on the activities of the early champions (Giddens, 1984); subsequent members of the partnership then react to this structure, either reifying it or advocating for changes.

Because champions are also part of a home organization, these structures influence their agency as well. The agency of champions does not substitute for the agency of followers (Reicher, Haslam, & Hopkins, 2005) because the process of collective agency in groups is interactive. Indeed, Reicher et al. (2005) found that leadership is dependent on the existence of a shared social identity, that leaders are not passive onlookers, that they actively intervene in creating and redefining identities, thereby creating and transforming followers, and that initiation of structures helps to enact the ideas that leaders and followers generate. The type of partnership formed also dictates the role of agency and structure. In strategic partnerships, champions might represent a variety of levels of position or a collective that focuses on looking for partners that help complement organizational strategic goals. Here, agency is strongly linked to actions that support the strategic goals. In this case, partnership structure ultimately may reflect the home organization's structures or may be more formal (Denis, Lamothe, & Langley, 2001). Traditional partnerships may have less initial reliance on home institutional structure and may be more informal in design. When champions are more cognizant of the levers for change at their disposal, they may have more influence on jump-starting partnerships and, ultimately, in sustaining them, too.

Ongoing learning and using feedback loops are critical for champions. Cultural proficiency (Lindsey, Robins, & Terrell, 2003) is a useful construct for thinking about this learning and adaptive response. "Acquiring cultural proficiency is a component of continuous learning that changes the way an organization functions by institutionalizing cultural knowledge in its policies, practices, and organizational culture" (Hickman, 2010, p. 60). Champions adept at cultural proficiency are able to read the cultural context and understand how a change in perspective is needed. In particular, champions are able to tell the story of the partnership to others in such a way as to exert influence regarding the value of collaborating. Through collaborating, the system changes, and as a result, individual organizational members must adapt.

Champions may ponder a range of questions as partnerships are formed and develop, including:

- How will I advocate for the partnership?

    o Whom will I involve?
    o How does the structure of my home institution influence my advocacy?
    o How does my level of agency within my home institution influence my advocacy?

- What does collective leadership look like in the partnership?

    o What collective agency exists?
    o How do the partnership structures influence options?

- What type of cultural competency exists among the leaders in the partnership?

Leaders and Adaptive Change

Adaptation emerges when changes occur as a result of partnering. In this case, change influences the partnership itself, but also affects operations at each partner's organization. Because conflict and differences in values emerge during the course of change (Morgan, 2006), leaders play a critical role in orchestrating actions. Heifetz (1994) argues that these differences may be essential to adaptive success. Because we rely on our underlying schemas to guide our actions (Harris, 1994), our mental maps might blind us to other perspectives (Senge, 1990). The presence of multiple perspectives, then, serves a critical role in highlighting blind spots. Often, adaptive leadership means going against the grain. Table 6.2 shows how champions can use their authority to help support adaptive change. Differences emerge when considering leadership and adaptive change within a traditional partnership versus a strategic partnership.

Leaders within a traditional partnership may not have strong links between partner leaders and top-level positional leaders in the home institutions. As a result, the type of authority or power they have potentially operates differently from the leverage of leaders in strategic partnerships. Leaders of strategic partnership have the buy-in from leadership at multiple levels and with multiple partners, which represents a wider range of authority and power. Leaders can aid campus members in thinking about adaptations using

TABLE 6.2

Strategies for Leading Adaptive Change

Strategy*	Traditional Partnerships	Strategic Partnerships
Identify the adaptive challenge.	• Often seen as discrete goals or objectives • May involve multiple challenges—those for individual partners and those for partnership	• Unbundles challenge • Diagnoses underlying issues/causes • Links to strategic goals • Focuses on collective work of partnership
Keep the level of distress within a tolerable range for doing adaptive work.	• Partners protect individual vested interests • Leverages threat to argue banding together	• Identifies threat • Uses urgency to move collective to action
Focus attention on ripening issues and not on stress-reducing distractions.	• Leaders within the partnership may focus on issues, but those at the home institution may advocate withdrawal • Partner leaders may focus on reducing stress to evade too much attention by home institutions	• Questions underlying assumptions guiding actions • Reviews the interaction of issues among partners and at home institution relative to strategic objectives
Give the work back to people, but at a rate they can stand.	• Work vested with champions • Champions seek partners to help based on happenstance versus links established by intention or strategy	• Vests work in those most knowledgeable within the organization and the partnership • May involve leading upward where champion moves work to positional leaders

(Continues)

TABLE 6.2
Strategies for Leading Adaptive Change (Continued)

Strategy*	Traditional Partnerships	Strategic Partnerships
Protect voices of leadership without authority.	• Those with high levels of social capital help protect those with lower levels • Those with authority help protect those without	• Creates culture of trust • Builds shared norms • Focuses on organizational learning that values feedback loops

*Adapted from Heifetz, 1994, p. 128.

strategic thinking. In this case, it is critical to prepare organizational members in multiple manners—in both dialogue about changes and questioning underlying processes—to achieve the type of cultural adaptation of the organization to support best required changes (Chaffee, 1985).

Leading adaptive change requires creating space in which members of the organization can wrestle with problems, contemplate alternatives, and test solutions.

Undergirding the notion of adaptive leadership is the process of learning. Leaders help guide this process of change and can establish scaffolding that supports the required change as outlined in Table 6.2. "Adaptive leadership generates and sustains a context where people develop and use their capacity to pursue new opportunities, meet unknown conditions or threats, and solve problems that emerge from a complex, dynamic environment" (Hickman, 2010, p. 58). The concept of leaders as learners (Amey, 2005) highlights the roles leaders play as participants and observers. Heifetz (1994) advocates for leaders "getting on the balcony" (p. 252) to view the organization and actions of various organizational actors, because larger patterns are observable from this higher position. Leaders within the partnership and those at home institutions can find value in gaining this type of perspective. A view of how the partnership is seen at the home institution can emerge and brewing issues or current problems can be seen differently. Yet, "even from the balcony, people who lead never really get an objective picture because they never entirely dispense with the filters through which they perceive events" (Heifetz, 1994, p. 272). Thus, it is necessary to engage in collaborative leadership to bring multiple individuals to the balcony, to help provide a range of perspectives.

Leaders must pose a range of questions as they work to create adaptive change, including:

- What best supports the range of strategies for adaptive change?
  - o How might this look within my organization?
  - o How might this look within the partnership?
- How can I foster learning?
  - o Who is needed on the balcony?
  - o What feedback loops will get information to support learning?

Leading Second-Order Change

As outlined in chapter 2, a number of motivations spur partnering. Motivations to change include leader initiative, internal pressures, and external pressures (Astin & Astin, 2000). Second-order change requires questioning underlying assumptions rather than making mere incremental changes that build on the status quo (Bartunek & Moch, 1987). Kezar (2013) points out that colleges and universities are reluctant to engage in deep change because they are not accustomed to questioning their core purpose, yet the current climate suggests that the public and policymakers are pressing for changes in new ways. Second-order change might be recognized by changes in organizational culture or attitudes, or by changes in structure (Kezar, 2013). Leaders play a critical role in identifying when second-order change is needed.

Second-order change requires questioning underlying assumptions rather than making mere incremental changes that build on the status quo.

Leadership and change go hand in hand. Hickman (2010), who reviewed various types of change and associated leadership theories that best support the type of change required, notes that dialectical change applies to mergers or collaborations and requires second-order change. Collaborative leadership can support this change. Six components regarding this form of leadership and associated change have emerged:

1. Change in a pluralistic collective is more likely with the range of talents brought to bear from an assembly of leaders.
2. Collaborative leadership is fragile.

3. Change occurs in a cyclical fashion with advancements, retreats, and advancements based on feedback loops.
4. Leaders' actions are guided by competing forces; in the case of the partnership, the competition is between the home institution's needs and the partnerships' needs.
5. Stability during change occurs when sufficient resources create slack, when leaders are in a position to make decisions, and when time allows for the chance to create opportunities.
6. Increased pluralism increases the need for counterbalances because it is difficult for the collective leadership to unite all parties and remain grounded in fulfilling the needs of their home institution. (Denis et al., 2001)

As we have noted throughout this volume, tensions exist between loyalties to the partnership and to the home institution. The emergence of a distinctive entity within new partnerships helps shape the partnership as separate and distinct from, but tightly coupled to, the home institutions.

Because second-order change requires individuals to make sense of what is happening, leaders need to be adept at framing change efforts under way in partnerships. When everyone in the organization understands this new way of seeing things, institutional sensemaking occurs (Weick, 1995). As highlighted in the next chapter, organizational learning is evident in the creation of partnership capital. Leaders can aid in the development of organizational learning when feedback loops are in place to help create opportunities for dialogue and questioning past practices. Kezar (2013) identifies the following tools leaders can use to help in sensemaking and, ultimately, in creating second-order change:

- ongoing and widespread conversations;
- collaborative leadership;
- developing cross-departmental teams or working groups;
- drawing and discussing external ideas;
- sponsoring faculty and staff development;
- preparing and giving public presentations;
- flexible vision; and
- creating documents and concept papers. (p. 120)

Collaborative leadership can support the type of adaptive transformation needed to achieve second-order change. "Each one of us has the power and the opportunity to participate in collective work around the practice of transformative leadership" (Astin & Astin, 2000, p. 97). Thus, those operating at different levels within partnerships can influence change and contribute to sustainable partnerships.

In working to create second-order change, leaders need to consider several questions, including:

- How can we create collaborative leadership?
  - ○ Which strategies work for the home organization?
  - ○ Which strategies work for the partnership?
- How can we create opportunities for conversations that encourage deep change?
- How can we help organizational members and partners make sense of the change?

Leading Strategic Versus Traditional Partnerships

As noted throughout this chapter, leaders at different levels exert varying levels of influence on the partnering process, but all types of leadership are critical to the process. We have advocated for the role of collaborative leadership as a means to engage in successful partnering. Positional leaders have certain levers at their disposal to help enact change that those without formal authority do not. Just as the level of leadership matters in terms of action, so does the type of partnership. Strategic partnerships assume a level of intentionality and have ties to organizational strategic objectives. Leaders can use the mission and vision of the organization to help spur buy-in (Higgerson & Joyce, 2007). Through framing and communicating, support for the partnership can occur. How communication occurs builds on previous relationships between the leader and stakeholders.

Leading strategic partnerships requires navigating multiple cultures and norms that emerge from the different partners. Creating a holding environment in which building and crafting the partnership is critical to long-term success of adaptive change initiatives. Heifetz and Linsky (2002) describe a holding environment as "a space formed by a network of relationships within which people can tackle tough, sometimes divisive questions without flying apart" (p. 102). Boundary spanners in organizations are those who help bridge these gaps among partners and help create and participate in this holding environment. Boundary spanners are often initial champions for partnering, given their high levels of social capital and social network.

> Hence, the creation of organizational strategy will depend on the interpretations and sensemaking of the boundary spanners, as well as those within the organization (e.g., executive staff members) whose responsibility it is to

create a coherent strategy from the disparate impressions of the boundary spanners. (Bess & Dee, 2008b, p. 722)

Heifetz and Linsky (2002) emphasize that the types of adaptive challenges institutions face require involvement of all organizational members and that new solutions and ways of being require learning, on both the individual and organizational level. Leadership in strategic partnerships may involve individuals leading beyond their authority.

Current adaptive challenges require involvement of all organizational members—and this requires learning at the individual and organizational levels.

Leading traditional partnerships often means focusing on the problems at hand. Being in the midst of the action, however, results in a lack of perspective about the fit of the partnership in the overarching schema of the home organization (Heifetz & Linsky, 2002) and may mean missed opportunities for linking to strategic initiatives that can help ensure sustainability.

In both strategic and traditional partnerships, leaders may create a sense of urgency to get the attention of key stakeholders and obtain buy-in (Kotter, 2008). "Partnering on an issue means giving up some autonomy, causing both you and your potential partners some degree of reluctance about getting together" (Heifetz & Linsky, 2002, p. 78). What differs in the type of partnerships may be the leadership level involved. Positional Leaders may use urgency to frame the links of the partnership and strategic objectives, whereas leaders on the ground in traditional partnerships may use urgency to work with partners on more of a one-on-one level with no strong connections to the home institution.

Summary Points

- Leadership emerges in a variety of forms in partnerships.
- Both Leaders and leaders play critical roles in various stages of partnerships.
- Champions draw on their social network and position to support partnering.

- Collaborative leadership emerges by form and necessity in partnerships.
- Adaptive change is an outcome of partnering, and how leaders manage and create the context for this change matters.
- The metaphor of a kaleidoscope helps illustrate the dynamic interchange of leadership, levels, and phases within partnerships.
- Adaptive change acknowledges and takes into consideration changing contexts, using feedback loops to support organizational learning.
- Leading second-order change requires creating meaning for stakeholders and engaging in organizational learning.

CASE #6: A VIEW FROM THE MIDDLE

Individuals at different levels in the organization might initiate a partnership. The advantage of being embedded within the organization is the ability to start conversations without the specter of formal commitment. It is one thing for the president of an organization to investigate the possibility of a partnership and quite another for a director or program manager to explore an opportunity. When a top-level leader initiates a collaboration, those involved infer a particular meaning; if a mid-level leader is leading the collaboration, another type of meaning emerges. Who is involved in leading the partnership matters.

An international partnership emerged from relationships established by a Fulbright scholar exchange. A comprehensive college in the Northeast hosted Mitch Hamburg in 2010–2011. During his visit, he worked on developing a new consortium that involved partnering colleges and universities in New Zealand, Australia, and the United States, along with business and industry employers. The vision of the network was to create international learning and work experiences that provided individual employees with a skill base to cross international boundaries successfully. A focus on acquisition of twenty-first-century skills was part of the mission.

Hamburg was able to use his visiting time in the country to network with American colleges that wanted to establish international partnerships, but the colleges also focused on meeting local employer needs for hiring globally competent student graduates. Initial groundwork included hosting a series of workshops around the state. These first meetings gave Hamburg a chance to meet with other college leaders in formal positions of authority. From these initial relationships, other forms of connections emerged. Some of the college leaders moved on to other leadership positions in other states, but the connections remained that allowed for the expansion of the network in the states.

In 2012, Hamburg worked to establish the structure of the burgeoning partnership by creating a business plan and seeking nonprofit status for the new entity. He worked to build partnerships in the group and built on his existing network in his home country as well as expanding his U.S.-based network. As an outside consultant, he had different access to institutions from what he would have had if he had been part of the leadership hierarchy at a single institution. This position in the middle allowed him to cross borders—institutional, national, positional—in ways that others could not.

The process of formalizing the partnership involved creating a board of directors. Members included some of the key leaders at the institution where Hamburg's Fulbright sent him as well as other leaders in the host state. The partnership expanded beyond a single U.S. state because of Hamburg's national and international presentations on the project and the movement of out-of-state leaders to new institutions. The social network established as part of the Fulbright award continued to expand with new positions for leaders across the country. The official rollout of the new partnership occurred in April 2013.

The goal to provide authentic learning opportunities and training initially involved study abroad with member institutions. Orientation programs and a resource structure were established to support outbound mobility of study-abroad students. The second phase of the partnership involved internal evaluation of curriculum to ensure internationalizing learning in-house. Faculty involvement ensured that institutional efforts for internationalization were supported in degree programs and that this complemented student exchanges. Work on articulating course credits meant that institutional leaders needed to address how credit transfers would occur.

The platform for this partnership is unique in that it emerged because of an individual working in the middle of a process rather than because a single institutional leader contemplated creating an international partnership to aid in expanding global learning opportunities for students. Yet, Hamburg's location in the middle also presented limitations because he was an outsider; several fragile points of connections occurred in the developmental stages of the partnership that might have derailed the process.

Case Questions

- What is the advantage of leading from the middle to build a partnership versus leading from the top?
- What challenges to partnership creation emerge when leadership starts or is driven from the middle?
- In this case, how does outsider status help build the partnership in ways that it could not occur with internal leaders?
- What is the role of collaborative leadership when working between countries?
- How does context matter in building international partnerships? Consider the role of policy regarding awarding degrees, type of training or education needed, and differences in foci of educational learning.
- Given the reliance on the leader in the middle in this case, what needs to occur to embed this partnership institutionally so it does not fail if Hamburg leaves?

7

PARTNERSHIP CAPITAL
Sustaining Strategic Collaborations

L iterature on partnerships most often stops with a description of results
of the collaboration or recounting how partnering helped avert a dis-
aster such as closing a community center, student program, or college.
The belief is that these artifacts represent the intended benefit of the collaboration—namely, short-term goals. For many traditional partnerships, these
outcomes may be all that emerges from joining together. Strategic partnerships, however, can not only create tangible outcomes or objectives, but also
result in deep, lasting, organizational change and have the potential to form
partnership capital. Partnership capital represents a new form of relationship
potential that emerges when the collaboration becomes a separate entity that
is more than that of the individual partners. This form of capital helps create an adaptive space that is neutral but is still connected to the individual
partners. Partnership capital emerges as the collaboration evolves and brings
together the various forms of capital (social, resource, etc.) each member and
organization contributed to the partnership, though each one may not contribute equally or consistently over time.

The partnership becomes greater than the sum of its parts and evolves
to form a recognizable organization in itself with norms, values, networks,
synergies, and other resources upon which it operates. Here, weak ties
(Granovetter, 1983) and loose coupling (Weick, 1976) undergird creation
of the adaptive space that can nurture the collaboration as new partners
come together based on strategic goals, individual connections, and the
role of a champion in promoting the partnering opportunity. Partnership
capital helps institutionalize the partnership and creates a basis for sustainability, regardless of shifts in resource availability, leadership turnover, and

environmental turbulence. Strong partnership capital helps avert failure or helps provide the space and capacity to recognize when the partnership no longer meets the strategic goals of its member partners, signaling the time to end the collaboration.

Partnership capital emerges as a unique form of resource for collaborators that builds on the trust, shared meaning, and strategic alignment generated by partners.

Partnership capital might emerge from traditional partnerships and is not limited to outcomes of strategic partnerships. The challenges in generating partnership capital in traditional partnerships, however, include the initial motivation for collaborating (often short-term or linked to specific goals); the lack of a shared sense of meaning about the intentions of the partnership (meeting institutional needs versus partnership needs); and tenuous trust among partners (stronger ties to the institution create weaker ties with and trust in the partnership). A metaphor for thinking of the role of partnership capital in traditional partnerships is a joint bank account. It takes patience to grow a joint bank account, but this option leads to greater accumulation of (partnership) capital. Keeping tallies of individual contributions results in less gain over time but allows the individual contributor more control. The distinct and discrete roles of individual partners within the larger collaboration create a foundation that makes accumulating partnership capital more difficult.

Strategic partnerships, and the production of partnership capital in particular, provide a different potential for sustainability from traditional partnerships. Partnership capital from strategic partnerships is dynamic and blended. Continuing the banking metaphor, the accounts created are now "ours," not "yours" and "mine." The partnership capital that is created pulls from the individual entities involved to create a new organizational form that has its own language and meaning that are separate and distinct from those of the individual partners involved. The time spent together allows for the creation of shared meaning of terms, ideas, and concepts and allows trust to accrue among the group.

Motivations play into creating the backdrop for forming partnership capital. Stakeholder behavior is used to analyze conflicts that emerge over development of natural resources (Nakagawa, Bahr, & Levy, 2012). Working with community members, regional businesses, and other stakeholders helps to avert conflicts when taking natural resources from an area. Nakagawa et al. (2012) used agent-based modeling (ABM) to simulate alternative outcomes to a series of "what-if?" scenarios in a mining town in South America. The resulting outcomes show what occurs when stakeholders want to block resource development, when communication is more opened or closed, and when the mining company takes intentional actions. The value of this form of modeling is that stakeholders can see the range of outcomes from their actions and how group behavior can result in consensus—or not. This modeling technique holds promise for other types of partnerships that involve various stakeholders with differing levels of buy-in to a project. Knowing the potential outcomes allows partners an early litmus test to determine whether creating partnership capital is even possible.

> Initial motivations to partner create a foundation that can either support or detract from the establishment of partnership capital.

Grobe (1990) notes that the definitions of *partnerships* and *associated expectations* change over the course of time. Likewise, roles also shift over time. This chapter focuses on the latter stages of partnership development—after formation and development of the group. It is important to note, however, that the roots of the group influence the potential to create partnership capital. Hence, initial motivations and goals contribute to what is possible in the end. Likewise, the history of the development and activities of the partnerships promote (or hinder) creation of partnership capital.

We have offered the stages of partnership development in this volume, and others (Barnett, Hall, Berg, & Camarena, 1999; Gardner, 2011) offer typologies of partnerships as well. For example, Barnett et al. (1999) present a series of partnering options that range from simple to complex: independent agencies; vendor model; collaborative model; symbiotic partnership model; spin-off model; and creation of a new organization (p. 23). Gardner (2011) reviews a typology of partnership frameworks that includes single-tier; multi-tier; and complex-brokered partnerships. In the case of multi-tier partnerships, "effective middle level leaders understand the need to link partnership functions and collaborations, enabling technical expertise and support in schools and classrooms where teachers need them" (p. 75). The efforts of leaders in the middle are critical to sustaining partnerships as this level in the organization is often the most stable. The creation of partnership capital occurs when partnerships become more collaborative and symbiotic, when relationships are deeply embedded in the organization, and when collaborative networks are woven throughout the joint venture. In this case, trust is greater and buy-in to the larger goals of the group more established.

Several questions emerge that help determine whether the building blocks for partnership capital are evident in a collaboration. These include:

- How do the initial motivations for partnering influence the potential for the creation of partnership capital?
  - o Do institutional allegiances have a stronger pull on partners?
  - o How might these allegiances hamper creating partnership capital?
- What can be put in place to help foster building trust and creating shared meaning?
- What is the role of institutional leaders in creating incentives for partnership participation?

Creation of Partnership Capital

Previous research has often highlighted the steps required to develop a partnership, but falls short of explaining what happens in the sustainability stage (Kezar, Frank, Lester, & Yang, 2008). To address this gap in the literature, Amey et al. (2010) presented the concept of partnership capital and posited that this form of capital emerges when there are shared norms, shared beliefs, and networking that aligns processes and values among the individual partners. Trust (Vangen & Huxham, 2003) is created over time as partners create a shared understanding of the work they are doing and begin to see how the ethos of the individual partners and strategic objectives align. The creation of new and enhanced networks made possible through the partnering process helps build a foundation for sustainability and contributes to possibilities for the new entity to contribute to the partnership apart from what individual partners can do on their own. Strategic alignment of values and goals helps to strengthen these networks. Finally, for trust, shared meaning, and shared norms to blossom, adaptive space is critical (Heifetz, 1994). Providing a neutral adaptive space allows room for partners to nurture burgeoning partnerships and creates a strong environment of shared norms. The role of slack in the organizational system contributes to this space (Bourgeois, 1982) by enabling new processes to be created and the chance to see by trial and error what works best. The following sections explain each of these components; Figure 7.1 provides a conceptual model of how the factors of partnership capital interact.

Figure 7.1 Collaborative leadership and partnerships

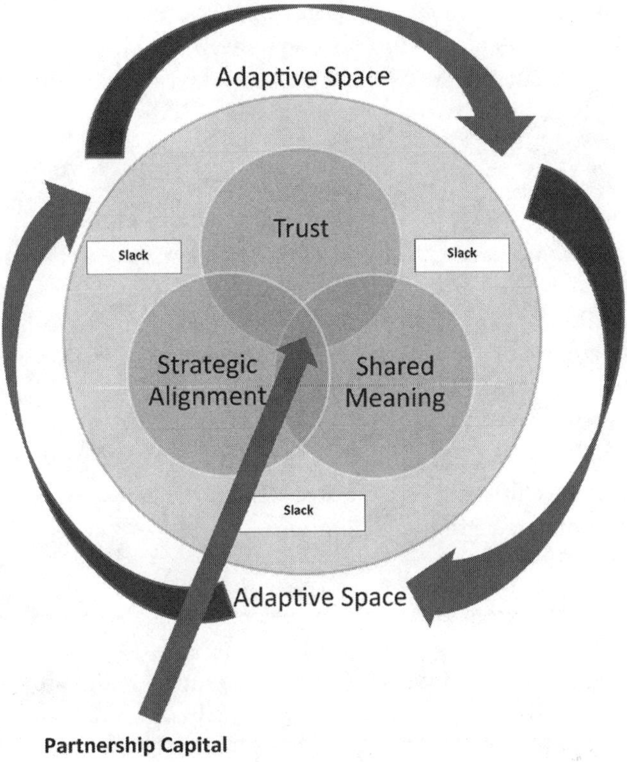

Trust

One of the central components of partnership capital is trust among partners. Yet, *trust* is a complex and difficult concept to define. Tschannen-Moran and Hoy (2000) reviewed four decades of research on trust, with a focus on trust and schools, and concluded that trust supports reform efforts and collaboration, but there are obstacles to building trust. These include different interpretations of and routes for communication in diverse settings, the existence of distrust, and rotating staff and leaders. "The hierarchical nature of relationships in a work setting complicates the study of trust because it affects the expectations of what people feel they owe to one another" (Tschannen-Moran & Hoy, 2000, p. 566). Further, the dynamic nature of trust means that its strength changes over time due to changing relationships, contexts, and needs.

As Zhang and Huxham (2009) report, studies over time emphasize the role of "trusting relationships to collaborative performance" (p. 187). Knowing the importance of trust in making partnerships work, Zhang and Huxham

(2009) sought to understand better the role of trust *building* and identity construction in international partnerships. They assume that "trust can exist between partners in collaboration if they *either* have confidence about each other's future behavior *or* are willing to accept the risk of possible opportunistic actions by a partner in the future" (Zhang & Huxham, p. 2009, 189; italics in original). Their case study research concluded that "trusting attitudes can be reinforced through recognition of deference action and adaptation of identity to fit with changing collaboration circumstances" (p. 206). Trust building occurs via reinforcement over time when relationships tap into the identity constructs of the individual partners. In the case of international partnering, acknowledgment of and sensitivity to cultural norms and relationships is critical. In both domestic and international partnerships, the context of the individual organizations, and the norms for individual roles within these institutions, influences how trust is built and maintained via relationships. Luo (2002) confirms this relationship and found that the trust-performance link is mediated by a variety of factors and may not demonstrate the same strength on all occasions.

Trust contributes to collaborative outcomes. The process of trust building occurs when partners know each other well or are willing to take a risk based on the assumption that the potential partner will follow through and fulfill promises.

Yet, the research on trust uses a variety of research methods, foci, and empirical approaches (Seppänen, Blomqvist, & Sundqvist, 2007). As a result, how trust is conceptualized and studied differs depending on the approach, focus of study, and data sources. A main issue is that trust is conceptualized on the organizational level, but measured on the individual level (Seppänen et al., 2007). Thus, operationalizing the concepts of trust proves illusive. A critical next step in the research on partnership capital includes more empirical research and data collection of building and sustaining trust.

Time plays a critical role in building trust and how trust is maintained or changes. Martenson, Newman, and Zak (2011) looked at school community partnerships with university extension and tribal partners. The framework explored involved listening, learning, and responding. In this instance, mutual trust was built over time, and joint identification of opportunities, solutions, and success occurred. Central here was a didactic dialogue that did not give privilege to one party or another and excluded individual egos.

Ratnasingam (2005) reviewed literature on trust and presented a typology that distinguishes four types of trust: technological perspectives of trust, economic perspectives of trust, behavioral perspectives of trust, and organizational perspectives of trust (p. 529). Her research of an e-commerce case study found that technology trust evolved into relationship trust due to "competence, predictability, and goodwill trust, that gradually evolved into relationship trust" (p. 541). The complexity of various facets of trust prompts us to include trust as an essential building block of partnership capital, with the understanding that it is not a single definition or type of trust and that trust builds over time as relationships become more established and reciprocal.

Different types of trust exist, with behavioral trust building on relationships nurtured over time through didactic communication.

The factor of trust in the model for partnership capital provides broad inclusion. As the research outlined in this section highlights, trust has various dimensions, but the foundational concept of trust to partnership success remains crucial. The ability to use relationships and organizational connections to build trust sets the stage for partnership capital to occur. Interaction with the other basic factors of strategic alignment and shared meaning is interactive. The context of partnering in a space that is adaptive and includes slack creates a fertile environment for creating and sustaining partnership capital.

As partners consider the role of trust in existing relationships and how to nurture trust building in burgeoning collaborations, several questions can help guide conversations:

- How does the length of time I've known my partner influence the level of trust I have in the partner and his or her word to follow through on promises?

    o Do experiences and outcomes provide evidence that I can count on my partner for our current initiative?
    o If I'm working with a new partner, do I think it is worth the risk to move forward on the current project?

- What type of communication networks are built into the partnership to help share information and build trust?
- Have I been a good partner in the past, and does my potential partner believe I will follow through in our new collaboration?

Strategic Aligning

Chapter 2 outlined how various motivations spur the formation of partnerships, with one motivating factor represented by value alignment. Alignment of values provides the basis from which strategic objectives emerge. When strategic objectives align for partners, it is easier to collaborate because they are seeking the same end goals. This type of alignment may emerge at various points of the collaboration. For example, part of a college's core mission and ethos may be a desire to provide open access to postsecondary education, and a local community agency may likewise desire to build bridges out of poverty for low-income students. These shared objectives can form the roots of a partnership and nurture the strategic alignment among the partners that existed individually at inception of the new collaboration. Or, a partnership may have formed initially based on a different set of motivating factors, such as the desire to achieve economies of scale, access funding, or achieve a defined objective. But, during the course of partnering, an alignment may emerge that bolsters the core strategic objectives of the partners involved. In this case, a partnership started by happenstance shifts to one that is strategic.

Over time, the educational sector has partnered increasingly with business and industry. Some argue that this form of academic capitalism (Slaughter & Rhoads, 2004) commodifies and taints the true focus of education. Neoliberals contend that a shift to a market-driven focus in education results in an emphasis on a narrow range of education objectives and draws attention, and resources, to these areas, thus ignoring other historically important topics (Letizia, 2013). The tension evident in the role of education in society is beyond the purview of this book, but it does contribute to thinking about how partners align based on strategic goals. The education sector increasingly looks to business for partners (Bennett & Thompson, 2011).

Using an organizational lens, Selznick (1957) "proposed that power relationships within organizations are the mechanism for the infusion of values" (as cited in Bennett & Thompson, 2011, p. 829). This finding underscores the role of the individual social capital of champions to instill in an organization a particular orientation, mission, and value system that ultimately translates to a strategic plan. Thus, leaders play a central role in casting internal strategy but also in influencing strategic alignment in newly formed partnerships. As Bennett and Thompson (2011) argue, "the efficacy of school-business collaboration also depends on the capacity of participants to sufficiently understand the management systems, resources, culture, jargon, limitations, accountability, and delivery systems of two separate organizational cultures" (p. 833). Forming a new culture from two or more distinct partnering organizations is easier when alignment exists.

Strategic alignment of goals and values among partners helps contribute to partnership capital. Leaders contribute to how institutional members *see* how a new partnership fits with organizational strategies.

The contextual nature of partnerships highlights the need for feedback loops to help assess the collaboration. Indeed, if

leaders intend development of a dynamic collaborative that truly intends to achieve and sustain reform beyond the tenure of key actors, they must deliberately pursue a partnership course associated with institutional change divergent from templates considered "legitimate and reputable." (Bennett & Thompson, 2011, p. 861; DiMaggio & Powell, 1991, p. 73)

The dilemma presented in this scenario is that the motivations and strategy that initially brought partners together needs to move beyond the historic organizational practices of each partner and transition to a new, unique form over time that includes norms for the new partnership. Yet, remaining central to the partnership are shared values that guide achievement of strategic objectives. Sanchez (2010) argues for thinking more complexly about the interconnections among the various systems and networks rather than focusing on traditional hierarchical modes of operation that discount levels of connection. The forms of network, creation of new ties within the partnership, and underlying strategy driving the partnership all contribute to how new meaning is made among partners and, more important, among stakeholders and followers.

As evident in this discussion, the role of the champion in guiding strategic alignment is critical. The champion must attend not only to issues of organizational structure but also to organizational meaning. The third component of partnership capital that ties in with building trust among partners is creating shared meaning. As we highlighted in chapter 4, framing and sensemaking are important elements throughout partnership development and take on a heightened role in forming partnership capital because at this stage new orientations and practices form.

Leaders can pose a range of questions as they consider the role of strategic alignment in creating partnerships, including:

- How can the partnership be linked to institutional strategic objectives?
- How does the form of communicating about the partnership influence how various stakeholders see the value of the collaboration?

- How does showing that strategic alignment exists within the partnership contribute to trust building?

Shared Meaning

Framing (Fairhurst & Sarr, 1996) and sensemaking (Weick, 1995) aid in the creation and ongoing support of the emergence of shared meaning in partnerships. In the process of change, particularly radical change, organizations are transformed and "frame bending" requires moving away from an "existing orientation" (Greenwood & Hinings, 1996, p. 1024). Here, breaks from known practices and understandings shift to include new, common experiences that occur through working together, holding committee meetings, and instituting programming. Dialogue and time together in these partnership contexts result in the creation of shared meaning. For example, GradCAM is a partnership among a variety of colleges and institutes of technology in Ireland that was formed to create programming in creative arts in higher education, with a particular focus on curriculum development to support a structured doctoral degree. At the inception of the partnership, the collective group created a logo to represent the new partnership, generated terms (including naming the new partnership GradCAM), and developed new meanings for degrees and associated curriculum over time. At the beginning of this partnership, faculty from the various colleges held institution-specific meanings for their own courses that changed to common meaning for the newly created degree programs.

As Kirby (2008) reports in her study of partnerships in Canada, those with more shared language, relationships over time, or shared mission saw higher levels of collaboration. The existing organizational culture and orientation of the individual partners sets the stage for how the joint collaboration will blend and morph to form a new entity with its own set of meanings, which in some respects represents its own code or language. Kezar (2013) underscores the importance of sensemaking during times of change.

Bolman and Deal (2008) present the concept of organizations as theater, underscoring how language and meaning are created through orchestrated action. Conflicts often emerge due to a lack of shared understanding or common terms (Morgan, 2006). Thus, it is important in sustaining partnerships and creating partnership capital to have a sense of shared understanding, not only about the words used to describe partnership actions, but also regarding shared direction. For this level of shared understanding to occur, and for shared meaning to emerge, the partners must create a space to allow for dialogue, provide time to allow feedback to occur, and allow slack in the system to support all of these factors.

Partners help create new language and shared meaning based on working with one another over time. Questions to ask regarding the level of shared meaning within the partnership include:

- What shared meaning exists among partners regarding terms, processes, and goals?
  - o How have partners adjusted their references and terms based on the partnership?
  - o What new processes were created that now constitute a shared understanding of how objectives are achieved?
- How much of the new shared understanding emerges from language/ practices unique to one partner or another? Does this tallying show that one partner has more "power" than another?
- What role have leaders taken in sharing the new meanings from the partnership with the rest of the institution?

Adaptive Space and Slack

Adaptive space in partnerships provides a neutral arena in which the partners have an opportunity to test new ideas and ways of operation. We link the concept of adaptive space to the notion of adaptive work. According to Heifetz (1994),

> Adaptive work consists of the learning required to address conflicts in the values people hold, or to diminish the gap between the values people stand for and the reality they face. Adaptive work requires a change in values, beliefs, or behavior. The exposure and orchestration of conflict—internal contradictions—within individuals and constituencies provide the leverage for mobilizing people to learn in new ways. (p. 22)

Bridging the demands of adaptive work to a space to think about the learning required for change requires viewing change as a process versus a mere outcome. In this case, organizational learning (reviewed in further detail later in this chapter) provides a mechanism for adaptation to individual and organizational thinking. Adaptive space might be physical or metaphorical. Heifetz (1994) refers to the term *holding environment* to define a "relationship in which one party has the power to hold the attention of another party and facilitate adaptive work" (p. 105). In partnerships, the champion may provide this type of holding environment or adaptive space as the new partners overcome their wariness regarding the collaboration.

An adaptive space creates a neutral environment to foster and nurture burgeoning partnerships.

Adaptive space might be represented by a physically distinctive location that provides neutral ground for the various partners. Borrowing from the idea of *third space*, used in community building to distinguish from the first space (home) and second space (work) (Oldenburg, 1989), a third space provides neutral ground that allows various actors a space to collaborate, with a reliance on conversation and dialogue to work on joint efforts. In partnerships, adaptive space provides a location where partners can meet that takes them out of their natural context and, one hopes, away from some of their historic assumptions. The mere availability of adaptive space does not automatically assume that adaptations are made, however. Instead, partners may opt to avoid required changes or the type of deep questioning that allows for change. In addition, partners may retreat to old practices and norms within their own organization and be unwilling to change practices or adapt to the needs required in the new partnership.

Adaptive space is represented in the model for partnership capital as the outer circle that encompasses the core elements of partnership capital (trust, strategic alignment, and shared meaning). This space may contract or expand depending on the needs of the partners. The more protection a burgeoning partnership can have from challenges, the better. This initial time can allow new partners to begin to work out initial differences, create shared meaning, and build trust. The move away from hierarchies of power typically associated with historic partners to new forms of reporting and relocation of power creates new frames of operation.

In her study of a partnership of an Early College Program involving 25 rural schools and a community college, Zuchelli (2010) concluded that several key characteristics are required to sustain and maintain the partnership, including "shared goals; shared policy; time; communication; rewards; action; cooperation; commitment; and, quality assurance" (p. 128). The space created to allow for partners to develop new relationships, and the web of inclusion for the partners, contributes to the formation of partnership capital. Key elements are trust, shared values, and networking.

In the partnership capital model, organizational slack is located within the adaptive space and represents the ability to absorb dramatic shifts or discontinuities in partnerships (Bourgeois, 1982). When slack is present, it reduces goal conflict, creates less need for information processing, and aids in negotiations within institutions (Bourgeois, 1982). Slack provides a useful cushion during periods of change. March (as cited in Bourgeois, 1982) notes how slack may accrue because of spare resources or unexploited opportunities, which creates a buffer that helps smooth out bad times. Slack in partnerships may occur due to extra resources that are created when partners pool their various forms of capital together. The presence of slack can provide some breathing space for partners as they work on building trust, creating networks for strategic alignment, and coming up with shared meaning. Having slack in the newly created adaptive space also provides additional leveraging for emerging partnership capital. The central features of slack and adaptive space provide both the resources required for change and the safe location in which to change.

New partners may consider the following questions about adaptive space and slack:

- What type of adaptive space is available for the partnership?
  - Does the physical space create a neutral environment?
  - Does the metaphorical space allow for enough separation from home institutions to create a neutral environment?

- What type of questions emerge that challenge assumptions due to the space and slack?
- How can partners work intentionally to create a neutral space and slack in the system to help foster the new collaboration or breathe new energy into an existing partnership?

Summary

Partnership capital occurs when a partnership uses feedback loops to question underlying assumptions and invests in organizational learning. This iterative change process uses the information gleaned from learning to change and adapt to current needs. The reliance of the foundation factors (trust, strategic alignment, and shared meaning) on changes due to dynamic behavior is central.

Sustainability of partnerships is of heightened interest as policymakers, individual partners, and organizations turn toward collaborating to build efficiencies and achieve shared strategic goals. Thune (2011) studied higher education-business partnerships and proposed three main factors that contribute to success (contextual, organizational, and process factors), which he then studied empirically using four case studies. This research determined that there were three central implications for practice:

- First, proximity matters for regional partnerships, but several aspects of proximity should be addressed in relation to particular goals and available resources. Being located in geographical proximity does not mean that the regional college is a relevant partner for regional industry. A thorough review of preconditions and common resources and motives is needed when forming collaborative relationships.
- Second, organizational commitment is often neglected after formal agreements have been signed. Collaborating with industry represents opportunities, but also costs, particularly in terms of the continuous attention of senior academic staff.
- Third, successful partnerships develop in a cumulative manner. Small, relatively risk free projects and activities help in building a stronger foundation for regional partnerships. Having available resources for coordinating small projects and collaborative activities is probably important for universities that want to play a central role in the regional innovation system. (p. 46)

Thune (2011) presents a model that highlights the process nature of partnering that leads to success. He notes the role of social capital, but falls short of suggesting the development of partnership capital. The model highlights success at the end of the process of partnering that is based on subjective goals (we think things are going well) and objective goals (we have met the strategic objectives we outlined at the beginning of the partnership). The view of success for the partnership is subjective and is in the eye of beholder. Typically, there is a lack of common or empirical data that evaluate partnerships, and the different metrics applied to different stakeholder groups makes comparisons difficult (see Figure 7.2).

Figure 7.2 Factors of success in university-industry collaboration

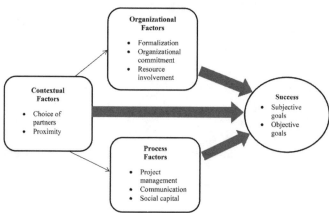

Thune, 2011, p. 37.

We argue that partnership capital is one measure of partnership success and a factor that contributes to sustainability. For strategic partnerships, partnership capital often emerges due to alignment of strategic objectives and the presence of shared norms, meaning, and ethos. Establishing the partnership often creates just the type of adaptive space that makes it possible to create partnership capital. Yet, several threats to sustainability threaten building this form of capital and can lead to failure. For instance, Waschak (2009) posits that current policies and grant funding promoting partnerships support a narrow definition of partnership options and unknowingly contribute to less sustainability. If, instead, the policy focus were on adaptive management and emphasized wider inclusion, networks and learning communities could emerge that would allow for longer success and sustainability.

Barriers to Creating Partnership Capital

A number of barriers may prevent creation of partnership capital. Changes in institutional needs may result in individual partners no longer finding the outcomes they need from the partnership. A study of partnerships in Ireland (Eddy, 2010b) showed that individual partners were torn between allegiance to the collaborative and loyalty to their institutions. The metaphor of the Roman god Janus provides a means for thinking of the struggle many partners face as a result of competing allegiances. Like the two-headed god Janus, who is looking in opposite directions, individuals are looking toward the goals and projects that are important for their home institutions and at the same time looking to those projects that benefit the partnership. In the case of strategic partnerships, alignment of strategic objectives makes it so the two heads are actually facing the same direction and are focused on similar goals. Where dissonance or conflict emerges, however, is when individual goals differ from those of the partnership. Typically in instances of difference or changes in direction, institutional needs trump those of the partnership. Thus, a key barrier to creation of partnership capital is conflicting objectives emerging from the individual partnering organizations. In a study of dual credit programming in Canada, Watt-Malcom (2011) found tensions due to stakeholders competing to gain and maintain control over their institutional territories. Here, the pull of the home institution threatened to overcome the benefits accrued from the joint collaboration.

Syam (2010) investigated a partnership formed as a result of a mandate in which multiple agencies collaborated to address health and wellness issues of teen girls in an alternative school. Contributing to the success of the partnership and the unexpected benefits was the learning that occurred for the individual partners during the process. Yet, barriers existed due to the different cultures present among the partners. As we identified in this book, issues of pull of institutional roles and giving up or changing power influenced the dynamics of the partnership. Practical implications include "framing practice in complex social domains; understanding of discourse and rhetorical framings in communicative action, and cultivation of practical intelligence and tacit knowledge in practice" (Syam, 2010, p. 216). The tensions operating against the formation of partnership capital may begin to be addressed through leadership framing, partner communication, and ongoing learning. The role of practice-based learning contributes to framing partnership capital.

Barriers to creating partnership capital include the strong pull of institutional loyalty, working competitively at cross-purposes, and changing power dynamics.

As noted in the previous chapter, leaders and champions play a central role in bringing individuals together for partnership and in prioritizing the partnership within strategic plans. When partnerships are built on individual contributions and a single person is the critical linchpin for smooth operations, the departure of one or several key players from the partnership can doom the alliance. When partnerships are person-centric, instability results when changes occur that draw the attention of the champion away to other projects or when the champion leaves the partnership. Thune (2011) points out that champions can serve as boundary spanners, which allows them to link with a number of key partners in disparate areas and across sectors. These networks may be used to help form new collaborations; however, dependence on a single person creates a vulnerable situation. Even if a formal agreement is signed, cooperation can break down if the champion is not available.

A lack of shared ethos behind the reasons for the partnership, its sought-after outcomes, or shared meaning and understanding of objectives creates additional barriers. Ikpeze, Broikou, Hildenbrand, and Gladstone-Brown (2012) found in their study of a professional development school (PDS) partnership that differences in experience within and among faculty and students resulted in poor communication "as well as divergent models of collaboration and philosophical goals between faculty and mentor teachers" (p. 275). When partners are not on the same page, conflicts and differences can emerge that threaten the partnership. On an individual level, difference in epistemology and philosophical underpinnings creates mental maps that may conflict when disparate team members are brought together (Vanasupa, McCormick, Stefanco, Herter, & McDonald, 2012). These individual-level issues are mirrored on a macro-institutional level as well and can create fissures in a partnership that threaten failure and sustainability.

The greater macro issues also involve the larger regional and national context in which partnerships occur. For instance, Piazza (2010) points out that the push for learning economies in Europe is often thwarted by barriers created by a focus on neoliberal stances on education that value individualism and a market approach to education. Focusing on a common goal of improving learning through partnership thus becomes difficult in an environment that values products and economies of scale over the public good of learning that is not tied to a specific commodity outcome.

On a micro-level, Thune (2011) points out that a concern with burgeoning partnerships is taking into consideration any negative consequences for academic staff and students. Partnerships may evolve that have a long-term impact on curriculum and college programming. Programs that result in tailored academic programs or curricula to meet partner needs might do so at the expense of developing general scientific knowledge or new areas of learning. A trade-off exists. Unintended effects of partnerships might occur if resources are distributed differently and if one discipline over another is able to garner external partnership support, thus further strengthening the strong diversification between academic fields in access to resources and students (Thune, 2011, p. 49). Disciplinary differentiation already exists within colleges based on market demands in which engineering faculty earn higher salaries than English faculty. A focus on particular partnership opportunities may exacerbate these differences and calls into question the larger underpinnings of education and the battle of neoliberal orientations to markets and commodities. A barrier to partnership capital exists if one area is valued over another.

In contemplating how to address barriers to creating partnership capital, partners might pose the following questions:

- How do institutional goals align with partnership goals?
- Does the partnership rely too much on one champion?
- What type of disciplinary or paradigm orientations exist among the various partners?
  - How might these differences be discussed to come up with a shared approach?
  - How can a new orientation be created based on the goals and needs of the partnership?

Organizational Learning

Organizational learning involves learning and unlearning. When experiences are irrelevant to current needs, a process of unlearning must occur (Mezirow, 1990). Individuals bring mental maps to new learning settings (Argyris & Schön, 1974); how these mental models manifest in action occurs along two domains. Theories-in-use describe what occurs in practice, whereas espoused theories reflect how individuals envision or describe to others what is happening (Argyris & Schön, 1974). The norms and habits underlying actions guide what happens daily and can differ from what individuals in an organization say is happening. For example, leaders of organizations may say they want to partner to improve student learning, but the deeper rationale is to share resources. Reconciliation of these two perspectives occurs via reflection and questioning the assumptions that guide actions. Learning occurs when the disconnection between reality and espoused values is addressed.

> Partners bring mental models to the new collaboration, and the use of organizational learning can help create a new, shared mental model for the partnership.

According to Doz (1996), successful alliance projects use organizational learning and evolve over time. The interactive cycle of learning involves evaluation, adjustments, and reevaluation, whereas failing alliances "were highly inertial, with little learning, or divergent learning between cognitive understanding and behavioral adjustment, or frustrated expectations" (p. 55). Of import are the initial conditions for establishing the partnerships as the orientation to organizational learning is set early on. "Organizational learning is the study of whether, how, and under what conditions organizations can be said to learn" (Kezar, 2005, p. 10). Complicating the thinking and application of organizational learning is the concept of learning organizations. Kezar (2005) argues that learning organizations represent a management fad that lacks empirical research and "focuses on creating organizations that can be adaptable, flexible, experimental, and innovative" (p. 11). According to Kezar, "Organizational learning focuses more on the study of threats to and limitations with organizational learning, while the learning organization focuses on the processes for overcoming threats to learning; it overpromises success, as Birnbaum notes of fads" (p. 13). The process of using feedback loops in creating partnership capital in particular, involves organizational learning. Organizational learning can occur on multiple levels and to varying

TABLE 7.1
Forms of Organizational Learning

Single-Loop Learning	Double-Loop Learning	Triple-Loop Learning
• Corrective action • Improves efficiencies • Metaphor—thermostat	• Questions underlying assumptions and rationale • Changes underlying norms, policies, and objectives	• Deepens learning • Links together a range of local levels toward action • Collective mindfulness

degrees. Being aware of underlying mental models (Senge, 1990) influences the process of learning. The following sections discuss the notion of single-loop learning, double-loop learning, and triple-loop learning (see Table 7.1).

Single-Loop Learning Versus Double-Loop Learning

Single-loop learning corrects deviations using existing systems and iterative actions, whereas double-loop learning involves critical questioning of underlying systems of operation (Argyris & Schön, 1974). Efficiencies are improved using a single-loop learning process, but the deeper learning involved in double-loop learning questions the rationale for the way operations occur. In the case of partnerships, single-loop learning might apply when potential partners court one another with an eye toward creating economic efficiencies of operations. Double-loop learning would be evident instead when new partners confront traditional modes of operation and work to create new ways to operate. In this case, the means of improving efficiencies emerges only when partners question underlying norms and values. The shift to alternative forms of delivering learning (e.g., online, distance learning, weekend classes, etc.) requires questioning the historic assumptions of the three-hour class and semester format. When linked to strategic partnerships, one assumes that the alignment of strategic objectives and the environmental scanning that occurs to identify likely partners implicitly imply that the partners are willing to question together how they might form a new entity.

Leaders work to resolve incongruence in the organization using different levels of learning applications. Argyris and Schön (1978) describe the differences in the learning processes as follows:

> When the error detected and corrected permits the organization to carry on its present policies or achieve its present objectives, then that error-and-correction process is *single-loop* learning. Single-loop learning is like a thermostat that learns when it is too hot or too cold and turns the heat on

or off. The thermostat can perform this task because it can receive informa-tion (the temperature of the room) and take corrective action. *Double-loop* learning occurs when error is detected and corrected in ways that involve the modification of an organization's underlying norms, policies and objec-tives. (pp. 2–3)

Taking the thermostat metaphor one step further, in the case of double-loop learning, the corrections might focus instead on the need for a particular form of heating or cooling, adjusting the norms of what a "typical" tempera-ture should be, and questioning the role of temperature control in overall quality of life. Yet, barriers often prevent double-loop learning from occurring.

Single-loop learning corrects deviations using existing systems and iterative actions, whereas double-loop learning involves critical questioning of underlying systems of operation.

Challenges to double-loop learning align with Model I theories-in-use practices (Argyris, Putnam, & McLain Smith, 1985). In Model I, Argyris et al. (1985) posit that individuals are predominantly defensive about ques-tioning errors. In this model, little questioning exists regarding actions and actors are quick to point out why their actions are most appropriate; these excuses seem rational at the time. Using the alternative delivery of course example, a defensive response might be that new forms of classes are not possible because they do not result in the highest level of deep learning for students. Model II (Argyris et al., 1985) instead uses data to create a reality informed by information and uses dialogue and shared leadership to sur-face conflicting views without trying to control the outcome. Here, norms are questioned and understood differently as a result of reflection. Within the partnership capital model, incorporating feedback loops contributes to the use of Model II processes; this mode of feedback is leveraged when partnership capital exists as common meanings, norms are shared via stra-tegic alignment, and trust exists to support this level of internal scrutiny.

Triple-Loop Learning

Triple-loop learning (Romme & van Witteloostuijn, 1999) moves from identification of the assumptions and underlying rationale that needs to be changed to actually changing operations.

As such, triple loop learning is about increasing the fullness and deepness of learning about the diversity of issues and dilemmas faced, by linking together all local units of learning in one overall learning infrastructure as well as developing the competences and skills to use this infrastructure (Flood & Romm, 1996). (as cited in Romme & Van Wittelootuijn, 1999, p. 439)

Ameli and Kayes (2011) refer to triple-loop learning as "learning to learn together" (p. 186). The move from the local level to one that combines all levels results in a sense of "collective mindfulness" that links past operations to modern day as a result of reflecting on what worked and what did not, ultimately resulting in the creation of new structures and strategies for learning (Romme & van Witteloostuijn, 1999, p. 440). Romme and van Witteloostuijn (1999) present the concepts of the various levels of organizational learning by positing the following questions:

- "Are we doing things right (single-loop learning)?"
- "Are we doing the right things (double-loop learning)?"
- "Can we participate in making well-informed choices regarding strategy, objectives, etc. (triple-loop learning)." (p. 452)

Specifically, Ameli and Kayes (2011) researched a cross-sector partnership asking, "How can cross-sector partners learn from each other and develop their partnership capabilities, while creating value for society?" (p. 179). (See Figure 7.3 for a view of their model.) The research site was the DC Central Kitchen (DCCK), an innovative cross-sector partnership. The study concluded that the DCCK was a learning organization and that its flat organizational structure and shared decision making supported a shared vision. Feedback was easy to obtain given the organizational structure and underlying value system based on joint processing. Both single-loop and double-loop learning occurred in this organization as changes occurred in the process (single-loop changes) and on the process (deeper-level changes). Triple-loop learning was emerging at the DCCK as the organization changed its culture due to interactions with its various partners. Yet, interorganizationally, the constellation of the DCCK and its various partners resulted in different levels of learning. Triple-loop learning did not emerge throughout the partnership, but individuals were challenging their underlying assumptions and changing their behaviors.

Triple-loop learning moves beyond identifying and questioning underlying assumptions to actually creating a strategy for change.

Ameli and Kayes (2011) posit that triple-loop learning is similar to reciprocal learning in which cocreation of knowledge occurs. "Reciprocal learning

Figure 7.3 Organizational learning in partnerships

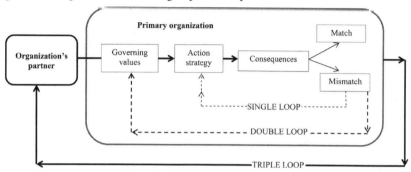

Adapted from Ameli & Kayes, 2011, p. 177

requires that both partners willingly disclose aspects of their knowledge valuable to the partnership. . . . This requires an environment primed for internal learning first" (Ameli & Kayes, 2011, p. 186). Thus, the generation of partnership capital can occur when triple-loop learning is evident between and among partners. The occurrence of strategic alignment and shared values creates a context ripe for this level of learning to occur in partnerships. The presence of shared meaning among partners, built on a foundation of trust, creates an environment in which partners can share information and really question assumptions.

Summary

The concept of partnership capital builds on core building blocks and a set of assumptions. First, partnerships that evolve to include high levels of trust, shared meaning, and alignment of strategic objectives are more successful (Bennett & Thompson, 2011). The presence of these three components confirms that partners are invested in the process and are willing to work through challenges. Second, creation of partnership capital relies on a commitment to the tenets of organizational learning, in particular more advanced stages of double- and triple-loop learning. Partners must be willing to challenge historic assumptions of how things get done and how relationships are built and be willing to change practices based on the information gleaned in this self-reflection process. Moving beyond a series of local-level feedback loops to a larger, more encompassing view of the partnership helps in creating the collective mindfulness noted earlier. This level of mindfulness then permeates the organizational culture and helps sustain the long-term practice of questioning assumptions and using feedback to make changes. The following section reviews a particular type of partnership that involves organizations from different sectors and demonstrates how partnership capital may emerge in this model.

Partners can pose a range of questions to understand better the type of organizational learning occurring within the partnership:

- What institutional mental models have we brought to the partnership?
  - What types of assumptions have we made as a result?
  - How does questioning these assumptions move us toward double-loop learning?
- What new mental models have emerged for the partnership?
- How can we foster organizational learning?
- What processes are in place to help us move from questioning assumptions (double-loop learning) to acting (triple-loop learning)?

Triple Helix Model and Partnership Capital

A triple helix model of partnership involves the interaction of industry, government, and universities (Kitagawa, 2005). This type of partnering may emerge from the bottom up as a result of grassroots efforts (Kezar & Lester, 2009) or from the top down as a result of policy mandates or dictates from leaders (McDonnell & Elmore, 1987). Viale and Ghiglione (1998) outline the three levels of interaction in the triple helix model: micro, meso, and macro. At the micro level, individual faculty researchers engage in entrepreneurial activities regarding technology transfers emerging from their research, often in coordination with industry. University advisory boards consist of industry experts and local government representatives. In this case, the changes typically influence the local and regional level. At the meso level, institutions rather than individuals are the central actors. For example, colleges, businesses, and government create innovation or technology centers that provide a space for spin-off businesses. Finally, the macro level in the triple helix model involves state or national policies that support university/business partnerships. For example, the 2011 Higher Education Act in Virginia included policy to help support college completion to address industry needs in high-demand areas of employment, in particular targeting STEM (science, technology, engineering, and mathematics) employment. Incentives were included to encourage education and business collaboration to help increase the pipeline to technical careers.

Positioning higher education to foster entrepreneurial universities creates new forms of organizational interactions among partners. Kitagawa (2005) outlines the following characteristics of institutions found in a triple helix model:

- "New incentives need to be balanced against traditional university functions."
- "Universities have to strategically deploy resources to create new institutional mechanisms in line with their long-term missions and objectives in relation to their surrounding regions."
- "Universities need to acknowledge the complementarity of activities among different institutions, and consider the sustainability and accountability of their own activities as individual places as well as a distributed knowledge space as a whole."
- "Entrepreneurial universities and regions operate beyond local and regional levels to attract resources. There are growing interactions between the local and the global, blurring the boundaries between local and non-local actors."
- "Increasingly, universities serve as a talent magnet in attracting highly skilled workers to a region. As such, they can leverage this role by creating new curricula to meet local needs." (p. 82)

When policymakers understand the intermediary roles of universities in connection with regional and state economies, they can leverage resources and build system capacity (McDonnell & Elmore, 1987).

Higher education institutions are physically situated in a community. This concrete location provides a basis for creating partnerships based on proximity, but also on shared values that seek to support and improve regional social issues (Pasque, Smerek, Dwyer, Bowman, & Mallory, 2005). The creation of partnerships that help improve the public good can result in new initiatives with potential for partnership capital, especially in forming a culture of support for community engagement. Leveraging of educational partners, community businesses, and government policy can lead to higher levels of organizational learning and can create the type of adaptive space required to nurture partnership capital.

Summary Points

- Foundational elements for the creation of partnership capital include:
  - trust
  - shared meaning
  - strategic alignment
- Adaptive space serves as a context that supports the creation of partnership capital.

- Organizational slack provides additional opportunities for partnership capital to emerge.
- Barriers to the creation of partnership capital include:
  o a focus on individual organizational goals rather than partnership objectives
  o reliance on a single champion
  o lack of shared ethos or philosophy regarding the partnership
  o unintended consequences for curriculum development and faculty rewards
- Higher levels of organizational learning (double-loop and triple-loop) support the creation of partnership capital.
- Cross-sector collaboration is becoming more of a norm as policy-makers seek ways to leverage limited resources.

CASE #7: THE SUM IS GREATER THAN THE PARTS

Ireland's 2011 *National Strategy Report 2030* (Higher Education Authority [HEA], 2011) advocated for mergers and consolidation of its tertiary system of higher education. A follow-up document, *Toward a Future Higher Education Landscape* (HEA, 2012), articulated details of criteria for a submission to create a new type of institution—a technological university—through mergers of existing institutions. In July 2012, a proposal was put forth for the creation of the Technological University of Dublin Alliance. The three Institutes of Technology (IoTs) involved were Dublin Institute of Technology (DIT), Institute of Technology Tallaght (ITT), and Institute of Blanchardstown (ITB). The proposal (HEA, 2012) argued that these institutes "already share this vision for higher education [to be globally competitive] and have an agreed strategy for its implementation" (p. 1). The proposal stated that "TU Dublin, as part of its strategy, will be proactive in initiating collaborations for the benefit of the region" (p. 6).

IoTs in the Dublin region were well known to one another and had a history of cross-fertilization of personnel, collaborations, and interests. As one of the presidents commented, "We were in each other's orbit." What changed as a result of the National Strategy (Department of Education and Skills, 2011) was moving from informal partnerships to formal partnerships.

The informal conversations occurring among the Dublin-based institutes since 2009 provided a forum for discussing ideas, mapping out expectations, and arguing for institutional roles. Initial dialogue regarding the proposal for TU-Dublin included the Institute of Art and Design Technology (IADT). Before the criteria were spelled out in the guidelines for proposing a TU, much speculation existed. During this period, exploration occurred among the four Dublin based IoTs regarding the potential to partner. Even during this stage, the IADT had concerns about the strategic fit of aligning with the other institutes due to its specific mission foci, student demographics, and size. As in other types of partnerships, participants were concerned about preserving institutional identity. Ultimately, IADT opted out of the partnership.

The acknowledgment in Ireland of the need for system changes to create a new organizational structure recognizes the need for attention to the interconnections among the partners and the role of relationships. Appreciative Inquiry is one method used during this change process. Yet, as in any new venture, concerns existed. Members of the two smaller institutes worried that they would be subsumed by the largest institute—DIT. The economies of scale made it evident, however, that pairing with other institutes was the path to long-term survival. DIT had made two failed attempts to seek university status, and the prospect of working with the smaller institutes on a proposal to become a TU provided an opportunity to obtain the long-sought recognition; without the collaboration, they would not qualify.

The small size of Ireland contributes to high levels of social capital among college leaders. Long-standing alliances among programs, movement of personnel among the IoTs, and informal conversations created a context ripe for change. The social networks within the country are tight. The time gap between the announcement of the National Strategy in 2011 and publication of the criteria for submission of proposals for TU designation created slack in the system. This period allowed the leaders of the IoTs in the Dublin region to have informal conversations to discuss options for partnering, problem solve anticipated challenges, and determine alignment of strategic objectives. The HEA primed the pump for these discussions with the National Strategy report, and the time lag between this report and the call for proposals allowed the institutional leaders to engage campus and community members in the conversation to generate greater buy-in. The social capital of the individual presidents provided leverage internally to engage in these conversations and provided a period to build trust among the final partners and create the framework and communication vehicles that guided communication about TU-Dublin.

Case Questions

- How does the size of Ireland influence relationship building and contribute to the ability to create partnership capital?
- Given the withdrawal of IADT from the partnership, what long-term challenges might the remaining partners face?
- How might the size differential among the partners influence the overall partnership and the creation of partnership capital?
- What type of organizational learning is occurring in this case? What supports/challenges this process?

8

STRATEGIES FOR CREATING
LASTING PARTNERSHIPS

T his volume highlights how a number of changing factors contribute
     to the act of partnering. The antecedents to partnership are embed-
     ded on individual and organizational levels. What motivates an
individual to buy into the partnership may differ from what motivates an
organization to seek out or begin a partnership, yet both sources contribute to partnership formation. The organizational positions of stakeholders
involved in forming, developing, and sustaining a partnership contribute to
the complex dynamics of the process and illustrate the fragility of the many
areas of the partnership process and ultimate arrangements made for collaboration. This final chapter provides a template for individuals, collaborators,
and organizations to help inform and guide their own partnership endeav-
ors. To illustrate the process, we use a case study involving the community
colleges in Massachusetts throughout this chapter to highlight the various
levels of leadership, motivators for partnership formation, and development
of partnership capital.

Central points of the partnership model are highlighted, in particular,
the role of relationships, communication, organizational capital, and leadership. In addition to the levels of leadership involved, we offer suggestions for
both state and federal policymakers on how best to leverage collaborations to
achieve public policy goals. Partnering occurs both domestically and internationally, yet these settings invoke some differences. Partners within a state or
region are dealing with a particular context and may be seeking partnership
to address regional challenges, whereas partners operating across national
borders may be seeking a particular type of outcome from the partnership

that is not possible with local partners, such as increasing global competencies in student learning outcomes.

Case Example—Massachusetts

As part of national attention on community colleges at the cusp of the twenty-first century, a variety of policies were proposed to help build bridges between educational institutions and business needs. One of the outcomes of these policy efforts was funding by the U.S. Department of Labor for the Trade Adjustment Assistance Community College and Career Training (TAACCCT) grant program, which is coadministered by the Department of Education (see www.dol.gov/opa/media/press/eta/eta20101436.htm). A total of $2 billion was allotted for grant funding for fiscal years 2011–2014, with $500 million in award funding granted over each cycle in the five-year program. The policy goal was to build community college capacity by expanding and improving education delivery options, with completion of career training in two years or less required. Student participants in the program should then be ready for immediate employment in high-wage, high-skill occupations.

Building on the momentum of this grant program, the Bill and Melinda Gates Foundation and Lumina Foundation supported an exploratory program, titled Transformative Change Initiative (a joint project of the Office of Community College Research and Leadership [OCCRL] at the University of Illinois at Urbana-Champaign and the Collaboratory; see http://occrl.illinois.edu/projects/transformative_change). Achieving the Dream also collaborated on this support programming. Round 1 winners of TAACCCT funding included 49 organizations with partnerships occurring in all 50 states. From this first group, eight project teams were invited to participate in the exploratory program on Transformative Change. Round 2 winners, announced in September 2012, included another 27 projects.

One of the Round 1 TAACCCT award winners, and a pilot participant in the Transformative Change Initiative, was a program created in Massachusetts—a program that illustrates how to instigate a successful partnership and how to sustain a collaboration that results in transformational change. Early outcomes indicate that this collaboration has begun to produce partnership capital and lasting impact. In 2011 the community colleges in Massachusetts were awarded a $20 million, three-year grant from the U.S. Department of Labor that was part of the initial year of the TAACCCT grant program. The project, Massachusetts Community Colleges and Workforce Development Transformation Agenda (MCCWDTA), involves a number of key stakeholders: community colleges, the Commonwealth's adult basic education and workforce development systems, and industry stakeholders. The focus of the MCCWDTA is to transform the delivery of education and training programs in Massachusetts and serve as a model for others. Massachusetts ranks 19th in the nation for manufacturing job loss, and almost half of the displaced workers are deficient in basic skills (Quinsigamond Community College [QCC], 2011). The partnership is meant to create or redesign career-focused certificate and degree programs in the state. Four key priorities drive the overarching Transformation Agenda are to:

1. accelerate progress for low-skilled, and other workers;
2. improve retention and achievement rates; reduce time to gain industry recognized credentials, certificates, and degrees;
3. build programs that meet industry needs, including developing career pathways; and
4. strengthen online and technology-enabled learning. (QCC, 2011, abstract)

The partners sought to build programming based on best practices from research and concentrated their attention on how to compress course material to accelerate learning and focus educational content and training on strategies that meet individual student needs. Critical to student success are scaffolds in place that help support student learning, in particular study strategies, career planning, and acquisition of appropriate learning skills. Ultimately, "the Transformation Agenda will serve 4,000 students and place 2,800 in employment throughout the three year period" (QCC, 2013, p. 1).

The MCCWDTA identified several barriers to students even gaining access to community college programs. Lack of information about community college options, low literacy rates, inflexible campus policies and course offering formats, disconnected noncredit and credit courses, faculty expertise, funding for changes, and lack of career counseling all create barriers for students (QCC, 2011). The consortium identified three statewide initiatives to address these challenges:

1. design of a modularized and industry-specific contextualized curriculum for Adult Basic Education through developmental education;
2. a networked case management strategy that integrates student support services provided by college and Career Center staff; and
3. a unified methodology for both shared statewide curriculum development and implementation of education and career training pathways that aligns competencies from basic skills to the associate degree attainment in six high growth industry sectors. (QCC, 2011, p. 10)

Use of evidence-based best practices and research provide a model for programming and the creation of effective strategies for students, faculty, and consortium leaders to overcome identified barriers.

> Additional services include: establishment of virtual resource centers to support adaptation, evaluation and refinement of evidence-based acceleration practices; online community of practice and professional development for employees; and design and execution of a statewide marketing campaign to build public awareness of community colleges as responsive and high quality workforce trainers. (QCC, 2011, p. 14)

Dale Allen, vice president of community engagement at QCC is project director. In addition, the grant allowed hiring of numerous personnel to fulfill the goals and objectives for the partnership.

The Massachusetts partnership built on interactions of the 15 community college presidents through association with the Massachusetts Community Colleges Executive Office (MCCEO, www.masscc.org). An early champion of the partnership was Gail Carberry, president of QCC. Carberry noted, "I was fortunate to have Dale [Allen] on my team who has a record of teambuilding. The project was brought together using the strength of each campus; we were not competing against one another." The funding potential of $20 million was a critical source of motivation for the group as they knew the only way to obtain the grant was by working together. Yet, it was the ability to build on existing relationships at multiple levels of the colleges, state organizations, and industries that provided the linchpin for forward movement.

Initially, not all campuses embraced the prospect of collaborating—several participants likened this to "herding 15 cats." Initial resistance ultimately succumbed to peer pressure to participate, but not necessarily total buy-in. Confidence in staff and the decision to allocate the funds in even proportional shares, which gave campuses flexibility to use the funding based on their needs, helped early resisters turn the corner. Approximately 100 people were involved in the four-month intensive planning and grant-writing period. All-day meetings occurred once a week during this time, with specific group meetings scheduled throughout the day. Concepts from the Breaking Through model (see www.breakingthroughcc.org) helped frame conversations. Trust among partners and relationships grew as a result of this early period of face-to-face meetings.

QCC provides project direction in coordination with the MCCEO. The project office and the presidents' council through MCCEO are a source of communication to the 15 campuses. In addition to involvement of key stakeholders from each of the campuses and the MCCEO, connections occurred with the state's workforce development, economic development, adult basic education and department of higher education, and leaders in six major industry sectors.

Contributing to universal participation among the colleges was how the grant plans aligned with individual campus strategic plans—in particular the desire to shorten the distance for students to get into the workforce using stackable certificates. The missions of the one-stop centers, work on developmental education, and meeting workforce needs helped cut across sectors. The Breaking Through model helped provide a framework for thinking of how to aid low-skilled adults with a pathway to college and a career. Team meetings focused first on creating a list of shared objectives for the grant, and then addressed how the funds would be distributed. The attention paid to accomplishing shared goals helped alleviate perceived competition among partners, and equitable allocation of grant funds underscored the value of collaboration. Buy-in was apparent because the implementation was driven by local choice. In addition, the availability of seasoned grant writers supported the submission process.

The time committed to writing the grant and the initial implementation steps helped create shared language for talking about the partnership. Relationships were stronger because of the time spent together, and the shared goal of transforming workforce education in Massachusetts served as a rallying point. Creation of statewide systems for data collection helped align how campus leaders evaluated programming and assessed future needs. Even with the collaborative efforts, campuses relied on their contextual needs and strengths. The ability to retain some independence of campus service areas allowed flexibility within the system. The campus-centered programming built into the grant required a great deal of coordination, and a fear of change still exists. Because the people involved in the partnership are at different positional levels, it may be that 75% of the presidents are supportive of the changes and 75% of the chief academic officers are behind the new initiatives, but that these supportive leaders are not necessarily on the same campus. As a result, it means there is a champion of the project on every campus and in most cases two or more. The grant funding enabled some backfilling of funds to state agencies that had been cut during the recession.

Evidence of partnership capital is apparent after two years of MCCWDTA operations. First, momentum has built among the colleges with increased buy-in to the partnership. Early gains have helped spur this level of enhanced engagement. Second, a liaison director was hired to work with the state secretaries of state, economic development, and labor. This liaison position created opportunities for improved communication, shared understanding of issues, shared data about workforce skills, and pooling of resources. Workforce development is now on the radar in the state. The MCCEO supports adaptive space, and system capacity and programming are the biggest indicators of the partnership's ability to achieve results. Enhanced awareness of the contributions of the community colleges to state goals and workforce needs symbolically supports the partnership. Finally, the high visibility of the grant contributed the focus on system transformation—the stakes were high. The use of shared language provided a common way to view the grant; in particular, the use of the terms *we* and *team* help to underscore that this is a joint effort.

Despite the positive forward motion, resistance to change is human nature. Trying to change operating systems to a more flexible format that moves beyond taking courses in semester format to alternative modes of delivery meant that offices and staff had to change historical ways of operating. Typical responses such as, "This isn't how the system works" had to shift to accommodate new modes of operation. Pointing out examples where system changes were successful provided models. The mantra, "The future is not the past," and a focus on collective action aided in creating partnership capital. Trust among partners was strong, networks developed, and shared goals and language are evident.

The Case Viewed Through the Strategic Partnership Model

The essential argument in this volume builds on the notion that strategic alignment among partners creates stronger motivations to partner and enhances the probability of long-term, sustainable success. For strategic partnerships to emerge, awareness of the organization's mission and values is critical (Kezar, 2013). The underlying mission guides the formation of the strategic plan and identification of strategic objectives. Once these goals and guiding factors are known, leaders of institutions can engage in proactive environmental scanning to determine the best options for partnering that allow them to leverage internal resources, both human and capital.

The advancement of the organization's strategic objectives creates more buy-in to the partnering process and builds on a sense of shared values. The common direction helps initially, but it is important to realize that the initial reasons for partnering may change over time. On the one hand, this change does not necessarily mean that the partnership must be abandoned. If the change in objectives creates too large a chasm between joint goals, ending the partnership is a good option. On the other hand, if the partnership still sees positive gain for all parties, continuation is possible.

The following sections discuss in more detail how strategic partnerships form, how they may change over time, and how the role of the champion influences the process. The case example in Massachusetts provides a means to highlight the various stages of the strategic partnership.

Initial Formation

As we discussed in chapter 2, there are various motivations for partnering. In the case of Massachusetts, several motivations overlapped and provided the needed impetus for the group to pursue the TAACCCT funding. State budget cuts pressed all of the community colleges and state offices. This loss in funding meant that functional areas were not staffed, needs were going unmet, and loss of service was evident. The grant provided strong motivation to make this partnership work. Yet, funding alone could not pull the parties together; the policy outlining the funding required partnering. But, as history shows, mandates alone are not enough to guarantee either the formation of a partnership (Watson, 2007) or the sustainability of system changes (McDonnell & Elmore, 1987). The alignment of the partners' values that sought more efficient ways to educate students and to provide a trained workforce for the state proved to be a critical tipping point. The final piece to forming the partnership in Massachusetts was the presence of strategic leadership.

Funding alone is not enough to ensure successful partnerships.
Creating shared goals, using adaptive space, and framing the
partnership as a joint effort help create a strong partnership foundation.

This leadership occurred at multiple levels. First, the buy-in from the presidents of all the community colleges, and in particular the championship of President Carberry, was essential. Carberry was able to advocate for the partnership in the presidents' council in a way that encouraged the other presidents to buy in to the effort but not view the collaboration as another form of competition. Second, Dale Allen served as an advocate for the collaboration's possible outcome. In his position as vice president of engagement, he worked in community circles and established relationships with many of the key stakeholders over his long career.

Once the grant was awarded, each community college hired a project director, placing local control on each campus. This individual was also a point person for connecting to the larger consortium. The colleges staffed career college navigators at the state's one-stop career centers, which helped create a network of connections between the colleges and the state offices. Also, these counselors were attuned to the needs of industry employers, despite initial uncertainty regarding the role of the navigators and their role in the centers.

Times of Change

Partnerships evolve over time. In the beginning, excitement runs high as partners are full of hope about the promise of a productive collaboration. Yet, tensions also exist as the partnership dance begins, given the uncertainty of the change process. Black and Gregersen (2003) point to the brain barriers that must be overcome for change to occur; these include the failure to see, to move, and to finish. As noted in the earlier case, it took time for all of the presidents to "see" the benefits of partnering. Even with the partnership under way, failure to see extends to those on the ground implementing the changes. For instance, those in the one-stop career centers are uncertain about the role and placement of the college-supported career counselors in the office. A sentiment of "us" and "them" currently exists. This failure to see the possibilities contributes to the failure to move—in this case to embracing the new colleagues and figuring out the best way to help move students through programs. The reporting metrics associated with the grant help contribute to moving programming forward. In this case, time will tell if there is a failure to finish.

Challenges always exist as new partnerships form and new mental models are created. How leaders throughout home institutions and within the partnership frame the partnership influences how others see and accept it.

The strategic planning model advocates that second-order or transformational change is required. The case in Massachusetts is moving forward in this area as questions about the way programming can be accomplished are posed throughout the process. Historic modes of operation and interactions are constantly challenged. Relationships are being built among a wide array of stakeholders, and the time spent together is creating trust. In addition, the group is forming a sense of shared meaning regarding the purpose of the grant and in the process is creating new terms and meaning. This sense of shared ethos contributes to a culture of questioning. The champions of the project help to frame the vision for others, and in turn, this framing is replicated throughout the larger system. Yet, as one president noted,

A great concern of campuses is that this is merely the initiative du jour. I'm reluctant to introduce another initiative on my campus; to the extent that this initiative can support and complement on things I'm already hammering home, great! It is not as a grant going to be transformational here, though it may help us transform as part of other things.

This point of view illustrates that framing is seen on multiple levels, with a campus lens ultimately being the one most members of the college community will use.

Role of Champion

As we noted earlier, a number of champions were involved in the initial stages of the MCCWDTA process. This initial involvement helped create the momentum to get the project off the ground. Yet, over time additional champions have provided critical contributions. These new champions are at various levels of leadership, in different partnering organizations, and have different roles. As early successes occurred, the state noted how the groups were collaborating and, in turn, created a new liaison for three central state offices. This person is able to champion the collaboration across formerly disparate agencies in a more productive fashion because she can "speak" the language of each area.

As directors are hired on each campus, they become localized champions of the process. How they talk about the partnership in light of other campus activities is central; as the president's commentary points out, there are several competing campus initiatives. Key to the long-term success of the strategic partnerships is the feedback loops built in. The use of common data sources helps bring similar information into the conversation, the creation of shared language builds buy-in on campus, and the time spent working together builds trust. To be successful, the partnership needs to move beyond reliance on a few key champions and create a sustainable foundation. Time will tell whether the MCCWDTA will have this staying power, but the early presence of partnership capital, as evidenced by shared vision, strategic alignment of goals, and emerging trust, in this case breeds hope.

Lessons Learned

The following sections provide a practical how-to guideline for those interested in forming, maintaining, or changing a partnership. As we have argued, there are different roles for those at varying levels of the organization. Knowing what you can do as an individual involved in a partnership is important because this knowledge can help you leverage your role and influence to enhance outcomes. Mid- and senior-level leaders have particular levers of influence on the process. Finally, policymakers can help shape how partnerships are formed and, more important, how they can be sustained. The orientation of this section allows readers to "see" the level and functions of roles at particular locations—for example, if you view this as an individual, you are going to observe the items identified because your vantage point is at the individual level. But knowing what is observed and enacted at other levels allows you to take into account these different perspectives.

Merely recognizing the other levels and what is observed from these points provides an insider's view and a way to think about how information needs to be presented so those at these other levels "see" and "hear" the points you desire to make. Advice and suggestions for these various stakeholders follows in the form of questions to consider regarding forming, developing, and maintaining partnerships. This multiframe view gives a peek into the dynamic moving parts of collaboration.

How-To for Individual Champions

As noted throughout this volume, partnerships often emerge due to the initiative of individuals (Amey, 2010). In the normal course of a job, individuals work with and interact with countless others. Building a social network (Carrington et al., 2005) includes both strong and weak ties to others. Opportunities to partner materialize through these interactions. For example, a college leader working out in the gym may encounter a professional working in a local industry and become friends. Over the course of a workout, it may come up that the industry needs some training and the college leader offers the services of one of the college departments to do this work. This initial contact grows into a partnership. If this collaboration aligns with strategic goals, it has a greater chance of success. If, however, the partnership is more one of convenience and happenstance, it is less likely to endure once the original champions are gone.

Likewise, the push for internationalization on college campuses often results in colleges hosting visiting scholars or in creating specialized offices, such as a Confucius Institute. These international exchanges may result in greater opportunities to partner with institutions overseas. With multiple options available, it is easy for an institution's international office and its staff to be overburdened and spread too thin in light of so many opportunities. Using strategic plans to decide how to pick partners provides judicious metrics for evaluating which opportunities to pursue and which to pass by.

Questions to consider on the individual level include:

- What core values guide my work? My organization?
- How do potential partners complement current needs?

- How does the work of potential partners align with our strategic plans?
- At what level will the partnership occur?
- Who benefits? What are the opportunity costs—both monetary and personal?
- What are the long-term expectations?

How-To for Mid-Level Leaders

Mid-level leaders serve in a unique organizational location. They typically have access to upper-level leaders, but also to those working in the trenches of the organization and in the field. These broad contacts provide multiple interaction possibilities and create the potential for a robust sense of social capital for those at this mid-level. The enhanced opportunity for relationship building means that those at this level are also often the "doers" of projects and initiatives. These leaders represent a stable portion of the organization as turnover here is not as high as in upper- or lower-level positions. Depending on their precise location in the organizational hierarchy, mid-level leaders also have access to various organizational resources. Even if these leaders do not have the authority themselves to allocate the requisite resources, they know the system well enough to know *whom* to ask and can use their position to advocate for them.

Another advantage for mid-level leaders is the ability to fly under the radar of public scrutiny. Top leaders are the symbolic representative of the institution, so they are the public face of the organization. In this capacity, their actions and communications are viewed more closely and with different interpretation (Pfeffer, 1977). Having some anonymity creates opportunities for mid-level leaders, and they also may have different sources of power (Bolman & Deal, 2008). Power is available to a certain extent through their position, but also in what they know, their ability to work the boundaries of the organization, and a comfort with uncertainty (Morgan, 2006). This type of social capital is unique and, as a result, is often overlooked.

Questions to consider for mid-level leaders include:

- How can I seek out partners that align with the strategic objectives of my organization?
- Who in my network would complement our current organizational needs?
- How can I leverage the power I have to entice our organization to support a partnership that aligns with our goals?
- How can I serve as an intermediary to partners and upper-level leaders?

- How does my area benefit? What are the opportunity costs—both monetary and personal?
- What are the long-term expectations and commitment?

How-To for Campus Leaders

As noted, campus leaders are the symbolic representation of the organization, so their seal of approval on a partnership is critical to long-term success. Buy-in and support by the leader not only provides access to a different range of resources for the partnership, it also symbolizes for others that they should pay attention to the project. How the campus leader frames the partnership matters. On the one hand, a leader might provide feint support for a project. On the other hand, a leader may show a deep and lasting commitment to the collaboration by talking about it constantly, putting information in public forums, and having subordinates reach out to their stakeholder to show support.

Campus leaders will have different questions depending on the phase of the partnership. For instance, actions might differ during the initial exploration phase from when putting the partnership into action. Of importance at this level is how the partnership withstands changes in upper-level positions. Typically, presidents serve in a position at a college for approximately seven years (American Council on Education, 2012). It is important to have a sustainable plan for transitions and to have champions at multiple levels to withstand these types of personnel changes (Watson, 2007). During the process of the partnership formation, development, and implementation, different questions emerge for leaders, which include:

- What are our institutional motivations to partner?
- How does the partnership help meet our strategic goals?
- How can we best leverage our organizational resources in the partnership?
- What are we looking for in a partner to help achieve our objectives?
- Who can help champion this partnership in-house?
- How can top campus leaders best frame the partnership to campus members?
- What feedback loops are in place to make corrections over time to the partnership?
- What can we as leaders do to help sustain the partnership?

How-To for Policymakers

Policy can create a strong motivating force for individuals and organizations to seek partnering opportunities. Increasingly, state and federal funding requires collaboration. An underlying premise of this requirement is that efficiencies will be gained by partnering, knowledge will be leveraged and created in ways that cannot be done on an individual basis, and greater capacity occurs when parties work together. Yet, the history of partnership failures (Eddy, 2007; Farrell & Sarr, 2007; Watson, 2007) highlights how collaboration does not guarantee success.

The stages of policy development provide a platform for creating policy that best supports partnerships. Each stage is reviewed briefly and links to partnership support are provided. *Issues* definition (Fowler, 2012) generates from varying needs observed by the public. When enough support is garnered, and these issues begin to gain traction, they enter the larger policy agenda. At these early stages of policy development, a number of competing ideas and concepts are presented. Because those that receive lobbying support or have large funding sources available to enhance advocacy draw the most attention, it is important to analyze which options are, indeed, best not only for the individual partners but also for obtaining policy objectives. Perhaps the most critical stages are policy formation and policy implementation (Fowler, 2012). Here, the way the policy is written matters. Wording is crucial as a simple "may" instead of "should" can change the options available to partners. Because different stakeholder groups understand terms differently, it is important to provide as much clarity in the policy document as possible. For instance, using "enhanced learning" or "student outcomes" may have different interpretations depending on the role of the stakeholder. Implementation may be held up if those who need to put the policy into place resist it. Providing necessary supports and anticipating barriers (recall Black and Gregersen's [2003] "failure to move") can make the difference between early adoption and no action. Finally, it is important to have evaluation procedures in place (Fowler, 2012). Understanding how the partnership will be evaluated will help in designing the program, providing feedback loops for organizational learning (Argyris & Schön, 1996), and documenting achieved outcomes.

Questions for policymakers to consider include:

- Do the desirable policy goals require partnerships?
- What types of partnerships create the best scenario for reaching policy goals?
- What motivates those with whom we want to partner?
- How can the partnership be sustained beyond the initial funding period?
- What policy formation best supports capacity expansion in the system?

- What is required to create systemic or transferable change?
- What metrics do we need to know to determine whether the partnership, and thereby the policy, is successful?

Revisiting the Strategic Partnership Model

This chapter provides tools for partners, organizations, and policymakers as they make decisions about whether to partner. The distinctions between traditional partnerships and strategic partnerships showcase the benefits of careful consideration of partnering based on aligned interests rather than mere opportunity. As resources grow increasingly scarce, it is tempting to view all partnership opportunities as positive. Taking the time to analyze underlying values and mission foci and how partnering allows for levering strategic objectives pays in the end.

The goal of this book is to provide a toolkit for picking partners, nurturing partnerships, and evaluating those partnerships over time. As we have shown throughout this volume, multiple levels of operation are at play in putting together partnerships; the process is dynamic. The concepts presented (motivations, relationships, framing and communication, organizational resources, leadership, and partnership capital) are present in various forms during different phases of partnership development. As a result, relationships look one way when seeking partners, but these relationships appear differently during the actual partnership or when partnership capital is evident. Recognizing the amorphous nature of the component parts during the various phases of the partnership is critical, as is knowing that each of these components is operationalized differently, depending on the level at which one works. A college president will see the relationships differently from a community director or faculty member. All of these views are important to recognize and understand to appreciate what is taking place in the partnership. The stakes are high in education at this point, and partnering can provide just the leverage needed to achieve success.

Summary Points

- Successful strategic partnerships involve multiple levels and motivations simultaneously.
- Champions use a variety of sources of social capital to help create strategic partnerships.
- Motivations for partnering may vary, but a central component of strategic partnerships is value alignment.

- Time changes partnerships—and evaluation must occur to determine whether the partnership is achieving its intended goals.
- The creation of partnership capital provides a foundation for sustainable partnering that outlives the roles of any one or two individual champions.
- Framing of strategic partnerships is continuous; the creation of shared meaning emerges through successful framing efforts.
- Different questions must be addressed depending on the level of involvement in the partnership process.

CASE #8: HINDSIGHT IS A BEAUTIFUL THING

It is often helpful to investigate failed partnerships to figure out what went wrong as a means to anticipate problems in advance and help forestall a similar fate for a burgeoning collaboration. At Hinterland High School (HHS), a collaboration evolved during the building of the new high school. Here, the school superintendent, a mid-level community college administrator, and a high-level university administrator were the central actors involved in moving the partnership forward.

The opportunity to create a new space provided a way to rethink how the space could be used, how to create links among the public school environment and higher education, and how to involve community members. The high school was planned to provide access to community college and university courses; the plan involved creating building wings that afforded the opportunity to offer segmented or specialized opportunities in different locations. For instance, one wing of the building was dedicated to a ninth-grade academy that supported student transition to high school. Another wing accommodated students in their junior and senior years taking college-level courses taught by community college and university faculty using a flex-scheduling option. The belief was that the presence of college faculty would demonstrate to high school students that college was possible and would reinforce high standards throughout the building in ways that were not possible when advanced students took college courses off-site.

Inherent in this partnership were unequal power bases among the central partners. The superintendent had more formal authority as he controlled resources and key decision-making regarding the building's construction. Both of the college administrators had high levels of social capital, which allowed them to move the partnership forward in their institutions and benefitted the group in ways that other individuals with less social capital could not. Yet, upper-level college leaders at the partner institutions with more formal authority than the college administrators involved on the ground with the partnership could trump decisions or withdraw commitment from the project. Trust was a central characteristic of this collaboration because each key player needed to trust that the others would follow through on agreements made, since none held all of the leverage and resources necessary to accomplish the goals independently, and each knew the partnership could be overridden by outside forces beyond their control. In addition, the case highlights how alignment with institutional strategic goals is critical. For the college partners, as long as the collaboration continued to meet the goals of student access and entrepreneurial approaches to course delivery, the program was on solid ground. If resources shifted, top-level leaders transitioned, or new goals were established that did not align with the partnership objectives, however, the collaboration could be in jeopardy.

The best-laid plans often go awry. The charismatic superintendent of HHS, Tom Butler, encountered push back from Peggy Smith, the president of the school board, as the building was opening. Smith questioned having the community college and social services in the school, thinking that this took away from the central mission of K–12 education. The sentiment in the community was that Smith was using her board position to catapult into state politics, and that her stance showed where she would stand on educational issues.

The college administrators involved believed in the services being offered to high school students but had different levels of motivation for their involvement. For the community college administrator, the partnership helped fulfill the mission of the two-year college by doing outreach into high schools to give high-ability students access to more advanced work. On the surface, his motivations were to help students. The four-year college administrator, on the other hand, was faced with financial pressures to increase the service area and catchment for off-site delivery of courses and to build the online presence of the college. The high school provided a convenient location to do this.

The swirl of motivations guiding the creation of the new learning space provided both an opportunity for change and a platform for conflict. After two years of meetings, negotiations, and public forums, the new high school opened. Yet, the initial plans did not produce the new changes initially imagined. The superintendent left in a cloud of board disapproval, few courses were offered, and the school board president continued to seek limits on external partnering.

Case Questions

- What actions might have prevented the problems faced in this case?
    o What could the individuals have done differently?
    o How might use of organizational learning have circumvented this ending?
    o What would have been different if this partnership had been built on strategy?

- Challenges abound over time for partnerships. What type of advance planning helps avert problems down the road?

Chapter Summary Points

Prologue: The Increasing Role of Partnerships in Education

- Pressures to partner are increasing, due to both policy mandates and economics.
- Grant funders, foundations, and donors are calling for more collaborations to increase efficiencies and scale up innovations.
- Motivations to partner differ among participants; however, most successful partnerships are built on a shared value system and alignment of goals.
- Top-level leaders are important champions for partnering.
- Partners most often operate from different organizational frameworks, which complicate collaborations.
- Framing the reasons to partner and the rationale for dedication for resources toward the partnership is critical for campus and community buy-in. How leaders help frame change matters to ultimate success.

Chapter 1: Creating a Strategic Partnership

- Partnerships are becoming increasingly critical to campus operations.
- Traditional and strategic partnerships differ in terms of the initial motivations and intentions.
- Traditional partnerships based on individuals historically have had limited shelf lives and long-term sustainability.
- Strategic partnerships differ from traditional partnerships in the rationale for startup. Strategic partnerships require goals aligned with institutional mission and vision. Intentionality and alignment are cornerstone features of strategic partnerships, which provide greater leverage for change.
- Change occurs in both forms of partnerships, but the type of change differs. Traditional partnerships create first-order (surface) change, whereas strategic partnerships create second-order (deep) change.

Chapter 2: Partnership Motivations and Roles

- The initial source of motivation or rationale to partner influences ultimate outcomes.
- Partnerships based on shared beliefs and values have a greater chance of long-term success.
- Traditional partnerships may shift to strategic partnerships when leaders recognize the alignment of institutional goals with potential emerging from the partnering relationship.
- The roles of the partners in both their home institution and within the partnership affect what type of power individuals use in the newly formed partnership and what type of power or influence they have in their home institution.
- Complex cognitive teams provide more flexibility and tap into a wider range of expertise and experience.
- Organizational culture influences alignment for partners—challenges may emerge when partners lack shared understandings of ideas, processes, or structures.

Chapter 3: Relationships and Partners

- Relationships provide a critical building block in the formation of partnerships.
- An individual's level of social capital influences who is asked to partner, the level of resources available, centrality to decision making, and the type of knowledge accessible to partners.
- Traditional partnerships are coupled more loosely to an organization's core mission and planning efforts.
- Relationships change over the course of the partnerships, either expanding the social capital of those involved or spending this capital.
- Relationships influence the decision-making process within partnerships and within the home institution.
- Institutional operations and policy influence relationships within organizations and among partners.

Chapter 4: Communication and Framing

- How leaders communicate and frame change influence how change is interpreted by campus members.

- Sensemaking must occur for leaders before they can help frame meaning for others.
- Leaders frame traditional partnerships and strategic partnerships differently.
- How partnerships are understood on campus affects sustainability of the partnership.
- Links exist between approaches to leadership and approaches to framing.
- Communication in traditional partnerships has a more technical orientation, with the focus on processes, tactics, and existing terminology.
- Framing in strategic partnerships involves the creation of shared terms and language and takes on a multidisciplinary orientation.
- The types of boundaries that exist among organizations either create barriers to partnering or foster collaboration.

Chapter 5: Organizing Partnerships: The Role of Structure and Resources

- Institutions entering partnerships often have different underlying organizational frameworks.
- The type of paradigm and frameworks in place dictates how partnerships are formed and what elements receive priority.
- The level of organizational capital, in its wide variety of forms, can create power imbalances among partners.
- All partners bring different forms of resources and power to the collaboration.
- How power differentials are negotiated sets the stage for long-term sustainability or partnership failure.
- Individuals and organizations enter partnerships with different mental models, and these orientations may be based on role, network within the institution, and underlying philosophical orientation.

Chapter 6: Leadership and Partnering

- Leadership emerges in a variety of forms in partnerships.
- Both Leaders and leaders play critical roles in various stages of partnerships.

- Champions draw on their social network and position to support partnering.
- Collaborative leadership emerges by form and necessity in partnerships.
- Adaptive change is an outcome of partnering, and how leaders manage and create the context for this change matters.
- The metaphor of a kaleidoscope helps illustrate the dynamic interchange of leadership, levels, and phases within partnerships.
- Adaptive change acknowledges and takes into consideration changing contexts, using feedback loops to support organizational learning.
- Leading second-order change requires creating meaning for stakeholders and engaging in organizational learning.

Chapter 7: Partnership Capital: Sustaining Strategic Collaborations

- Foundational elements for the creation of partnership capital include:
  - trust
  - shared meaning
  - strategic alignment
- Adaptive space serves as a context that supports the creation of partnership capital.
- Organizational slack provides additional opportunities for partnership capital to emerge.
- Barriers to the creation of partnership capital include:
  - a focus on individual organizational goals rather than partnership objectives
  - reliance on a single champion
  - lack of shared ethos or philosophy regarding the partnership
  - unintended consequences on curriculum development and faculty rewards
- Higher levels of organizational learning (double-loop and triple-loop) support the creation of partnership capital.
- Cross-sector collaboration is becoming more of a norm as policymakers seek ways to leverage limited resources.

Chapter 8: Strategies for Creating Lasting Partnerships

- Successful strategic partnerships involve multiple levels and motivations simultaneously.
- Champions use a variety of sources of social capital to help create strategic partnerships.
- Motivations for partnering may vary, but a central component of strategic partnerships is value alignment.
- Time changes partnerships— and evaluation must occur to determine whether the partnership is achieving its intended goals
- The creation of partnership capital provides a foundation for sustainable partnering that outlives the roles of any one or two individual champions.
- Framing of strategic partnerships is continuous; the creation of shared meaning emerges through successful framing efforts.
- Different questions must be addressed depending on the level of involvement in the partnership process.

APPENDIX B

Considerations in Developing Strategic Partnerships Using the Partnership Model

- Stage 1: Determining Motivations

  - What are our strategic goals?
  - What do we need in a partner to help us achieve our strategic goals?
  - Can we achieve these goals with one partner or are multiple partners beneficial?
  - What does an environmental scan show regarding potential partners?
  - What are the motivations of these potential partners?

- Stage 2: Picking Partners

  - Once our environmental scan identifies potential partners, what is our decision-making rubric for final selection?
  - What type of organizational structure exists with these potential options?
  - What type of resources, both human and capital, will the potential partner bring to the enterprise?
  - Can this partner create or open up new networks and relationships for us?
  - Do we share a value system and ethos of operation that align?

- Stage 3: Forming the Partnership

  - Who is critical to have on the guiding team that starts the partnership?
  - What type of structure will best support this new partnership? How does this align with the existing cultures of the partners?
  - Who will develop the operating procedures and provide guidance on the ground?
  - What types of resources are required upfront? On a regular basis?
  - Who will champion the partnership during this formation stage?

- Stage 4: Nurturing Relationships and Telling the Story

  - What best supports the creation of shared meaning?
  - How do we create trust among the partners?

- o How do we tell the story among the partners? Within our organization?
- o What nurtures and motivates those working at various levels of operation within the partnership?
- o How do we focus on talking about the partnership in a way that does not detract from other institutional initiatives?
- o How do we make sense of the role of the partnership with these other goals?
- o What do we do when the pull for institutional needs runs counter to partnership needs?

- Stage 5: Fostering Partnership Capital

  - o How do we sustain trust in the partnership?
  - o What processes are in place to evaluate the partnership to determine whether the shared meaning created initially still fits our needs and our partners?
  - o What metrics of success show that the partnership is beneficial for us? For our partners?
  - o How has the partnership been institutionalized?
  - o When is it best for the partnership to spin off from the initial partners?

REFERENCES

Abramo, G., D'Angelo, C. A., & Di Costa, F. (2011). University-industry research collaboration: A model to assess university capability. *Higher Education, 62*, 163–181. doi: 10.1007/s10734-010-9372-0

Altbach, P., & Knight, J. (2007). The internationalization of higher education: Motivations and realities. *Journal of Studies in International Education, 11*(3–4), 290–305. doi: 10.1177/1028315307303542

Ameli, P., & Kayes, D. C. (2011). Triple-loop learning in a cross-sector partnership: The DC Central Kitchen partnership. *The Learning Organization, 18*(3), 175–188. doi: 10.1108/09696471111123243

American Council on Education. (2012). *The American college president: 2012.* Washington, DC: Author.

Amey, M. J. (2005). Leadership as learning: Conceptualizing the process. *Community College Journal of Research and Practice, 29*(9–10), 689–704.

Amey, M. J. (2010). Administrative perspectives on international partnerships. In P. L. Eddy (Ed.), *International collaborations: Institutional frameworks and faculty roles. New Directions for Higher Education*, no. 150 (pp. 59–69) San Francisco: Jossey-Bass.

Amey, M. J. (2012). Leadership. In J. S. Levin & S. T. Kater (Eds.), *Understanding community colleges* (pp. 135–151). New York: Routledge.

Amey, M. J., & Brown, D. F. (2004). *Breaking out of the box: Interdisciplinary collaboration and faculty work.* New York: Greenwood Press/Information Age Publishing.

Amey, M. J., Eddy, P. L., & Ozaki, C. K. (2007). Demands for partnerships and collaboration in higher education: A model. In M. J. Amey (Ed.), *Collaborations across educational borders. New Directions in Community Colleges, no.139* (pp. 5–14). San Francisco: Jossey-Bass.

Amey, M. J., Eddy, P. L., & Campbell, T. (2010). Crossing boundaries: Creating partnerships to promote educational transitions. *Community College Review, 37*(4), 333–347.

Andrews, R., & Entwistle, T. (2010). Does cross-sectoral partnership deliver? An empirical exploration of public service effectiveness, efficiency, and equity. *Journal of Public Administration Research and Theory, 22*(4), 679–701.

Argyris, C., Putnam, R., & McLain Smith, D. (1985) *Action science: Concepts, methods, and skills for research and intervention.* San Francisco: Jossey-Bass.

Argyris, C., & Schön, D. (1974). *Theory in practice: Increasing professional effectiveness.* San Francisco: Jossey-Bass.

Argyris, C., & Schön, D. (1978). *Organizational learning: A theory of action perspective.* Reading, MA: Addison Wesley.

Argyris, C., & Schön, D. (1992). *Organizational learning: A theory of action perspective*. Reading, MA: Addison Wesley.

Argyris, C., & Schön, D. (1996) *Organizational learning II: Theory, method and practice*, Reading, MA: Addison Wesley.

Astin, A. W., & Astin, H. S. (2000). *Leadership reconsidered: Engaging higher education in social change*. Battle Creek, MI: W. K. Kellogg Foundation.

Baber, L. D., Castro, E. L., & Bragg, D. D. (2010). *Measuring success: David Conley's college readiness framework and the Illinois College and Career Readiness Act*. Champaign, IL: Office of Community College Research and Leadership, University of Illinois at Urbana-Champaign.

Baldridge, J. V. (1971). *Power and conflict in the university*. New York: John Wiley.

Baldridge, J. V., Curtis, D. V., Ecker, G. P., & Riley, G. L. (1977). Alternative models of governance in higher education. In G. L. Riley & J. V. Baldridge (Eds.), *Governing academic organizations* (pp. 11–27). Berkeley, CA: McCuthan,

Barnes, T. (2011a). Intentionality in international engagement: Identifying potential strategic international partnerships. In S. Buck Sutton & D. Obst (Eds.), *Developing strategic international partnerships: Models for initiating and sustaining innovative institutional linkages* (pp. 1–6). New York: Institute for International Education.

Barnes, T. (2011b). Beyond handshakes and signing ceremonies: Leveraging institutional agreements to foster broad and deep international partnerships. In S. Buck Sutton & D. Obst (Eds.), *Developing strategic international partnerships: Models for initiating and sustaining innovative institutional linkages* (pp. 177–181). New York: Institute for International Education.

Barnett, B. G., Hall, G. E., Berg, J. H., & Camarena, M. M. (1999). A typology of partnerships for promoting innovation. *Journal of School Leadership, 9*(6), 484–510.

Bartunek, J. M., & Moch, M. K. (1987). First-order, second-order, and third-order change and organization development interventions: A cognitive approach. *Journal of Applied Behavioral Science, 23*(4), 483–500. doi: 10.1177/002188638702300404

Bastalich, W. (2010). Knowledge economy and research innovation. *Studies in Higher Education, 35*(7), 845–857.

Bauman, Z. (2001). *The individualized society*. Cambridge, UK: Polity.

Baus, F., & Ramsbottom, C. A. (1999). Starting and sustaining a consortium. In L. G. Dotolo & J. T. Strandness (Eds.), *Best practices in higher education consortia: How institutions can work together. New Directions for Higher Education*, no. 106 (pp. 3–18) San Francisco: Jossey-Bass.

Belenky, M. F., Clinchy, B. M., Goldberger, N. R., & Tarule, J. M. (1997). *Women's ways of knowing: The development of self, voice, and mind* (10th ann ed.). New York: Basic Books.

Bennett, J. V., & Thompson, H. C. (2011). Changing district priorities for school-business collaboration: Superintendent agency and capacity for institutionalization. *Educational Administration Quarterly, 47*(5), 826–868.

Bensimon, E. M. (1989). The meaning of "good presidential leadership": A frame analysis. *Review of Higher Education, 12*(2), 107–123.

Bensimon, E. M., & Neumann, A. (1993). *Redesigning collegiate leadership: Teams and teamwork in higher education.* Baltimore, MD: Johns Hopkins University Press.

Berger, P. L., & Luckmann, T. (1966). *The social construction of reality: A treatise in the sociology of knowledge.* New York: Doubleday.

Bergquist, W. H., & Pawlak, K. (2008). *Engaging the six cultures of the academy.* San Francisco: Jossey-Bass.

Berman, J. (2008). Connecting with industry: Bridging the divide. *Journal of Higher Education Policy and Management, 30*(2), 165–174. doi: 10.1080/13600800801938762

Bernstein, B. (2000). *Pedagogy, symbolic control, and identity: Theory, research, critique.* New York: Rowman & Littlefield.

Bess, J. L., & Dee, J. R. (2008a). *Understanding college and university organization: Theories for effective policy and practice. Vol. I—Theories for effective policy and practice.* Sterling, VA: Stylus.

Bess, J. L., & Dee, J. R. (2008b). *Understanding college and university organization: Theories for effective policy and practice. Vol. II—Dynamics of the system.* Sterling, VA: Stylus.

Birnbaum, R. (1988). *How colleges work: The cybernetics academic organization and leadership.* San Francisco: Jossey-Bass.

Birnbaum, R. (1992). *How academic leadership works: Understanding success and failure in the college presidency.* San Francisco: Jossey-Bass.

Birnbaum, R. (2000). The life cycle of academic management fads. *Journal of Higher Education, 71*(1), 1–16.

Black, J. S., & Gregersen, H. B. (2003). *Leading strategic change: Breaking through the brain barriers.* Upper Saddle River, NJ: Pearson Education.

Black, J. S., & Gregersen, H. B. (2008). *It starts with one: Changing individuals changes organizations.* Upper Saddle, NJ: Prentice Hall.

Bliss, T., & Lisi, P. (1990). *The effect of state initiatives on school/university partnerships in Connecticut.* 2011 Connecticut Code, Title 10a State System of Higher Education, Chapter 185 Board of Governors; Department of Higher Education, Sec. 10a–17a. Institute for Effective Teachers.

Bolman, L. G., & Deal, T. E. (2008). *Reframing organizations: Artistry, choice, and leadership* (4th ed.). San Francisco: Jossey-Bass.

Bourdieu, P. (1986). The forms of capital. In J. G. Richardson (Ed.), *Handbook of theory and research for the sociology of education* (pp. 241–258). New York: Greenwood Press.

Bourgeois, L. J., III. (1982). On the measurement of organizational slack. *The Academy of Management Review, 6*(1), 29–39.

Brass, D. J. (1995). A social network perspective on human resources management. In G. R. Ferris (Ed.), *Research in personnel and human resources management* (pp. 39–79). Greenwich, CT: JAI Press.

Brinkerhoff, J. M. (2005). Partnership as a means to good governance: Towards an evaluation framework. In P. Glasbergen, F. Biermann, & A. P. J. Mol (Eds.), *Part-*

nerships, governance, and sustainable development: Reflections on theory and practice (pp. 68–92). New York: Edward Elgar Publications, Inc.

Browne-Ferrigno, T. (2011). Mandated university-district partnerships for principal preparation: Professors' perspectives on required program redesign. *Journal of School Leadership, 21*(5), 735–756.

Bruffee, K. A. (1999). *Collaborative learning: Higher education, interdependence, and the authority of knowledge.* Baltimore, MD: John Hopkins University Press.

Burns, J. M. (1978). *Leadership.* New York: Harper and Row.

Burrell, G., & Morgan, G. (1979). *Sociological paradigms and organizational analysis.* London, UK: Heinemann.

Burriss, A. H. (2010). *One mission-centered, market-smart globalization response: A case study of the Georgia Tech-Emory university biomedical engineering curricular joint venture.* University of Pennsylvania. *ProQuest Dissertations and Theses.* Retrieved from http://search.proquest.com/docview/839308973?accountid=15053

Carrington, P., Scott, J., & Wasserman, S. (2005). *Models and methods in social network analysis.* New York: Cambridge University Press.

Casion, J. G., & Gewolb, J. E. (2013). In online partnerships, compliance is key. *Chronicle of Higher Education.* Retrieved from http://chronicle.com/article /In-Online-Partnerships-Legal/139837/?cid=at&utm_source=at&utm_medium=en

Center for Higher Education Policy Analysis (CHEPA). (2005). *The opportunities and challenges of partnering with schools.* Los Angeles: CHEPA, University of Southern California, Rossier School of Education.

Chaffee, E. (1983). *Rational decision making in higher education: An NCHEMS executive overview.* Boulder, CO: National Center for Higher Education Management Systems.

Chaffee, E. E. (1985). Three models of strategy. *The Academy of Management Review, 10*(1), 89–98.

Clark, S. C. (2000). Work/Family Border Theory: A new theory of work/family balance. *Human Relations, 53*(6), 747–770. doi:10.1177/0018726700536001

Chesson, J. P., Jr., & Rubin, S. (2003). *Toward rural prosperity: A state framework in support of rural community colleges.* Chapel Hill, NC: MDC, Inc.

Clifford, M., & Millar, S. B. (2008). *K–20 partnerships: Literature review and recommendations for research.* Madison: Wisconsin Center for Education Research, School of Education, University of Wisconsin-Madison.

Cochran-Smith, M. (2005). Presidential address: The new teacher education: For better or for worse? *Educational Researcher, 34*(7), 3–17.

Cohen, M. D., & March, J. G. (1986). *Leadership and ambiguity: The American college president.* Cambridge, MA: Harvard Business Press.

Cohen, M. D., March, J. G., & Olsen, J. P. (1972). A garbage can model of organizational choice. *Administrative Science Quarterly, 17*(1), 1–25.

Coleman, J. S. (1988). Social capital in the creation of human capital. *The American Journal of Sociology, 94*: S95.

Coleman, J. S. (1990). *Foundations of social theory.* Cambridge, MA: Harvard University Press.

Comrie, A. (2011). Future models of higher education in Scotland: Can collaborative, technology-enhanced learning offer solutions? *Campus-Wide Information Systems, 28*(4), 250–257.

Connolly, M., Jones, C., & Jones, N. (2007). Managing collaboration across further and higher education: A case in practice. *Journal of Further and Higher Education, 31*(2), 159–169.

Cooper, J. & Mitsunaga, R. (2010). Faculty perspectives on international education: The nested realities of faculty collaborations. In P. L. Eddy (Ed.), *International collaborations: Institutional frameworks and faculty roles. New Directions for Higher Education*, no. 150 (pp. 69–81). San Francisco: Jossey-Bass.

Correia, T. (2010). *Sustaining partnerships between community colleges and the extended healthcare industry in Massachusetts.* Unpublished dissertation. Johnson & Wales University, Providence, RI.

Creamer, E. G. (2004). Assessing the outcomes of long-term research collaboration. *Canadian Journal of Higher Education, 34*, 24–41.

Daft, R. L. (1995). *Organization theory and design* (5th ed.). Minneapolis, MN: West Publishing.

Daniel, D. E. (2002). Partnerships are essential to fundraising. *Community College Journal, 72*(4), 15.

Daniels, H. (2011). The shaping of communication across boundaries. *International Journal of Educational Research, 50*(1), 40–47. doi:10.1016/j.ijer.2011.04.008

Denis, J., Lamothe, L., & Langley, A. (2001). The dynamics of collective leadership and strategic change in pluralistic organizations. *Academy of Management Journal, 44*, 809–837.

Department of Education and Skills, Ireland. (2011). *National strategy for higher education to 2030– Report of the strategy group.* Retrieved from http://www.hea.ie/files/files/DES_Higher_Ed_Main_Report.pdf

DePree, M. (2004). *Leadership is an art.* New York: Doubleday.

Dhillon, J. K. (2009). The role of social capital in sustaining partnership. *British Educational Research Journal, 35*(5), 687–704.

DiMaggio, P. J., & Powell, W. W. (1983). The iron cage revisited: Institutional isomorphism and collective rationality in organizational fields. *American Sociological Review, 48*(2), 147–160.

Dionne, E. J., West, D. M., & Whitehurst, G. J. (2009). *Invisible: 1.4 percent coverage for education is not enough.* Washington, DC: Brookings Institution. Retrieved from http://www.brookings.edu/~/media/research/files/reports/2009/12/02%20education%20news%20west/1202_education_news_west

Doz, Y. L. (1996). The evolution of cooperation in strategic alliances: Initial conditions or learning processes? *Strategic Management Journal, 17*(Special Issue), 55–83.

Duffy, F. M. (2008). Strategic communication during times of great change. *School Administrator, 65*(4), 22–25.

Eckel, P. D., & Hartley, M. (2008). Developing academic strategic alliances: Reconciling multiple institutional cultures, policies, and practices. *The Journal of Higher Education, 79*(6), 613–637.

Eddy, P. L. (2003). Sensemaking on campus: How community college presidents frame change. *Community College Journal of Research and Practice, 27*(6), 453–471.

Eddy, P. L. (2007). Alliances among community colleges: Odd bedfellows or lasting partners? In M. J. Amey (Ed.), *Collaborations across educational sectors. New Directions for Community Colleges,* no. 139 (pp. 59–68). San Francisco: Jossey-Bass.

Eddy, P. L. (2010a). *Partnerships and collaborations in higher education.* ASHE Higher Education Report, 36(2). San Francisco: Jossey-Bass.

Eddy, P. L. (2010b). Institutional collaborations in Ireland: Leveraging an increased international presence. In P. L. Eddy (Ed.), *International collaborations: Institutional frameworks and faculty roles. New Directions for Higher Education,* no. 150 (pp. 19–29). San Francisco: Jossey-Bass.

Eddy, P. L. (2010c). *Community college leadership: A multidimensional model for leading change.* Sterling, VA: Stylus.

Eddy, P. L., & Garza Mitchell, R. (2012). Faculty as learners: Developing thinking communities. *Innovative Higher Education, 37*(4), 283–296.

Eisenhardt, K. M., & Zbaracki, M. J. (1992). Strategic decision making. *Strategic Management Journal, 13*(S2), 17–37.

Fairhurst, G. T. (2001). Dualisms in leadership research. In F. M. Jablin & L. L. Putnam (Eds.), *The new handbook of organizational communication: Advances in theory, research, and methods* (pp. 349–439). Thousand Oaks, CA: Sage.

Fairhurst, G. T. (2011). *The power of framing: Creating the language of leadership.* San Francisco: Jossey-Bass.

Fairhurst, G. T., & Sarr, R. A. (1996). *The art of framing: Managing the language of leadership.* San Francisco: Jossey-Bass.

Farrell, P. L., & Seifert, K. A. (2007). Lessons learned from a dual-enrollment partnership. In M. J. Amey (Ed.), *Collaborations across educational sectors. New Directions for Community Colleges,* no. 139 (pp. 69–77) San Francisco: Jossey-Bass.

Fear, F., Creamer, N., Pirog, R., Block, D., & Redmond, L. (2004). Higher-education-community partnerships: The politics of engagement. *Journal of Higher Education Outreach and Engagement, 9*(2), 139–156.

Ferman, B., & Hill, T. L. (2004). The challenges of agenda conflict in higher-education-community research partnerships: Views from the community side. *Journal of Urban Affairs, 26*(2), 241–257.

Fielder, F. E. (1967). *A theory of leadership effectiveness.* New York: McGraw-Hill.

Flora, B. H., & Hirt, J. B. (2010). Educational consortia in a knowledge economy: Collaboration, competition, and organizational equilibrium. *Review of Higher Education, 33*(4), 569–592.

Flores, B. B., & Claeys, L. (2011). Academy for teacher excellence: Maximizing synergy among partners for promoting college access for Latino teacher candidates. *Urban Review, 43*(3), 321–338.

Fluharty, C. W. (2007). *Written statement for the record before the United States House of Representatives, Committee on Agriculture, Subcommittee on Specialty Crops,*

Rural Development, and Foreign Agriculture. Washington, DC. Retrieved April 15, 2008, from http://rupri.org/Forms/testimony032107.pdf

Forcier, M. F. (2011). Innovation through collaboration: New pathways to success. *Trusteeship, 19*(5), 8–12.

Foucault, M. (1982). The subject and power. In H. Dreyfus & P. Rabinow (Eds.). *Michel Foucault: Beyond structuralism and hermeneutics* (pp. 208–226). Chicago: University of Chicago Press.

Foucault, M. (1986). *Care of the self: Volume III of the history of sexuality* (translated by Robert Hurley). New York: Random House.

Foucault, M. (2001). *Michel Foucault: Fearless speech.* Los Angeles, CA: Semiotext.

Fowler, F. (2012). *Policy studies for educational leaders: An introduction* (4th ed.). Boston: Allyn & Bacon.

Friedman, T. H. (2005). *The world is flat.* New York: Farrar, Straus, and Giroux.

Fullan, M. (2005). *Leadership and sustainability: System thinkers in action.* Thousand Oaks, CA: Corwin Press.

Fullan, M. (2006). *Change theory: A force for school improvement.* Victoria, Canada: Centre for Strategic Education. Retrieved from http://www.michaelfullan.com/media/13396072630.pdf

Galbraith, J. R. (2002). *Designing organizations: An executive guide to strategy, structure, and process.* San Francisco: Jossey-Bass.

Gardner, D. C. (2011). Characteristic collaborative processes in school-university partnerships. *Planning and Changing, 42*(1–2), 63–86.

Gazley, B., & Brudney, J. L. (2007). The purpose (and perils) of government-nonprofit partnership. *Nonprofit and Voluntary Sector Quarterly, 36*(3), 389–415. doi: 10.1177/0899764006295997

Ghosh, S. (2011). Participation in the green power partnership: An analysis of higher education institutions as partners in the program. *International Journal of Sustainability in Higher Education, 12*(4), 306–321.

Giddens, A. (1984). *The constitution of society.* Berkeley: University of California Press.

Gino, F., & Margolis, J. D. (2011). Bringing ethics into focus: How regulatory focus and risk preferences influence (un)ethical behavior. *Organizational Behavior and Human Decision Processes, 115*, 145–156.

Gladwell, M. (2005). *Blink: The power of thinking without thinking.* Boston: Little, Brown.

Goffman, E. (1974). *Frame analysis: An essay on the organization of experience.* Cambridge, MA: Harvard University Press.

Gomez, M. N., & de los Santos, A. G., Jr. (1993). *Building bridges: Using state policy to foster and sustain collaboration.* Denver, CO: Education Commission of the States.

Googins, B. K., & Rochlin, S. A. (2000). Creating a partnership society: Understanding the rhetoric and reality of cross-sectoral partnerships. *Business and Society Review, 105*(1), 127–144. doi: 10.1111/0045-3609.00068

Gourville, J. T. (2004, April). *Why consumers don't buy: The psychology of new product adoption.* Harvard Business School Background Note 504-056. (Revised from original November 2003 version). Retrieved from http://hbr.org/product/why-consumers-don-t-buy-the-psychology-of-new-product-adoption/an/504056-PDF-ENG

Granovetter, M. (1983). The strength of weak ties: A network theory revisited. *Sociology Theory, 1,* 201–233,

Gray. B. (1989). *Collaborating: Finding common ground for multiparty problems.* San Francisco: Jossey-Bass.

Greenwood, R., & Hinings, C. R. (1996). Understanding radical organizational change: Bringing together the old and the new institutionalism. *Academy of Management Review, 21,* 1022–1054.

Gregersen, J., Sowa, M., & Flynn, H. K. (2011). Evaluating form and function of regional partnerships: Applying social network analysis to the "Network for A Healthy California." *Journal of Nutrition Education and Behavior, 43*(4), S67–S74.

Grobe, T. (1990). *Synthesis of existing knowledge and practice in the field of educational partnerships.* Washington, DC: Office of Educational Research and Improvement.

Gross, T. L. (1988). *Partners in education: How colleges can work with schools to improve teaching and learning.* San Francisco: Jossey-Bass.

Gross, N. C., Mason, W. S., & McEachern, A. W. (1958). *Explorations in role analysis.* New York: John Wiley & Sons.

Hammond, J. S., Keeney, R. L. L., & Raiffa, H. (2001). Even swaps: A rational method for making trade-offs. In *Harvard Business Review on Decision Making* (pp. 21–44). Cambridge, MA: Harvard Business School Publishing Company.

Harris, S. G. (1994). Organizational culture and individual sensemaking: A schema-based perspective. *Organization Science, 5*(3), 309–321.

Harris, S. (2005). Professionals, partnerships and learning in changing times. *International Studies in Sociology of Education, 15*(1), 71–86.

Hatch, M. J., & Cunliffe, A. L. (2006). *Organizational theory: Modern, symbolic, and post-modern perspectives.* New York: Oxford University Press.

Hebel, S. (2007). Partnership expands the college track. *Education Digest, 73*(2), 34–38.

Hebel, S., Stripling, J., & Wilson, R. (2012, June). University of Virginia board votes to reinstate Sullivan. *Chronicle of Higher Education.* Retrieved from http://chronicle.com/article/U-of-Virginia-Board-Votes-to/132603/

Heifetz, R. A. (1994). *Leadership without easy answers.* Cambridge, MA: Harvard University Press.

Heifetz, R. A., & Linsky, M. (2002). *Leadership on the line: Staying alive through the dangers of leading.* Boston: Harvard Business School Press.

Helms Mills, J., & Mills, A. J. (2000). Rules, sensemaking, formative contexts, and discourse in the gendering of organizational culture. In N. Ashkanasy, C. Wilderom, & M. Peterson (Eds.), *Handbook of organizational culture and climate* (pp. 55–70). Thousand Oaks, CA: Sage.

Hickman, G. R. (2010). *Leading change in multiple contexts: Concepts and practices in organizational, community, political, social, and global change settings.* Thousand Oaks, CA: Sage.

Higgerson, M. L., & Joyce, T. A. (2007). *Effective leadership communication: A guide for department chairs and deans for managing difficult situations and people.* Bolton, MA: Anker.

Higher Education Authority. (2011). *National strategy for higher education to 2030.* Dublin, Ireland: Author. Retrieved from http://www.hea.ie/files/files/DES_ Higher_Ed_Main_Report.pdf

Higher Education Authority. (2012). *Towards a future higher education landscape.* Dublin, Ireland: Author. Retrieved from http://www.hea.ie/en/policy/national-strategy/implementation

Holland, D. (2010). Notes from the field: Lessons learned in building a framework for an international collaboration. In P. L. Eddy (Ed.), *International collaborations: Institutional frameworks and faculty roles. New Directions for Higher Education,* no. 150 (pp. 31–41) San Francisco: Jossey-Bass.

Honeycutt, T. (2009). Making connections: Using social network analysis for program evaluation. *Mathematica Policy Research, 1,* 1–4.

Hora, M. T., & Millar, S. B. (2011). *A guide to building education partnerships: Navigating diverse cultural contexts to turn challenge into promise.* Sterling, VA: Stylus.

Hosking, D. M., & Morley, I. E. (1988). The skills of leadership. In J. G. Hunt, B. R. Baglia, H. P. Dachler, & C. A. Schrisheim (Eds.), *Emerging leadership vistas* (pp. 89–106). Lexington, MA: Lexington Books.

Huber, G. P. (1991). Organizational learning: The contributing processes and the literatures. *Organization Science, 2,* 88–115.

Humphreys, D. (2013, Winter). Deploying collaborative leadership to reinvent higher education for the twenty-first century. *Peer Review, 15*(1). Retrieved from http://www.aacu.org/peerreview/pr-wi13/Humphreys.cfm

Ikpeze, C. H., Broikou, K. A., Hildenbrand, S., & Gladstone-Brown, W. (2012). PDS collaboration as third space: An analysis of the quality of learning experiences in a PDS partnership. *Studying Teacher Education, 8*(3), 275–288.

Jablin, F. M., Putnam, L. L., Roberts, K. H., & Porter, L. W. (Eds.). (1987). *Handbook of organizational communication: An interdisciplinary perspective.* Newbury Park, CA: Sage.

Johnson, C. (2007). *The role of social capital in creating sustainable partnerships.* Unpublished dissertation. Mt. Pleasant, MI: Central Michigan University.

John-Steiner, V. (2000). *Creative collaboration.* New York: Oxford University Press.

Jolly, D. V., & Deloney, P. (1996). *Integrating rural school and community development: An initial examination.* Austin, TX: Southwest Educational Development Lab.

Kajner, T., Fletcher, F., & Makokis, P. (2011). Balancing head and heart: The importance of relational accountability in community-university partnerships. *Innovation in Higher Education.* Published online December 2011. doi: 10.1007/ s10755-011-9206-8

Kansas Register. (2012, March 29). Board of Regents Permanent Administrative Regulations. K.A.R. 88-Article 29, vol. 31, no. 13.

Kanter, R. M. (1983). *The change masters: Innovation for productivity in the American corporation.* New York: Simon & Schuster.

Kearney, K. S., & others. (2007). Building an academe and government partnership in workforce education: Challenges and possibilities. *Journal of Industrial Teacher Education, 44*(3), 71–91.

Kelman, H. (1961). Process of opinion change. *Public Opinion Quarterly, 25*(1), 57–78.

Kentucky House Joint Resolution 14 (HJR 14). (2006). *Learning-centered leadership: The preparation and support for the next generation of Kentucky's school and district leaders.* Frankfort, KY: Education Redesign Taskforce. Retrieved from http://www.kyepsb.net/documents/ExecOffice/ELRReport.pdf

Kentucky House Joint Resolution 16 (KAR 3:050). (2008). *Professional certificate for instructional leadership—school principal, all grades.* Frankfort, KY: Education Professional Standards Board. Retrieved from http://www.lrc.state.ky.us/kar/016/003/050.htm

Kezar, A. (2005). What campuses need to know about organizational learning and the learning organization. In A. Kezar (Ed.), *Organizational learning in higher education. New Directions for Higher Education,* no. 131 (pp. 7–22). San Francisco: Jossey-Bass.

Kezar, A. (2013). *How colleges change: Understanding, leading, and enacting change.* New York: Routledge.

Kezar, A., & Eckel, P. (2002). Examining the institutional transformation process: The importance of sensemaking, interrelated strategies, and balance. *Research in Higher Education, 43*(3), 295–328.

Kezar, A., Frank, V., Lester, J. & Yang, H. (2008). *Strategies for IDA practitioners to create partnerships with postsecondary institutions.* Los Angeles: Center for Higher Education Policy Analysis, USC Rossier School of Education.

Kezar, A., & Lester, J. (2009). *Organizing higher education for collaboration: A guide for campus leaders.* San Francisco: Jossey-Bass.

Kezar, A. J., & Lester, J. (2011). *Enhancing campus capacity for leadership: An examination of grassroots leaders in higher education.* Stanford, CA: Stanford University Press.

Khan, S., Castro, E., Bragg, D. D., Barrientos, J. I., & Baber, L. (2009). *The College and Career Readiness Act: Findings from evaluation-year one.* Champaign, IL: Office of Community College Research and Leadership, University of Illinois at Urbana-Champaign.

Kirby, D. (2007). Change and challenge: Ontario's collaborative baccalaureate nursing programs. *The Canadian Journal of Higher Education, 37*(2), 29.

Kirby, D. (2008). Advancing articulation: Models of college-university collaboration in Canadian higher education. *College Quarterly, 11*(4), 1–14.

Kisker, C. B. (2005, November). *Creating and sustaining community college-university transfer partnerships: A qualitative study.* Paper presented at the annual meeting of the Association for the Study of Higher Education, Philadelphia, PA.

Kitagawa, F. (2005). Entrepreneurial universities and the development of regional societies: A spatial view of the Europe of knowledge. *Higher Education Management and Policy, 17*(3), 59–86.

Knowles, M., Holton, E. F., III, & Swanson, R. A. (2011). *The adult learner: The definitive classic in adult education and human resource development* (6th ed.). New York: Taylor & Francis.

Kolowich, S. (2009, September). Another one bites the dust. *Inside Higher Education, 1–2.* Retrieved December 10, 2009, from http://www.insidehighered.com/news/2009/09/03/globalcampus

Koprucu, S. (2009). Raising global citizens: Focus on cultural competency. *School Business Affairs, 75*(4), 30–32.

Kotter, J. P. (2008). *A sense of urgency.* Boston: Harvard Business Press.

Kotter, J. P., & Cohen, D. S. (2002). *The heart of change: Real-life stories of how people change their organizations.* Cambridge, MA: Harvard Business School Press.

Kruss, G. (2006). Working partnerships: The challenge of creating mutual benefit for academics and industry. *Perspectives in Education, 24*(3), 1–3.

Kuhnert, K. W., & Lewis, P. (1989). Transactional and transformational leadership: A constructive/developmental analysis. *Academy of Management Review, 12*(4), 648–657.

Kuk, L., Banning, J. H., & Amey, M. J. (2010). *Positioning student affairs for sustainable change: Achieving organizational effectiveness through multiple perspectives.* Sterling, VA: Stylus.

Laferriere, T., Montane, M., Gros, B., Alvarez, I., Bernaus, M., Breuleux, A., . . . Lamon, M. (2010). Partnerships for knowledge building: An emerging model. *Canadian Journal of Learning and Technology, 36*(1), 1–20.

Lane, J., & Kinser, K. (2011, October). Another one bites the dust. *Chronicle of Higher Education.* Retrieved from http://chronicle.com/blogs/worldwise/another-one-bites-the-dust/28769

Lattauca, L. R., & Creamer, E. G. (2005). Learning as a professional practice. In E. G. Creamer & L. R. Lattuca (Eds.), *Advancing faculty learning through interdisciplinary collaboration. New Directions in Teaching and Learning,* no. 102 (pp. 3–11) San Francisco: Jossey-Bass.

Laver, M. S. (2008). Shared mission: Catholic higher education in partnership with Catholic NGOs. *Journal of Catholic Higher Education, 27*(1), 159–170.

Le Ber, M. J., & Branzei, O. (2010a). (Re)forming strategic cross-sector partnerships: Relational processes of social innovation. *Business Society, 49*(1), 140–172. doi: 10.1177/0007650309345457

Le Ber, M. J., & Branzei, O. (2010b). Towards a critical theory of value creation in cross-sector partnerships. *Organization: The Interdisciplinary Journal of Organization, Theory, and Society, 17*(5), 599–629. doi: 10.1177/1350508410372621

Leonard, J. (2011). Using Bronfenbrenner's ecological theory to understand community partnerships: A historical case study of one urban high school. *Urban Education, 46*(5), 987–1010.

Leslie, D. W., & Fretwell, E. K., Jr. (1996). *Wise moves in hard times: Creating and managing resilient colleges and universities.* San Francisco: Jossey-Bass.

Letizia, A. (2013). Dialectical constellations of progress: New visions of public higher education for the twenty-first century. *Journal of Critical Thought and Praxis, 2*(1), 55–82. Retrieved from http://www.education.iastate.edu/wp-content/uploads/2013/05/06_FINAL_SP13_Letizia.pdf

Levin, J. S. (2001). Public policy, community colleges, and the path to globalization. *Higher Education, 42*(2), 237–262

Lewin, K. (1951). *Field theory in social science: Selected theoretical papers.* New York: Harper.

Lindsey, R. B., Robins, K. N., & Terrell, R. D. (2003). *Cultural proficiency: A manual for school leaders* (2nd ed.). Thousand Oaks, CA: Corwin.

Lipman-Blumen, J. (1996). *Connective leadership: Managing in a changing world.* San Francisco: Jossey-Bass.

Liu, J., Elliott, E., Loggins, J., & Nayve, C. (2006). Toward common unity: From silent to more equitable partnerships. *Metropolitan Universities, 17*(1), 104–115.

Luft, J., & Ingham, H. (1955). The Johari window: A graphic model of interpersonal awareness. *Proceedings of the Western Training Laboratory in Group Development.* Los Angeles: UCLA Extension Office.

Lumina Foundation. (2012). *A stronger nation through higher education: A special report from Lumina Foundation.* Indianapolis, IN: Author. Retrieved from http://www.luminafoundation.org/publications/A_Stronger_Nation-2012.pdf

Luo, Y. (2002). Building trust in cross-cultural collaborations: Toward a contingency perspective. *Journal of Management, 28*(5), 669–694.

Macionis, J. J. (2006). *Society: The basics.* Englewood Cliffs, NJ: Prentice Hall.

Mactaggart, T. (2011). *Leading change: How boards and presidents build exceptional academic institutions.* Washington, DC: AGB Press and Association of Governing Boards of Universities and Colleges.

Maletzke, G. C. (2009). *Reconciling good intentions: The university-USAID partnership.* Michigan State University. *ProQuest Dissertations and Theses.* Retrieved from http://search.proquest.com/docview/304950510?accountid=15053

Martenson, D. M., Newman, D. A., & Zak, D. M. (2011). Building community-university partnerships by listening, learning, and responding. *Journal of Extension, 49*(5), 1–7.

McDonnell, L. M., & Elmore, R. F. (1987). Getting the job done: Alternative policy instruments. *Educational Evaluation and Policy Analysis, 9*(2), 133–152.

Mead, G. H. (1934). *Mind, self, and society: From the standpoint of a social behaviorist.* Chicago: University of Chicago Press.

Mezirow, J. (1990). How critical reflection triggers transformative learning. In J. Mezirow & Associates (Eds.), *Fostering critical reflection in adulthood* (pp. 1–20). San Francisco: Jossey-Bass.

Miller, M. T., & Kissinger, D. B. (2007). Connecting rural community colleges to their communities. In P. L. Eddy & J. Murray (Eds.), *Rural community colleges: Teaching, learning, and leading in the heartland. New Directions for Community Colleges,* no. 137 (pp. 27–35). San Francisco: Jossey-Bass.

Mintzberg, H. (1979). *The structuring of organizations: A synthesis of the research.* Englewood Cliffs, NJ: Prentice Hall.

Mintzberg, H. (1987). The strategy concept II: Another look at why organizations need strategies. *California Management Review, 30*(1), 25–36.

Monahan, E. J. (2004). *Collective autonomy: A history of the Council of Ontario Universities, 1962–2000.* Waterloo, Ontario, Canada: Wilfrid Laurier University Press.

Monge, P. R., & Contractor, N. S. (2001). Emergence of communication networks. In F. M. Jablin & L. L. Putnam (Eds.), *The new handbook of organizational communication: Advances in theory, research, and methods* (pp. 440–502). Thousand Oaks, CA: Sage.

Moore, T. L. (2008). *Placing engagement: Critical readings of interaction between regional communities and comprehensive universities.* Doctoral dissertation. Washington State University, Pullman, WA. Retrieved from ProQuest.

Morgan, G. (2006). *Images of organization.* Thousand Oaks, CA: Sage.

Mundell, L. (2003, April). *Faith partnerships and public schools in Philadelphia: Rewards and perils.* Paper presented at the Annual Meeting of the American Educational Research Association, Chicago, IL.

Nakagawa, M., Bahr, K., & Levy, D. (2012). *Scientific understanding of stakeholders' behavior in mining community.* Unpublished paper. Golden, CO: Colorado School of Mines.

National Commission on Excellence in Education. (1983). *A nation at risk. The imperative for educational reform: A report to the nation and the Secretary of Education, United States Department of Education.* Washington, DC: Author.

Neumann, A. (1995). On the making of hard times and good times. *Journal of Higher Education, 66*(1), 3–31.

Nilson, L. B. (2010). *Teaching at its best: A research-based resource for college instructors.* San Francisco: Jossey-Bass.

Nippert-Eng, C. E. (1996). *Home and work: Negotiating boundaries through everyday life.* Chicago: University of Chicago, IL Press.

No Child Left Behind (NCLB) Act of 2001. (2002). Pub. L. No. 107-110, § 115, Stat. 1425.

Nowell, B. (2010). Out of sync and unaware? Exploring the effects of problem frame alignment and discordance in community collaboratives. *Journal of Public Administration Research and Theory, 20*(1), 91–116.

Oldenburg, R. (1989). *The great good place: Cafes, coffee shops, community centers, beauty parlors, general stores, bars, hangouts, and how they get you through the day.* New York: Paragon House.

Parmigiani, A., & Rivera-Santos, M. (2011). Clearing a path through the forest: A meta-review of interorganizational relationships. *Journal of Management, 37*(4), 1108–1136. doi: 10.1177/0149206311407507

Pasque, P. A., Smerek, R. E., Dwyer, B., Bowman, N., & Mallory, B. L. (Eds.). (2005). *Higher education collaboratives for community engagement and improvement.* Ann Arbor, MI: National Forum on Higher Education for the Public Good.

Pathways to College Network. (2004). *A shared agenda: A leadership challenge to improve college access and success.* Boston: Author.

Peterson, M. (1997). Using contextual planning to transform institutions. In M. Peterson, D. Dill, L. A. Mets, & Associates (Eds.), *Planning and management for a changing environment* (pp. 127–157). San Francisco: Jossey-Bass.

Pfeffer, J. (1977). The ambiguity of leadership. *Academy of Management Review, 12*(1), 104–112.

Pfeffer, J., & Salancik, G. R. (1978). *The external control of organizations: A resource dependence perspective.* New York: Harper and Row.

Piazza, R. (2010). The learning region between pedagogy and economy. *European Journal of Education, 45*(3), 402–418.

Pidduck, A. B., & Carey, T. (2006). Partner power: A study of two distance education consortia. *International Review of Research in Open and Distance Learning, 7*(3), 1–13.

Portes, A. (2000). Social capital: Its origins and applications in modern sociology. In E. Lesser (Ed.), *Knowledge and social capital: Foundations and applications* (pp. 43–68). Woburn, MA: Butterworth-Heinemann.

Putnam, L. L., Phillips, N., & Chapman, P. (1996). Metaphors of communication and organization. In S. R. Clegg, C. Hardy, & W. R. Nord (Eds.), *Handbook of organization studies* (pp. 375–408). Thousand Oaks, CA: Sage.

Quinsigamond Community College (QCC). (2011). *Grant application to the Department of Labor.* Retrieved from http://webapps.dol.gov/DOLGrantData/GrantInformation.aspx?appid=12359

Rabe, B. (2007, Spring). Race to the top: The expanding role of US state renewable portfolio standards. *Sustainable Development Law & Policy, 7*(3), 10–16.

Radwan, A. B. (2011). Managing partnerships of strategic importance. In S. Buck Sutton & D. Obst (Eds.), *Developing strategic international partnerships: Models for initiating and sustaining innovative institutional linkages* (pp. 7–10). New York: Institute for International Education.

Ratnasingam, P. (2005). Trust in inter-organizational exchanges: A case study in business to business electronic commerce. *Decision Support Systems, 39*, 525–544. doi:10.1016/j.dss.2003.12.005

Reicher, S. D., Haslam, S. A., & Hopkins, N. (2005). Social identity and the dynamics of leadership: Leaders and followers as collaborative agents in the transformation of social reality. *Leadership Quarterly, 16*, 547–568.

Rochford, K. A., O'Neill, A., Gelb, A., & Ross, K. J. (2005). *P–16: The last education reform. Book one: Reflections on school restructuring and the establishment of local preschool through college compacts.* Canton, OH: Stark Education Partnership.

Rochford, K. A., O'Neill, A., Gelb, A., & Ross, K. J. (2007). *P–16: The last education reform. Book two: Emerging local, regional, and state efforts.* Canton, OH: Stark Education Partnership.

Romme, A. G. L., & van Witteloostuijn, A. (1999). Circular organizing and triple loop learning. *Journal of Organizational Change Management, 12*(5), 439–454.

Rowley, D., Lujan, H., & Dolence, M. (1997). *Strategic change in colleges and universities: Planning to survive and prosper.* San Francisco: Jossey-Bass.

Sanchez, L. (2010). *Partnering from the heart: Developing an ethic of care through inquiry with urban students and teachers.* Unpublished dissertation. Indiana University, Bloomington, IN.

Sandy, M., & Holland, B. A. (2006). Different worlds and common ground: Community partner perspectives on campus-community partnerships. *Michigan Journal of Community Service Learning, 13*(1), 30–43.

Schein, E. H. (2010). *Organizational culture and leadership* (4th ed.). San Francisco: Jossey-Bass.

Scott, W. R. (2008). *Institutions and organizations: Ideas and interests* (3rd ed.). Thousand Oaks, CA: Sage.

Selsky, J. W., & Parker, B. (2005). Cross-sector partnerships to address social issues: Challenges to theory and practice. *Journal of Management, 31*(6), 849–873. doi: 10.1177/0149206305279601

Selznick, P. (1957). *Leadership in administration.* New York: Harper and Row.

Senge, P. M. (1990). *The fifth discipline: The art and practice of the learning organization.* New York: Doubleday.

Seppänen, R., Blomqvist, K., & Sundqvist, S. (2007). Measuring inter-organizational trust—A critical review of the empirical research in 1990–2003. *Industrial Marketing Management, 36,* 249–265. doi:10.1016/j.indmarman.2005.09.003

Slaughter, S., & Rhoades, G. (2004). *Academic capitalism and the new economy: Markets, state, and higher education.* Baltimore, MD: Johns Hopkins University Press.

Slimbach, R. (2010). *Becoming world wise: A guide to global learning.* Sterling, VA: Stylus.

Smircich, L., & Morgan, G. (1982). Leadership: The management of meaning. *Journal of Applied Behavioral Science, 18*(3), 257–273.

St. George, E. (2006). Positioning higher education for the knowledge-based economy. *The International Journal of Higher Education and Educational Planning, 52*(4), 589–610.

Stevens, A. P. (2010). *The role of public universities in workforce development: Assessing public-private partnerships in the California state university system.* University of La Verne). *ProQuest Dissertations and Theses.* Retrieved from http://search.proquest.com/docview/858866550?accountid=15053

Stogdill, R. M., & Coons, A. E. (Eds.). (1957). *Leadership behavior: Its description and measurement.* Columbus, OH: Ohio State University, Bureau of Business Research.

Syam, D. S. (2010). *Learning in collaboration: A case study of a community-based partnership program.* Unpublished dissertation. The University of Wisconsin-Milwaukee.

Tatro, C. N., & Hodson, J. B. (2011). Partners in student success. In J. B. Hodson & B. W. Speck (Eds.), *Entrepreneurship in student services. New Directions for Higher Education,* no. 153 (25–34). San Francisco: Jossey-Bass. doi:10.1002/he.423

Taylor, J. (1993). *Rethinking the theory of organizational communication: How to read an organization.* Norwood, NJ: Ablex.

Tedrow, B., & Mabokela, R. (2007). An analysis of international partnership programs: The case of an historically disadvantaged institution in South Africa. *Higher Education, 54*, 159–179.

Thayer, L. (1988). Leadership/communication: A critical review and a modest proposal. In G. M. Goldhaber & G. A. Barnett (Eds.), *Handbook of organizational communication* (pp. 231–263). Norwood, NJ: Ablex.

Thune, T. (2011). Success factors in higher education-industry collaboration: A case study of collaboration in the engineering field. *Tertiary Education and Management, 17*(1), 31–50.

Todeva, E., & Knoke, D. (2005). Strategic alliances and models of collaboration. *Management Decision, 43*(1), 123–148.

Tompkins, P. K. (1967). Organizational communication: A state-of-the-art review. In G. Richetto (Ed.), *Conference on organizational communication* (pp. 4–26). Huntsville, AL: National Aeronautics and Space Administration.

Tompkins, P. K., & Wanca-Thibault, M. (2001). Organizational communication: Prelude and prospects. In F. M. Jablin & L. L. Putnam (Eds.), *The new handbook of organizational communication: Advances in theory, research, and methods* (pp. xvii–xxxi). Thousand Oaks, CA: Sage.

Tschannen-Moran, M., & Hoy, W. K. (2000). A multidisciplinary analysis of the nature, meaning, and measurement of trust. *Review of Educational Research, 71*, 547–593.

Tubbeh, L., & Williams, J. (2010). Framing issues of international education. In P. L. Eddy (Ed.), *International collaborations: Institutional frameworks and faculty roles. New Directions for Higher Education*, no. 150 (pp. 7–16). San Francisco: Jossey-Bass.

Tuckman, B. W. (1965). Developmental sequence in small groups. *Psychological Bulletin, 63*, 384–399.

U.S. Department of Education. (2006). *A test of leadership: Charting the future of U.S. higher education.* Washington, DC: Author.

Vanasupa, L., McCormick, K. E., Stefanco, C. J., Herter, R. J., & McDonald, M. (2012). Challenges in transdisciplinary, integrated projects: Reflections on the case of faculty members' failure to collaborate. *Innovative Higher Education, 37*(3), 171–184.

Vangen, S., & Huxham, C. (2003). Nurturing collaborative relations: Building trust in interorganizational collaboration. *Journal of Applied Behavorial Science, 39*(1), 5–31. doi: 10.1177/0021886303039001001

Viale, R., & Ghiglione, B. (1998). The triple helix model: A tool for the study of European regional socio economic systems. *The IPTS Report 29.* Retrieved from www.jrc.es/home/report/english/articles/vol29/REG1E296.htm

Violino, B. (2011). Community abroad: International partnerships generate revenue, opportunity for colleges in tough fiscal times. *Community College Journal, 82*(1), 14–16, 18–21

Warmington, P., Daniels, H., Edwards, A., Brown, S., Leadbetter, J., Martin, D., Middleton, D. (2004). *Interagency collaboration: A review of the literature.* Bath,

UK: Learning in and for Interagency Working. Available from http://www
.bath.ac.uk/research/liw/resources/Microsoft%20Word%20-%20Interagency_
collaboration_a_review_of_the_literature_initial.pdf

Waschak, M. R. (2009). *Evaluating the impacts of partnership: An electronic panel study of partnering and the potential for adaptive management.* Unpublished dissertation, Georgia Institute of Technology, Atlanta, GA.

Watson, J. S. (2007). Stepping outside the big box high school: A partnership influenced by goals, capital, and decision-making. In M. J. Amey (Ed.), *Collaborations across educational sectors. New Directions for Community Colleges*, no. 139 (pp. 49–57). San Francisco: Jossey-Bass.

Watt-Malcolm, B. (2011). Dual credit: Creating career and work possibilities for Canadian youth? *Canadian Journal of Education, 34*(2), 256–276.

Weber, M. (1948). *From Max Weber: Essays in sociology.* C. Wright Mills & H. H. Gerth (Eds. & trans.). New York: Routledge.

Weerts, D. J., & University of Wisconsin-Madison, Wisconsin Center for the Advancement of Postsecondary Education. (2011). *"If we only told our story better . . ." Re-envisioning state-university relations through the lens of public engagement. WISCAPE viewpoints.* Wisconsin Center for the Advancement of Postsecondary Education.

Weick, K. E. (1976). Educational organizations as loosely coupled systems. *Administrative Science Quarterly, 21*(1), 1–19.

Weick, K. E. (1995). *Sensemaking in organizations.* Thousand Oaks, CA: Sage.

Wepner, S. B. (2011). Defining collaborative leadership. In S. B. Wepner & D. Hopkins (Eds.), *Collaborative leadership in action: Partnering for success in schools* (pp. 121–144). New York: Teacher's College Press.

Wergin, J. (Ed.). (2007). *Leading in place: How academic professionals can find their leadership voice.* San Francisco: Jossey-Bass.

Wheatley, M. J. (1999). *Leadership and the new science.* San Francisco: Jossey-Bass.

Yendol-Hoppey, D. (2010, summer). The promise of transformative partnerships. *Teacher Education and Practice, 23*(3), 326–330.

Young, C. K. (2010). *Vital collaboratives, alliances, and partnerships: A search for key elements of an effective public-private partnership.* East Tennessee State University. *ProQuest Dissertations and Theses.* Retrieved from http://search.proquest
.com/docview/848643699?accountid=15053

Zakocs, R. C., Tiwari, R., Vehige, T., & DeJong, W. (2008). Roles of organizers and champions in building campus-community prevention partnerships. *Journal of American College Health, 57*, 233–241.

Zhang, Y., & Huxham, C. (2009). Identity construction and trust building in international collaborations. *Journal of Applied Behavioral Science, 45*(2), 186–211. doi: 10.1177/0021886309333327

Zuchelli, B. (2010). *Early college partnerships: Relationships and success elements of an early college program between 25 rural school districts in Southwestern Pennsylvania and a community college.* Unpublished dissertation, Indiana University of Pennsylvania, Indiana, PA.

and, second, the author's thoughtful inclusion of vignettes and case studies provides the day-to-day grounding to make her model relevant to readers of all professions. Yes, community college readers have the advantage of knowing many of the leadership challenges firsthand and will be more interested than most in sections such as 'Challenges of Community College Leadership,' but this book adds sufficiently to leadership literature that it should find itself on the bookshelves of professionals across education and the private sector."

—The Department Chair

"Pamela Eddy has done seminal work in creating a multidimensional model for leading change in the community college. This is an excellent resource for all aspiring community college leaders as well as those serving as senior leaders in our institutions. The book is well written and contains an exceptional combination of theory to practice ideas and thoughts. It is sure to become required reading in community college leadership development programs."

—Larry H. Ebbers,
Community College Leadership Programs, Iowa State University

Sty/us

22883 Quicksilver Drive
Sterling, VA 20166-2102

Subscribe to our e-mail alerts: www.Styluspub.com

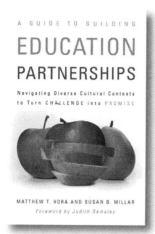

A Guide to Building Education Partnerships
Navigating Diverse Cultural Contexts to Turn Challenge Into Promise
Matthew T. Hora and Susan B. Millar
Foreword by Judith A. Ramaley

"Useful artifacts in the book help make this a true guide to the work of partnership. There is a glossary, because shared language is an important aspect. There are schematics that communicate the complexity of new developing relationships. Bibliographic references are also helpful and could point to additional experts and resources."

—Education Review

"This book is helpful for any leader involved in designing or managing a partnership with an outside group. The book's mini-summaries, partnership action points, core ideas and bibliographic notes in each chapter highlight useful points and provide resources for further research."

—The School Administrator

"Partnerships spanning K–12 and higher education institutions represent one approach to marshalling the intellectual capacity and resources necessary for effective education reform. The authors draw from their experiences as evaluators of one large partnership and extensively from the research and applied literature on partnerships to offer detailed and practical advice on the do's and the don'ts. They have produced a very pragmatic and practical book that should be valuable to those in K–12 and higher education considering entering into new partnerships for school improvement. It will also be of interest to people who have been in such partnerships but aren't currently, helping them to figure out what they did right and wrong."

— Andy Porter,
Dean, Graduate School of Education, and George and Diane Weiss Professor of Education, University of Pennsylvania

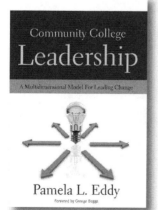

Community College Leadership
A Multidimensional Model for Leading Change
Pamela L. Eddy
Foreword by George R. Boggs

"Pamela L. Eddy's *Community College Leadership: A Multidimensional Model for Leading Change* deserves our time for two simple reasons: first, the multidimensional model for leading change transcends community colleges and is applicable broadly within and beyond education;